DUTRA'S WORLD

Diálogos
A series of course-adoption books on Latin America:

*Independence in Spanish America:
Civil Wars, Revolutions, and Underdevelopment* (revised edition)
—Jay Kinsbruner, Queens College

Heroes on Horseback: A Life and Times of the Last Gaucho Caudillos
John Chasteen, University of North Carolina at Chapel Hill

The Life and Death of Carolina Maria de Jesus
Robert M. Levine, University of Miami, and José Carlos Sebe Bom
Meihy, University of São Paulo

The Countryside in Colonial Latin America
edited by Louisa Schell Hoberman, University of Texas at Austin,
and Susan Migden Socolow, Emory University

The Faces of Honor: Sex, Shame, and Violence in Colonial Latin America
edited by Lyman L. Johnson, University of North Carolina at
Charlotte, and Sonya Lipsett-Rivera, Carleton University

The Century of U.S. Capitalism in Latin America
Thomas F. O'Brien, University of Houston

Tangled Destinies: Latin America and the United States
Don Coerver, Texas Christian University,
and Linda Hall, University of New Mexico

*Everyday Life and Politics in Nineteenth Century Mexico:
Men, Women, and War*
Mark Wasserman, Rutgers, The State University of New Jersey

*Lives of the Bigamists:
Marriage, Family, and Community in Colonial Mexico*
Richard Boyer, Simon Fraser University

*Andean Worlds: Indigenous History, Culture, and Consciousness Under
Spanish Rule, 1532–1825*
Kenneth J. Andrien, Ohio State University

Series advisory editor:
Lyman L. Johnson, University of North Carolina-Charlotte

DUTRA'S WORLD

Wealth and Family
in Nineteenth-Century Rio de Janeiro

ZEPHYR L. FRANK

University of New Mexico Press ◈◈ Albuquerque

10 09 08 07 06 05 04   1 2 3 4 5 6 7

Library of Congress Cataloging-in-Publication Data

Frank, Zephyr L., 1970–
Dutra's world : wealth and family in nineteenth-century
Rio de Janeiro / Zephyr L. Frank.
p. cm. — (Diálogos)
Includes bibliographical references (p.   ) and index.
ISBN 0-8263-3410-5 (cloth : alk. paper) —
ISBN 0-8263-3411-3 (pbk. : alk. paper)
1. Wealth—Brazil—Rio de Janeiro—History—19th century.
2. Social mobility—Brazil—Rio de Janeiro—History—19th century.
3. Social structure—Brazil—Rio de Janeiro—History—19th century.
4. Slavery—Brazil—Rio de Janeiro—History—19th century.
5. Family—Brazil—Rio de Janeiro—History—19th century.
6. Rio de Janeiro (Brazil)—Economic conditions—19th century.
7. Rio de Janeiro (Brazil)—Social conditions—19th century.
8. Dutra, Antonio José, d. 1849. I. Title. II. Diálogos (Albuquerque, N.M.)
HC189.R4F72 2004
305.5'234'09815309034—dc22

2004015734

Design and composition: Maya Allen-Gallegos
Typeset in Palatino 10/13
Display type set in Bremen and Tiepolo

FOR PAULO AND TRAM-ANH

TABLE OF CONTENTS

LIST OF ILLUSTRATIONS

Tables

Figures

Map

Illustrations

PREFACE

This book is the result of serendipity. While researching for an extensive study of wealthholding in nineteenth-century Brazil, my assistant, Silvana Jeha, called my attention to the extraordinary case of Antonio José Dutra. The original project, still in motion, called for the collection of great amounts of quantitative data—minimal attention was to be placed on the nominal characteristics of individual observations. We collected names, places of residence, civil status, and not much else. What we were after, and still are, were numbers. We wanted to test a hypothesis about economic and institutional change and patterns of wealthholding over the nineteenth century, so apparent oddities like Dutra did not enter into our original research agenda. Yet this former slave, barber, and musician called to me; I found myself wondering about him and how to tell his story when I should have been worrying about the big picture.

I see now that Dutra and the big picture have a great deal in common. Telling Dutra's story in the context of a large dataset covering wealthholding in Rio de Janeiro allows us to begin to answer three major questions. The first is a question of method and rhetoric. How can quantitative history serve to elucidate the lives of ordinary people in the past? The second is more substantive. How did social structure in Rio de Janeiro change during the nineteenth century and what, in particular, happened to the middle groups in society? This question is doubly important because we cannot understand the history of slavery in Rio without understanding the social group that owned nearly half of the slaves and depended on them for the accumulation of wealth, and because this social group has been neglected in favor of studies of slaves themselves or political and economic elites. Finally, there is a philosophical question embedded in Dutra's case. Is it possible for an ambivalent character like Dutra to play the role of the hero in our narrative? On the one hand, he overcame slavery to become a singularly interesting and successful entrepreneur. On the other, he owned slaves himself and built his fortune on their labor.

The ambivalence we are bound to feel toward Dutra is salutary. The history of slavery and society in Brazil has too often been distorted by our anachronistic preferences. Because the subject is so hard to grasp from our present-day perspective, scholars have tended to shy away from confronting its sheer ubiquity in nineteenth-century Brazil. In this sense, the past really is "another country." As with many painful subjects, the tendency has been to focus on the aspects of slavery that resonate with our own deeply negative feelings about the institution: slaves and their canny forms of resistance, large landowners and their exploited minions. The basic fact that perhaps half of all slaves lived under the roof of small-to-middling owners and that many accepted the institution of slavery itself in so natural a way as to think nothing of obtaining their freedom and buying their own slaves has been commented on before. Yet no detailed and systematic treatment has been offered on the history of middling slaveholders over time, and on the former slaves among them in particular. This book is intended as a modest beginning in this direction.

I have accumulated many debts in the course of researching and writing this book. To begin with, it would not have been possible to write Dutra's story and place it in the world of slavery in nineteenth-century Rio de Janeiro without reference to Mary Karasch's monumental study, *Slave Life in Rio de Janeiro*. To Professor Karasch, I owe a vast debt of gratitude from a distance. Although never a pupil of hers in the traditional sense, I am nonetheless her student.

The collection of large amounts of quantitative data from manuscript sources is time consuming and expensive. This work could not have been done without the generous support of grants from Stanford's Office of Technology Licensing, Latin American Studies Center, Social Science History Institute, and Department of History. Time and space, two rare commodities in academic life, were provided by a fellowship in the Stanford Humanities Center during the final period of revising and preparing the manuscript for publication. Impeccable research assistance in Rio de Janeiro was provided by Silvana Jeha, Elsa Marie Campos, and Fabíola Camargo. Similarly, my team of researchers, colleague Afonso de Alencastro, and assistants Renata Kosuinski and Edriana Nolasco, in São João del Rei provided key data with which to compare my results from Rio de Janeiro. In both Rio and Minas, I owe a debt of gratitude to the many helpful archivists who allowed me and my associates to work unimpeded. At Stanford, I was assisted by an able team including: Aldo Musacchio, Ian Read, Marcelo Bucheli, Robert Walker, Lise Sedrez, Celso Castillo (of UC Berkeley), Kari Zimmerman, Veronica Aoki Santarosa (of the University of São Paulo), and Heather Flynn.

Members of my Brazilian social history seminar contributed pointed criticism on the whole manuscript, as did generous colleagues in the Stanford community. Richard Roberts and Carl Degler read early versions of the manuscript and pushed me to think about slavery in a broad, comparative perspective. Gavin Wright set me straight on some of the quantitative aspects of the analysis in reading drafts of related material. Outside of Stanford, many colleagues assisted me in the completion of this book. Joseph Love read drafts of related work on wealthholding and supplied his usual blend of substantive commentary and editorial expertise. Long e-mail exchanges with Lyman Johnson refined my sense of the possible when working with estate inventories. Stuart Schwartz read an early draft and encouraged me to continue with Dutra's story. Jeffrey Needell came through with apt criticism on key aspects of the book on short notice. Finally, the anonymous reviewer assigned by the University of New Mexico Press helped catch mistakes and omissions. The errors and infelicities that remain are all my own.

Note on Orthography

Readers of Portuguese will know that the orthography of the language has changed dramatically over the years. In particular, the guardians of the language have tended to change what are considered redundant consonants or archaic spellings: thus, Matto Grosso becomes Mato Grosso, and telephone becomes telefone. In this book, I have sought to maintain, in the references and the text where appropriate, the names of individuals as they were indicated in the original documents. Thus: Ignacia, not Inácia. With regard to place names, spellings and accents conform to current Brazilian practice with a few minor exceptions. My decision to maintain the original spellings of names was guided by a desire to conserve period authenticity as well as to avoid dissonance between text and notes. In most cases, individuals are presented with their full names when first introduced in the text; subsequently, they are referred to by their first name(s). The major exception to this rule is Antonio José Dutra himself, whom I refer to by his last name in order to differentiate him from the many other Antonios in the text.

Readers should take note that the city of Rio de Janeiro, also known as the Corte (royal seat) during the period of the empire, shares its toponym with the province of the same name. Throughout this book, Rio de Janeiro refers to the city, not the province, unless otherwise indicated.

Note on Currency

Throughout the period covered by this book, the main unit of currency in Brazil was the *mil-réis*, denoted numerically as 1$000. One thousand mil-réis made up one *conto de réis*, the largest unit of the time, which was written 1:000$000 and was worth about 580 U.S. dollars in 1850.

Note on Measures

Archaic measures of length cited in the text include the *braça*, the *pé*, and the *palmo*. The braça measured 2.20 meters and corresponded to the English fathom. A pé signified an English foot. A palmo measured 0.22 meters, or an English span. The most common unit of measure for the dimensions of urban properties was the palmo. Thus, to get an idea, a residence listed with the dimensions 50 by 50 palmos would correspond to a living area of 121 square meters. The most common measure of length for rural property and undeveloped urban lots was the braça.

1

INTRODUCTION

On July 19, 1849, Antonio José Dutra, a barber and small-time entrepreneur resident in Rio de Janeiro, died leaving six heirs. On September 9 of the same year, his eldest daughter, Ignacia Antonia Maria de Jesus Dutra, renounced her role as her father's executor, claiming that her own husband, a spendthrift womanizer, was unfit to oversee the disposition of the estate. Antonio's death and Ignacia's renunciation mark the beginning of a series of legal disputes and ensuing records that inspired this book by providing a window through which to view wealth and family in nineteenth-century Brazil in a new light.[1]

Antonio was no simple barber: he pulled teeth, set bones, and applied leeches as well as performing the mundane offices of his trade. He was also an extraordinarily diversified entrepreneur for a man of his social background, owning thirteen slaves at the time of his death—six of which comprised a band of musicians for hire. Beyond slaves, he owned two urban residences, a varied collection of musical instruments, and a hodgepodge of furniture and sundries. These facts alone make Antonio interesting; that he was born in Africa and brought to Brazil as a slave makes him an irresistible subject.[2]

What kind of world gave rise to someone like Antonio Dutra, and what kind of changed world would his headstrong daughter Ignacia face after his death? Was he really all that different from hundreds or thousands of other middling wealthholders in Rio de Janeiro circa 1850? In order to answer these questions, this book connects quantitative data on patterns of wealth and social structure with an analysis of the political economy and institutions of Brazil during the nineteenth century—from the time Dutra arrived in Brazil to the period of rapid economic and institutional change that took place in the years after his death. The central argument is this: Dutra was not a particularly unusual wealthholder for his time—in fact, with the important exception of his slave background, he was representative in many other ways—but his world itself was ephemeral. Created in the aftermath of Brazilian independence and reaching its zenith around the time of his death, it was altered during the next decades by sweeping economic and institutional change with the repression of the international slave trade and the transformation of Rio de Janeiro's economy into a huge, modern financial center filled with sophisticated enterprises and bursting at the seams with new immigrants.

The literature on social structure and the Brazilian economy has typically accorded little space to this intermediate world and "oddities" like Dutra. This is understandable: the 1830s and 1840s do not lend themselves easily to traditional narratives, and Dutra and his ilk represent an ambivalent and hard-to-define category of persons. The scholars perhaps most likely to appreciate Dutra's world, colonial specialists, do not often venture into the 1800s; when they do, their insights are most valuable.[3] Those interested in the decline of slavery and the process of abolition generally begin in 1850 with the ending of the Atlantic slave trade.[4] Economic historians wanting to explain Brazil's development in the nineteenth century tend to focus on the expansion of coffee and the post-1850 period.[5] Historians seeking signs of agency among slaves and subalterns are unlikely to focus on the likes of Dutra as historical subjects.[6] Students of politics and elites tend to focus their attention on a different, much more restricted stratum of society or emphasize vertical relations of power embodied in patronage.[7] Perhaps the literature that comes closest to touching on Dutra's world is that which concerns itself with the ambiguous lives of freedmen and the free colored.[8]

Dutra's world is the world of the striving, upwardly mobile but tenuously positioned urban middle groups at a critical juncture in Brazil's history. The slave trade is about to end; railroads and export growth are about to transform the economy; the city of Rio de Janeiro has doubled in population in the course of a generation. Meanwhile, wealthholders have seen their primary assets—slaves and urban real estate—explode in value in a few short decades. His is the world of the majority of wealthholders for whom slaves made up a substantial part of their estates; for whom wealth was accumulated in a lifetime and then dispersed; for whom social and economic standing was ambiguous in life and even more uncertain in death. The history of this world, when placed in the broader context of Brazil's social and economic development, provides an indispensable counterpoint to the well-known story of Brazil as a plantation society made up of rich slaveholders, their slaves, and poor free workers.

Several misconceptions persist about social structure and the place of Dutra and his world in the tapestry of Brazilian history. Foremost is the typical claim that elites were especially dependent on slavery. Some were. But then again, so were the vast majority of middling wealthholders.[9] It is now well established in the literature that slavery permeated all ranks of society throughout urban and rural Brazil. According to my research, the very wealthy in Rio de Janeiro city actually invested little in slaves relative to other assets (although, to be sure, they were often linked to kith and kin with large slaveholdings in the countryside). This finding, which will be developed at length in this book, is corroborated by Katia Mattoso's study of nineteenth-century Salvador. There, four of the five richest categories of wealth-holders invested between 2.5 and 8.7 percent of their wealth in slaves. Among the poorest classes inventoried, by contrast, 12 to 40.3 percent of wealth was held in slaves.[10]

The second problem that continues in the literature involves the extent to which the urban petite bourgeoisie was behind the burgeoning antislavery movement over the course of the nineteenth century. It is often suggested that the urban middle groups were at the forefront of the abolitionist movement, yet the close ties of this group to slaveholding are rarely made explicit.[11] Although it was certainly the case by the 1870s that urban groups were mobilizing against slavery, the evidence in this study paints a very different picture of this segment of society in the first six decades of the nineteenth century. Indeed, Viotti da Costa argues that, until the 1860s, abolitionist sentiment had minimal public exposure.[12] This was not because the middle groups were co-opted by the slaveholding elite; rather, they were for the most part committed slaveholders themselves. Likewise, while it is no doubt true that some freed slaves became abolitionists, many others accommodated themselves to the institution of slavery and sought to purchase slaves of their own.[13]

A third misconception turns on the question of social mobility. Slavery, for example, did not impede the ascent of urban middle groups; rather, it aided it. Because slaves were the most equally distributed of assets, the institution actually dampened inequality among the free population (cold comfort to the slaves, to be sure) and allowed aspirants to middling wealth a means to climb the social ladder. Indeed, as Richard Graham has argued, the limited but nonetheless palpable prospect of social mobility was part of the foundation of Brazil's remarkably stable hierarchy during the nineteenth century. Of course, as Graham insists, we should not mistake relative fluidity for a lack of hierarchy altogether.[14]

Fourth, and finally, by placing great store in the transformation of Brazil in the late nineteenth century—with the abolition of slavery and proclamation of the Republic—the traditional story often fails to register the profound transformation of Brazil a generation earlier in the 1850s. The fundamental argument of this book hinges on this transformation from a period of moderate economic growth, relatively inexpensive slaves, and rapid urbanization to a period of rapid export growth, railroad construction, high slave prices, and increasing inequality. The trend for the period from the 1820s through the 1840s was toward slightly greater equality among the free population and social mobility in Rio de Janeiro based largely on slaveholding; from the 1850s onward, this trend reversed as a consequence of Brazil's economic and institutional development. Independence did not transform Brazil's economy; coffee, railroads, and financial capital did. Herein lies the paradox of Brazil's nineteenth-century economy and society: for the denizens of Dutra's world, the 1830s and 1840s were the best of times, even though Brazil's economy was growing slowly in the aggregate; when growth accelerated, the benefits accrued to a smaller slice of the population with ties to the Atlantic economy or access to the expanding collar-and-tie world of Rio's commercial and administrative sectors.

The historical reconstruction of doomed or ephemeral social structures risks falling into antiquarianism unless grounded in broader questions of historical explanation. I am therefore interested not only in describing Dutra's world but also in explaining how it came to be and why parts of it disappeared while others persisted. The dynamics of historical change come into focus when we are able to juxtapose the familiar, in the standard literature and sources, with the unfamiliar. Such analysis often leads to further counterintuitive or unexpected results.

The descriptions of Dutra's world rendered in this book, and the explanations given for its rise and fall, are anchored, fundamentally, in one particularly rich set of sources: postmortem estate inventories. Although the analysis is enriched with other primary information and many secondary sources, the definition of Dutra's world in terms of wealthholding and the lens through which change in this world is measured derive from estate inventory (*inventário*) samples. All told, 1,109 estate inventories with usable quantitative information were coded and analyzed in order to trace out the structure of wealthholding in Rio de Janeiro during the nineteenth century. The systematic use of these documents is complicated, and I have attempted to explain their collection and analysis in detail in the appendix. Readers with particular interest in the creation of the samples and their reliability are encouraged to dip into the appendix early on.

Like all historical studies, there are limits to what can be asserted in this book on the basis of the sources and the methodological constraints imposed by the adopted approach. Beyond this, there are fields of historical inquiry that doubtless overlap the analysis attempted in this volume. Dutra's world obviously contained much more complexity than can be captured in an analysis of wealthholding, and it is conceivable that another historian, faced with the question of what to do with a seeming oddity like Dutra, would adopt another approach, perhaps emphasizing his cultural milieu. By limiting this study to wealth (as it intersected with social structure, economic growth, urbanization, institutions, and the family), I do not intend to suggest that everything that happened was somehow determined by material considerations. Dutra lived in a world filled with ideologies, superstitions, cultural formations, politics, and so forth. In the course of writing this book, I have tried to evoke these aspects of Dutra's world to greater or lesser degrees, but the core of the argument and documentation rests on a study of wealth.

In Rio de Janeiro, circa 1849, in spite of his diversified entrepreneurial activities, slave origins, unorthodox daughter, and wayward son-in-law, Dutra was actually close to the mean in terms of his wealth. He owned slightly more slaves, had slightly more children, and worked at slightly more jobs; otherwise, so far as his patrimony went, he was like thousands of other residents of Brazil's capital. We can infer a great deal about the standard of living, accumulation of wealth, sources of income, and family structure of the middle groups from records such as Dutra's; what is more, we can begin to see the subtle distinctions in wealth and social standing that divided the residents of Rio de Janeiro into a complex hierarchy of race and class.

The type and degree of wealth attained by Dutra and the social group he represents proved ephemeral in Brazil: the structure of society in Rio de Janeiro, circa 1849, was about to be radically transformed. Thus, this book is also the story of the end of an era. A generation later, wealth was more concentrated than ever, slavery was a dying institution, and the avenues for advancement were increasingly closed off for people of Dutra's ilk.[15] In this sense, the middle of the nineteenth century marks a watershed in Brazilian history. Far enough from its colonial roots to have developed a social structure and political economy distinctly its own, Brazil had yet to catch the fever of railroads and coffee, and with it, the associated (but not causally determined) growth of immigration, abolitionism, and republicanism.

The institution of slavery is central to understanding social and economic life in nineteenth-century Brazil. More Africans were transported as slaves to Brazil than any other part of the Americas. More than 4 million slaves were sent to Brazil over the course of the trade; in contrast, 661,000 slaves were transported to what became the United States.[16] In the decades preceding Brazilian independence, an average of 9,543 slaves per year entered the port of Rio de Janeiro alone.[17] By the 1820s, around the time Antonio Dutra probably arrived, slave imports to the Brazilian capital had increased to an astounding 36,224 per year.[18] Of course, many slaves who landed in Rio de Janeiro were shipped out to other parts of Brazil. Yet many stayed in the city, swelling the ranks of the enslaved in the capital from 40,376 in 1821 to 78,855 in 1849.[19] Demand was fueled by an expanding urban economy, high returns to slaveholding, lack of alternative investments, and the fact that the slave population did not reproduce naturally in most cases.

If the slave population was growing rapidly in the city, so too was the population of free colored. A minority of the free colored obtained their freedom through manumission, whether purchased or freely granted. The majority were born free to the already large and growing free-colored population. The salience of the free-colored population in Rio de Janeiro (and Brazil as a whole) cannot be overstated. Because manumission was relatively common in Brazil, especially in urban areas, and because the free-colored population was large to begin with, the social landscape in Brazil was quite removed from that found in the United States in particular.[20] With the partial exception of Louisiana, which had a different legal tradition (associated with the French and Spanish), the free-colored population was neither large nor economically salient in most of the southern United States.[21]

In the past thirty years a new understanding of Brazilian slavery has developed with a salutary emphasis on the diversity of the institution and the social complexity that it produced in both rural and urban settings. The bulk of recent research focuses on rural slavery. Stuart Schwartz, in a groundbreaking article in the mid-1980s, recast the research agenda on Brazilian slavery by synthesizing an emerging understanding of the diversity of slaveholding and the preponderance of smallholdings in Brazilian slavery.[22] Other scholars in the 1980s opened important debates concerning the viability of slavery as an economic system, challenging old chestnuts about its purported inefficiency and incompatibility with economic development.[23] Along the way, they also began to rewrite the economic history of nineteenth-century Brazil. In particular, the southeastern region of the country emerges in this literature as a dynamic and growing economy. Rio de Janeiro Province, in particular, grew rich on sugar and slavery during the late eighteenth and early nineteenth centuries, with coffee adding further stimulus from the 1800s onward.[24] This emerging picture of a relatively dynamic and diversified economy has major implications for our understanding of the social, as well as economic, role of slavery in Brazil. If the economy was not sclerotic in southeastern Brazil, and if slavery was a complex, diverse institution, we will need studies that examine the way in which social structures informed and were influenced by slavery in dynamic urban milieus such as Rio de Janeiro.

Understandings of urban slavery shifted over the past few decades as well. An abundance of excellent studies have shown how slaves lived and worked and resisted their subjugation. We now know, for instance, that urban slaves tended to receive wages, often lived outside of the direct control of their masters, and were a generally better skilled and more resourceful lot than previously imagined in the older literature that focused more heavily on their subjection.[25] The positive contributions of the social history revolution of the 1960s and 1970s are plainly evident here. There is, however, a blind spot in this approach. Because these scholars were determined to turn the tables on the old master-oriented narratives about slavery, they were less interested in the lives of slaveholders themselves.

The best of the literature on slave culture and resistance keeps the masters and their world in clear view; yet, a systematic appraisal of the class structure of slaveholding remains lacking. If we know that most slaveholdings were of middling size, and we know that the social structures within which slavery played such a prominent role were fluid and complex, then it becomes necessary to understand the lives and motivations of middling slaveholders. Who were they? How did they acquire slaves? To what end did they employ them? How important were slaves to their economic and social standing? How did slavery inflect their family relationships? Finally, what were the consequences of economic and institutional change for this middling group over the course of the nineteenth century?

This book is structured along two basic lines of analysis. First, it develops a quantitative portrait of slaveholding in nineteenth-century Rio de Janeiro. It is not enough to present summary data about the number of slaves per household and show that middling slaveholding predominated. Instead, the analysis is based on postmortem estate inventories, which allow for a much more detailed understanding of the kinds of people who owned slaves, the kinds of slaves they owned, the uses to which they were put, and their importance to their estates. This methodology also allows us to track the changes in the institution of slavery as it intersected with shifting social and economic structures in Rio de Janeiro. Other studies have utilized estate inventory data to good effect in the case of Rio; none has systematically studied the middling groups and their economic dependence on slavery.

At this point, it is necessary to say something about social class and the definitions used in this book. Although the terms middle groups and middling wealthholders sound less precise than "middle class," I have purposely avoided using the latter term for the following reason. Middle class connotes a form of class-consciousness for which evidence is scarce in Rio de Janeiro during the period covered by this book. Indeed, in his recent study of the emergence of the middle class in Brazil, Brian Owensby suggests that such a class only crystallized in the last years of the nineteenth century. Owensby's findings are compatible with my own: the institutional and economic transformation of Rio de Janeiro led to the rapid growth of a class he identifies as "literate, white-collar employees and professionals, who did not engage in manual labor and who were overwhelmingly white or light skinned."[26] From the beginning of the nineteenth century, white-collar work expanded in Rio de Janeiro as the result of growing bureaucracy and expanding professional services. Thus, the fortunes of Dutra's ilk and the urban professional classes marched in step through the 1840s, parting ways thereafter as the former experienced contracting opportunities and the latter expanded and grew into Brazil's middle class.

Middling wealthholders were a varied group, and there is no reason to suspect that a barber-surgeon like Dutra shared a sense of class with a similarly wealthy public servant.[27] Instead, in this book, the term middle group is used in the sense of economic standing, primarily determined by wealthholding. For the most part, in fact, I will refer to the subject of analysis as middling wealthholders, to make this distinction clear. The decision to focus on an economic definition of the middle groups for the purpose of this study is not meant to imply that other, alternative designations cannot be devised. Rather, the choice of definition arises from a conscious effort to focus the analysis on wealthholding, slavery, and social mobility as measured in economic terms.

What the middle groups did have in common was a generalized dependence on slavery as the basis of their wealth through at least the 1850s and, in attenuated form, even into the 1870s. It follows from this that the extent of their overlapping "class" concerns were typical of slaveholders in general, accentuated by their relatively greater dependence on the institution of slavery as a source of wealth and income. At the expense of nuance, I have defined these middle groups entirely on the basis of their wealth and have used a considered shorthand to identify what middling wealth means: for the purpose of this book, when referring to middling wealthholders, I refer to the middle 60 percent of the distribution of wealthholders in my estate inventory samples. Doubtlessly there were other important markers of "class" in Rio de Janeiro, color and education to name just two. Moreover, a person's place in the social hierarchy of the city also depended, to a degree, on the nature of their vertical relationships (clients and patrons) and their horizontal ties (brotherhoods, professional associations). To the extent possible, I try to incorporate these nuances into the details of my discussions of particular wealthholders, but when referring to the middle groups, I refer to the whole mass of individuals in the middle of the wealth distribution.

The second line of analysis draws inspiration from the extraordinarily rich case of Antonio José Dutra. In this regard, it provides the detailed narrative counterpoint to the quantitative analysis of social structures outlined above. Underlying this approach is my intention to show that Dutra, in spite of his seemingly bizarre characteristics, was in many ways representative of middling slaveholders who predominated among all wealthholders in Rio de Janeiro. In addition, a close reading of Dutra's case opens historical windows into the history of social mobility, death and dying, and family structure.[28] Dutra escaped slavery only to become a slaveholder. His daughter Ignacia traced out a double arc of emancipation: first as a child, obtaining freedom when her father paid for it; second as a young woman, when she sued for ecclesiastical divorce (legal separation) from her allegedly womanizing husband and sought to remove him as de facto executor of her father's estate. Dutra's third lover, Maria Mathildes, lost her man in 1849 but did not gain a share of his estate until the death of her own child, Fructuosa, in 1851. Relatively wealthy during his latter years, his family faced an uphill struggle to regain its middling status in the decades following his death. Although these aspects of social history in Rio de Janeiro (and elsewhere in Brazil) have been analyzed before, no study has sought to relate them systematically to quantitative data.

A study of wealthholding, by necessity, cannot fully explore much that is of interest to students of nineteenth-century Brazil. A breathtaking range of alternative sources exists for the study of social life in Rio during this time: criminal court records, notarial records, and newspapers all offer important insights. And yet, there is something special about estate inventories and testaments. They provide the historian with a reliable guide to the material conditions of life in the past; they offer detailed insights into family structures; and, in cases such as Dutra's, they provide hundreds of pages of documentation on lives otherwise lost to history. For these documents are not limited to appraisals of estates. They are concerned with the last wishes of the deceased; they involve deeply personal matters such as the recognition of children born out of wedlock; and they follow the fortunes of the surviving family for years or decades, providing us with an unparalleled source for tracking family history over time.

The Argument of the Book

Although this study was inspired by the case of Antonio Dutra, his family, and his class, it is not intended solely as an exercise in historical recovery. Reconstructing the microhistory of lived experience in nineteenth-century Rio is a worthy enterprise, but this book is concerned with more than this.

This book aims to clarify three unresolved questions regarding the interaction between social structures, on the one hand, and economic and institutional change, on the other. I wanted to understand Dutra's place in the larger social order in which he and his family were embedded. In order to do so, I began with three simple propositions. First, the colonial heritage of institutions and attendant social structures mattered a great deal in the aftermath of Brazilian independence. The level of initial inequality and the institutional framework underpinning it influenced the rate and extent of change in the ensuing decades. Brazil was born unequal, but with a relatively broad distribution of slaves, especially in urban areas. This fact greatly influenced outcomes in social and economic structure during the first thirty-odd years of independence. When these colonial structures were accompanied with slow but steady economic growth and a surfeit of cheap slaves, inequality diminished among the free population and social mobility was relatively high—this was Dutra's world.

The second proposition regards the effects of institutional change and the socioeconomic context within which they are imbedded. Institutions are the formal and informal rules of the game for a society and economy. When the rules change, some groups stand to gain and others to lose. Internal institutional change is largely driven by powerful social and economic interests as they reach negotiated positions among themselves and with subaltern groups, which may produce pressure for change from below. Changes can also be imposed by relatively autonomous state actors in conjunction with external forces. In Brazil, the institutional change critical to understanding the unraveling of Dutra's world occurred when the British and Imperial Brazilian authorities combined, in 1850, to suppress the Atlantic slave trade once and for all. Although most of the internal rules of the game of slavery remained the same after 1850, their effects on Brazilian social structure were radically altered. Overnight, Brazil shifted from an institutional environment of inexpensive and numerous slaves to one characterized by high prices and increasing scarcity—with profound effects on social structure and mobility. In this regard, the effect of institutions depends on the context within which they operate. Slavery remained as pernicious and pervasive as ever, but its meaning for society was transformed and, with this change, Dutra's world began to unravel for his children and their contemporaries.

The third piece of the puzzle is the relationship between economic change and social structure. The extent to which economic change affects different groups in society depends on the nature of the economic system itself. One possibility is that economic growth occurs without much social change. Growth can be outwardly oriented, as in the case of enclave economies. Old social arrangements can be adapted, with little change, to new economic opportunities. Another possibility, at the other end of the spectrum, is that the new economic system will revolutionize social relations. In any event, as Douglass North points out, economic change is shaped and constrained by underlying institutional arrangements.[29] Along these lines, then, institutions, created by politicians and mediated by ideology, interact with social and economic structures to create the rules of the game for a given society and economy.

The attentive reader probably notes, at this point, a circularity in the argument: the economy affects institutions, which are adapted by powerful interests in light of perceived economic opportunities and the desire to capture rents; institutions, in turn, have economic consequences. Although the belief in bases and superstructures, and linear causes and effects, dies hard, there is no theoretically or empirically satisfactory way to disentangle institutions, social structures, and economic systems. Social scientists, therefore, should cultivate some of what Keats referred to as "negative capability," that is, the ability to entertain more than one set of relationships and outcomes at once—to be at peace with doubt and uncertainty. This means, in turn, that our research agenda needs to be broader, omnivorous, and, at the same time, much more modest. We can hypothesize that institutions matter for economic growth, we can postulate that economic growth has consequences for social structures, and we can claim that social structures inform institutions, but we are unlikely, with the data available to us for the nineteenth century, to be able to say with certainty how these factors interacted.

Because Brazilian independence did not usher in a revolutionary set of new institutions, and because social structures tend to change slowly, colonial structures survived largely intact well into the nineteenth century.[30] So long as the foreign and domestic dimensions of the economy and the internal context of its institutions remained fairly stable, social change was limited to the internal dynamics of system: wealth tended to be concentrated in real estate and slaves; and social mobility for a fortunate minority was possible owing to the availability of inexpensive slaves and the expanding opportunities in the urban milieu.

As the economy in southeastern Brazil was increasingly transformed with the onset of export growth, beginning in the 1830s and picking up steam by the 1850s with the added impetus of Brazil's first railroads, social structures changed with the rise of new institutions, sophisticated financial wealth, and the arrival of European immigrants attracted by the opportunities for social ascent in the dynamic zones of the Atlantic economy.[31] Other forms of institutional change, more directly the result of politics, also shifted the rules of the game after 1830. Brazil's first emperor, D. Pedro I, abdicated in 1831, in part owing to his unpopular (and not enforced) agreement with the British to turn off the tap on the African slave trade. A weaker political regime held sway into the early 1840s, in part because the political landscape itself was unsettled and the emergence of ideologically coherent parties and a strong central authority were still some time off. By the 1840s, however, Emperor D. Pedro II emerged as a forceful political leader in his own right, paving the way for substantial institutional change in the 1850s regarding the slave trade (shut off), commercial law (updated), and land laws (written and implemented). What is more, as both Richard Graham and Jeffrey Needell have argued perceptively, by the 1840s the propertied elite had allied decisively with centralized authority—setting the stage for the sweeping changes of the 1850s.[32]

The colonial heritage bequeathed the city of Rio de Janeiro a specific institutional environment and social structure that, baring external shocks or internal transformations, developed in a way that elevated the relative status of middling social groups. An institutional shock, the suppression of the slave trade, changed the context within which the rules of the game operated in Brazil. Slavery, which had functioned perversely as a tool for social mobility and had dampened inequality among wealthholders, gradually took on a new cast as an institution with ever fewer and richer owners. At about the same time, the export economy boomed and capital flowed into Rio de Janeiro to finance railroads and the coffee plantations along the railway lines. This economic growth, unlike the slower, steadier growth of the preceding decades, tipped the balance toward greater inequality of wealth in Brazil's capital. As noted, entrepreneurs with ties to the Atlantic economy saw their wealth mushroom; middling wealthholders lost ground. Meanwhile, the confluence of institutional and economic change met with the rising authority of D. Pedro II and his more aggressive and activist government. Together, these changes rewrote the rules of the game in social, economic, and political terms by the end of the 1850s; in the process, the relative status of Rio de Janeiro's middling wealthholders was gradually eroded.

Even with these changing institutional contexts and economic growth, the social structure of Rio de Janeiro remained, on the whole, remarkably stable from the 1810s through the 1850s. From this finding, we are forced to admit that our second and third hypotheses about the effects of institutions and economic growth on social structures end up rendering less than was hoped for. Economic change and external shocks to institutions matter, a proposition we will see fully developed in this book; yet, it appears that the most powerful explanation for the form social structures took in Rio de Janeiro as late as the 1850s resides in the initial endowment of institutions and social structures circa 1820. A young person, seeing Rio for the first time in 1860, may have echoed Miranda and seen a brave new world taking shape. After all, slaves were worth five times as much as in the past, railroads were integrating the city to the surrounding region, and exports and financial wealth were booming. Yet the transformation had just begun. Slaves remained an especially important form of wealth for the middle groups; real estate wealth was of even greater importance; and the profound effects of the transformation of Rio de Janeiro by these economic and institutional changes were really only to be felt a generation or two later in the 1870s and beyond. Fundamentally, social structures evolve slowly, even in the face of major institutional, economic, and technological change. Yet evolve they do.

Beginning in the 1850s, and gaining steam as time went on, Rio de Janeiro's economic and social structures shifted toward the "modern" forms they would take by the 1890s. Three transformations were of particular significance: the gradual decline and eventual abolition of slavery; the rise of free, European immigration; and the institutional transformation of Brazil's credit markets with the creation of a modern banking system and stock market, which, although incipient in the middle years of the nineteenth century, nonetheless began to transform wealthholding in Brazil's capital city. Clearly there were other important processes and developments over the course of time. Railroad construction, intimately tied to capital markets and financial institutions, was one thing; the coffee boom, increasingly centered in São Paulo by the 1880s, was another.

For Antonio Dutra and his ilk, the enduring irony is that the inhumane and "backward" world of 1849 was better for him and his family than would be this new world of wealth and political change in the latter part of the nineteenth century. The callousness of his world, with slavery and the oppression of women, would not be replaced by a better, more inclusive Brazil. The dream of wealth, however brutally built on the backs of slaves, had been accessible to a relatively large slice of the population in Dutra's day, and the rules of that cruel game were known to him and many like him. When freedom came, in 1888, it arrived with a whimper, not a bang (so few slaves remained), and the promise of inclusion in the civil and economic fabric of the city was deferred. Voting became more restricted (although also somewhat more direct), not less. European immigrants crowded out the Afro-Brazilian population from employment and housing, and ideologies of race derived from social Darwinism and eugenics introduced new and virulent forms of discrimination against the Afro-Brazilian population. In short, the world of the 1890s was much better in normative terms without slavery, but, in practical terms for middling wealthholders and freedmen alike, it may have been indifferent or worse.

Permit me to conclude this introduction on a personal note. For a long time now, the discipline of history has drifted apart. Cultural historians and social historians often seem to have lost the ability or desire to communicate. It is my contention that social historians need to seek out sources that can speak across this divide as well as connect the microfoundations of history to macrostructures.[33] Fundamentally, this is what I believe an analysis based on estate inventories makes possible in this book: a history that is quantifiable and that generates falsifiable claims, yet also contains that smell of flesh that Marc Bloch so famously noted in the pages of History. In this, I know I am not alone.[34]

2

ECONOMY AND SOCIAL STRUCTURE IN RIO DE JANEIRO, CIRCA 1820

On the verge of independence, gained in 1822, Rio de Janeiro was home to more than 86,000 souls, including more than 40,000 slaves.[1] One of the largest cities in South America at the time, it was the center of political and economic life in late colonial Brazil. Home to the Portuguese court from 1808 to 1821, it was also an administrative and cultural center in a sea of smaller cities and villages that dotted the Brazilian coast and parts of the interior. Because of its size and central place in the political economy, Rio de Janeiro held a unique position in Brazil throughout the nineteenth century.

Famous for the natural beauty of its bay and surrounding hills, Rio de Janeiro itself garnered mixed reviews from travelers arriving in the city from Europe. In a typical description of the scenic panorama of the bay, the Irish-born traveler Robert Walsh wrote of his impressions circa 1828:

> Nothing could exceed the beauty of the place in which we lay. . . . On our left was a range of fantastic hills, receding behind each other; those in front rising into cones, and terminated by the great Sugar Loaf . . . and we entered the most magnificent harbor in the world.[2]

Upon disembarking in the port, however, Reverend Walsh tempered his enthusiasm by noting the prevalence of slaves and their demeaning condition. On further observation, Walsh found that not all blacks in Brazil were so downtrodden, and that, in fact, their condition depended on whether they were slaves or freed, and on their occupations.[3] Notwithstanding these mixed feelings, the weight and importance of slavery as an economic and social reality hit Walsh and other travelers as the single most noteworthy aspect of the city itself.

Illustration 1. *A panoramic view of Botafogo Beach, Rio de Janeiro. When this scene was drawn, in the 1820s, Botafogo was just beginning the process of urbanization. The large buildings in the background depict mansions of Rio de Janeiro's elite. (Johann Moritz Rugendas,* Voyage Pittoresque dans le Brésil, par Maurice Rugendas, *Paris, 1835).*

With regard to the physical layout of the city, Walsh was struck by the narrow streets and closed, barred-up houses that lined them.[4] Writing a century later, Gilberto Freyre suggested that, especially in the first half of the nineteenth century, urban life in Brazil exhibited a strong dichotomy between house and street: houses were like fortresses, at least for the middle and upper classes, built to protect valuables and women.[5] Aside from residential buildings, which varied greatly from two story mansions down to improvised hovels in the poorer districts, the city also boasted commercial districts and a growing number of public buildings, many associated with the presence of the Portuguese court in the city from 1808 to 1821 and others with the newly independent regime.

We will have occasion to revisit the architecture of the city and the interior of its houses and shops in subsequent discussions. For now, suffice it to say that Rio de Janeiro, in the 1810s and 1820s, was a fast-growing port city with narrow streets and limited public amenities. More important to the story we want to tell, however, are the diverse people of the city and their socioeconomic relationships. In this regard, the first impressions of travelers such as Walsh were right on

Illustration 2. *Street scene in the Rua Direita, Rio de Janeiro, during the 1820s.* (*Johann Moritz Rugendas,* Voyage Pittoresque dans le Brésil, par Maurice Rugendas, *Paris, 1835*).

the mark: Rio de Janeiro, more than anything, was a city built on the institution of slavery and practically no aspect of life went untouched by its influence.

The population of the city was divided into three major groups, each of which were further divided into a bewildering series of classifications according to wealth, education, race, ethnicity, and place of residence. At the top of Rio society were the rich few who controlled most of the wealth, filled the positions of political and legal authority, and looked to Europe for culture and consumption. This group, however, was not a cohesive class. Within it there were subtle divisions between the traditional landed elite and the emergent mercantile families growing up in the hothouse of the Atlantic economy.

Below this stratum, a mass of middling and lower-class families struggled up and down the social ladder. At the top of this group were successful businessmen, professionals, and high-level public servants. In the middle were government functionaries, small businessmen, skilled artisans, and a good number of sons and daughters of wealthier parents fallen on hard times owing to the vicissitudes of the economy and to the Portuguese custom of partible estates. At the bottom, comprising well over half of the city's entire population, workers, poor widows, and other unfortunates scraped by on limited resources in an increasingly costly city. The racial and ethnic composition of the middle and lower sectors of society was extremely heterogeneous: poor whites looked up the ladder at well-situated free-colored artisans; an occasional former slave rose to a moderate fortune; one's social position defined, in part, one's racial category.

At the bottom of the social and economic hierarchy stood Rio de Janeiro's slaves. United in their basic social condition of captivity, slaves were, themselves, an enormously varied group. Domestic servants attended on the rich and well-to-do, carpenters and stonemasons worked along side their free cousins; others bent their backs to the simple tasks of manual labor—hauling goods to and from the port, carrying the waste of the city for disposal in the bay. In this urban setting, slaves interacted on a daily basis with the free; their range of movement and social options were, generally speaking, greater than their brothers and sisters working in the cane fields, mines, and coffee groves of rural Brazil.[6] Because so many slaves worked outside of the direct purview of their masters, and because so many toiled in a monetary economy, there were also relatively greater prospects of purchasing freedom among urban slaves.[7] Self-purchase, although fairly common, was not, however, an easy transaction to conclude for slaves. Slaves had to worry about their savings being confiscated illegally by their owners or third parties and often had to trust freed companions to hold onto their money for them.[8] There was also the possibility of falling in arrears in payment of agreed upon sums to their owners. In such cases, masters could rescind the deal and force their slaves to return to service under their direct control. Indeed, up until a court decision of 1865, manumission was revocable on the purely subjective grounds of "ingratitude," and this practice was not completely banned until 1871.[9]

Proximity to their masters in domestic work also served to create personal ties and enhance the prospect of manumission. Although the distinction between urban and rural slavery must not be drawn too sharply, it is clear that mobility and opportunity were greater in the cities. Because slaves purchased their freedom or were manumitted, an important population of former slaves (*libertos*) was continually bubbling up into the lower and middle ranges of Rio's society. This population of freed persons was Antonio Dutra's first stop on the way from captivity to middling wealth.

The Slave Trade

Although we cannot be certain, Antonio Dutra probably arrived in Rio de Janeiro in the 1810s. Clues pointing to his arrival during this period include the age of his children at the time of his death and the size of his estate. Father of six children with three different women, Dutra's eldest daughter Ignacia was married at the time of his death in 1849. She was twenty-seven years old at the time, placing Dutra in Brazil no later than 1821.[10] This assumes, however, that he started a family immediately upon arrival. It is equally possible that he arrived some years earlier, obtaining his freedom before the birth of Ignacia.[11]

Slaves brought to Brazil in the early nineteenth century underwent a harrowing passage across the Atlantic after their capture and sale in Africa. Even before they were packed into the ships, slaves spent days or weeks crammed into barracoons in the major slave ports along the African coast. Dutra may have spent time in such a place in Luanda, a leading point of departure for slaves from the Kongo.[12] There, he would have been jammed into a crowded barracoon with no more than two square meters of space. Along with scores of fellow slaves, he would have shared this space with pigs and goats and human and animal waste. During this time, he would have subsisted on a diet of porridge (made from cassava) and small amounts of beans and fish. In Joseph Miller's compelling account, these slave ports were permeated with the "stench of death"—something reproduced on the other side of the Atlantic.[13]

At some point Dutra was sold to a slave trader and readied for the "voyage of no return."[14] Prices for young male slaves in Luanda were between 70$000 and 80$000 during the years Dutra was likely sold. He would fetch twice that on arrival in Rio de Janeiro.[15] Prior to embarking, Dutra and his fellow slaves were required to show evidence of having heard the catechism and being baptized. They were also branded with a hot iron (although this painful and humiliating procedure was suspended for five years from 1813 to 1818, and Dutra may have been lucky to avoid it).[16]

Although recent quantitative evidence tempers the horrific portrait of death and disease on the slave ships, there is no doubt that conditions on board these ships were atrocious and that many slaves died in transit or arrived in Brazil in poor physical and mental condition.[17] Slavers packed their human cargo into the holds of relatively small ships and permitted slaves little by way of fresh air, food and water, or freedom of movement. Contemporary accounts of what is known as the "Middle Passage" are rife with suffering. Sometimes ships were blown off course, and their passage extended for weeks beyond their supplies of food and water. In some cases, slaves rebelled on board, leading to deaths among slaves and crew.

In a remarkable document published in 1854, the slave Mahommah Baquaqua narrates the story of enslavement and transit on a slave ship. First, Baquaqua tells of his capture in Africa by fellow Africans. He then tells of his days aboard the slave ship, during which the slaves "were thrust into the hold of the vessel in a state of nudity" and crammed together. Water was scarce, and the slaves "suffered very much for want of water . . . a pint a day was all that was allowed." Discipline was brutal. According to his testimony, "when any one of us became refractory, his flesh was cut with a knife, and pepper or vinegar was rubbed in to make him peaceable."[18]

After suffering the Middle Passage, slaves were brought on shore and taken to market. Prior to 1830, slaves entering Rio de Janeiro usually went to the slave market of the Valongo. This is where Dutra himself probably was first sold to a Brazilian owner. The Rio slave market was a massive affair, with as many as two thousand slaves on display at any given time in the many warehouses along this street. Conditions for slaves in the market were little better than on board the ships, and many died before they could be sold.[19] Having survived the crossing and the conditions of the Valongo, Dutra would have been inspected and prepared for sale.[20] This horrible scene is captured in Walsh's description of 1828–29, written just before the slave trade was made illegal and the slave market moved to less conspicuous quarters:

> Almost every house in this place is a large ware-room, where the slaves are deposited, and customers go to purchase. . . . [T]he poor creatures are exposed for sale like any commodity. When a customer comes in, they are turned up before him; such as he wishes are handled by the purchaser in different parts, exactly as I have seen butchers feeling a calf; and the whole examination is the mere animal capability.[21]

Traders sorted slaves by age and gender, fed them in order to replace some of the weight lost in the voyage, and vaccinated them to increase their value. After all of this, Dutra was probably sold for about 141$000 (28 pounds sterling) to an urban buyer.[22]

Shortly after Dutra's arrival, the slave market in Rio de Janeiro changed substantially with the "legal" prohibition on slave imports

Illustration 3. *Slave Market in Rio de Janeiro during the 1820s. After 1831, when the slave trade was technically declared illegal, slave markets moved to less conspicuous quarters and to beaches on the periphery of the city. (Johann Moritz Rugendas,* Voyage Pittoresque dans le Brésil, par Maurice Rugendas, *Paris, 1835).*

to Brazil in November 1831. Thereafter, slave imports moved through clandestine (but hardly secret) markets located in specific neighborhoods in the city such as Rua Direita, in the heart of the city's commercial district.[23] Dutra himself, as he came to acquire his own slaves in the 1830s and 1840s, probably purchased them through auction houses or direct negotiations with other owners who often advertised their slaves in the local newspapers.

All told, there were more than forty thousand slaves in the city of Rio de Janeiro around the time of Dutra's arrival—making up nearly half of the population and, as we shall see, performing a vast array of tasks while forming the basis of wealth for many urban fortunes. In particular, urban slavery was critical to the formation of Rio de Janeiro's middle groups, providing income, collateral, and a source of social mobility for those who owned slaves. The many thousands of slaves entering Rio de Janeiro in the early nineteenth century were inserted into a complex and growing economy—where urbanization and specialization provided an impetus for internal growth and where exports of agricultural commodities from the province's hinterland generated additional prosperity.

Politics and Institutions

The arrival of the Portuguese court in Rio de Janeiro, in flight from Napoleon's armies on the Iberian Peninsula, hastened the process by which Rio de Janeiro emerged as the political and economic center of Brazil. Already the colonial capital of the domain, having been elevated to that status in 1763, Rio de Janeiro welcomed the arrival of João IV and his retinue with a mixture of excitement and consternation. What would this unprecedented move entail for the city? On the one hand, it clearly raised Rio's already high profile within Brazil. On the other, it highlighted the need, perceived by many among the elite, to refurbish and embellish the city along European lines. Along these lines, new public buildings were erected and new neighborhoods constructed to accommodate royal aspirations and a swelling population.[24]

Although scholars today emphasize the contingent nature of Brazilian independence and the subsequent constitutional monarchy, there is no doubting that the presence of the court influenced the direction Brazil was to take after 1822. When D. João IV returned to Portugal in 1821, leaving behind his son, D. Pedro I to rule Brazil, he set in motion the process of Brazilian independence. A year later, in 1822, Pedro declared an independent, monarchical Brazil.

As the legal prohibition of the slave trade in 1831 makes clear, politics played a significant role, beyond the transfer of the court to Rio and the achievement of independence, in shaping the institutions and the rules of the game for economy and society in newly independent Brazil. The 1830s, in particular, were marked by political unrest and a relatively weak state. By the 1840s, the Conservative party (first known as the Party of Order) had gradually constructed the foundation of an authoritarian, centralized nation-state. The limitations of state power were evident in the inability of the Brazilian authorities to suppress the illegal importation of fresh slaves from Africa. Of course, politicians and their elite backers were little disposed to enforce the ban from the outset; but whatever their sins of omission, there was really little the state could do with its weak authority and limited resources to prevent further importation.

Although independence came without bloodshed, Brazil's first ruler, D. Pedro I, enjoyed the briefest of honeymoons with his subjects. Throughout the 1820s, his position was continually under attack from political radicals and disgruntled members of the agrarian elite. Acceding to British pressure and preparing the way to declaring the slave trade illegal (the law itself came into effect after his abdication) broke the already weak back of his regime, which was roundly criticized for being too closely tied with Portuguese interests, autocratic, and, in the case of his personal conduct, immoral.[25]

In the ensuing decade and a half, Brazil was wracked by civil war and urban revolt as the authority of the state devolved to a series of regents who ruled in the name of Pedro's young son, D. Pedro II, aged just five at the time of his father's abdication. Notwithstanding the turmoil associated with this period, social and economic life continued in Rio de Janeiro in largely the same rhythms laid down during the late colonial era. The city continued to grow in population and trade; slaves continued to pour in from Africa. Indeed, the very weakness of the state limited its capacity to alter effectively the rules of the game.

The Economy

In keeping with its position as Brazil's main port and commercial entrepôt, Rio de Janeiro was the conduit of a significant volume of domestic and international trade. For the four-year period 1819 through 1822, an average of 333,447 arrobas of salt-beef, 194,284 arrobas of manioc flour, 163,115 arrobas of wheat, and 363,203 arrobas of sugar entered the port.[26] Mostly imported from other parts of southeastern and southern Brazil, some of this tide of food was consumed in the city itself and another portion was transported to towns in the interior of the province of Rio de Janeiro. Overland trade was equally important. Slightly out of the period under consideration, a reported 659 mule trains (*tropas*) entered Rio in 1829, the majority carrying dairy products, cloth, coffee, and tobacco from the neighboring Provinces of Minas Gerais and São Paulo.[27] Lastly, on the import side of the equation, Rio de Janeiro received an average of twenty thousand slaves per year circa 1820.[28] Most of these slaves were exported from Rio to the neighboring states of Minas or to the interior of Rio Province.[29] In any case, Rio de Janeiro was far and away the busiest slave port in the world in the nineteenth century.

Along with importing food, textiles, and slaves, Rio de Janeiro also exported large quantities of sugar and smaller quantities of coffee and other products to Europe and the United States. For Brazil as a whole, exports amounted to 20,119 contos in 1821—the equivalent of 4,324,000 pounds sterling. With an estimated population of 4,396,132 circa 1819, this implies exports of about 1 pound sterling per head—not much in aggregate terms.[30] However, keeping in mind that most of these products were exported from a restricted set of coastal cities and their hinterlands, the salience of exports in the lives of residents of Rio's rose dramatically.

How important was trade to Rio de Janeiro on the eve of Brazilian independence? Building on João Fragoso's meticulous research, we know that waterborne imports of sugar, aguardente (an alcoholic beverage made from sugarcane), salt-beef, wheat, and manioc flour (also known as cassava, a staple in slave and lower-class diets) added up to 1,604 contos in 1820. This implies a value of approximately 344,862 pounds sterling, or about 4 pounds per head.[31] Slave imports added another 3,000 contos, or another 8 pounds sterling per head, if we assume that imported slaves fetched the median price of slaves listed in contemporary inheritance records.[32] Added to this were the overland imports from Minas and São Paulo and substantial maritime imports from Europe and the United States. Although we lack specific data, it is likely that the total value of imports of goods and slaves into Rio de Janeiro in the 1820s amounted to well over 20 pounds sterling per head of population—or, put another way, the residents of Rio were twenty times as involved in trade as was the average Brazilian.

There was much more to the economy of Rio de Janeiro than long-distance trade. As an administrative and military center, Rio was home to thousands of government functionaries, sailors, and soldiers. John Luccock, an Englishman resident in Rio from 1808 to 1818 estimated that there were two thousand public officials and another two thousand military officers resident in the city circa 1818.[33] To the extent that Brazil had financial institutions, these too were concentrated in the capital. Finally, home to more than eighty thousand people, Rio was Brazil's most developed service economy—with upwards of two thousand merchants and businessmen and four thousand clerks.[34] Urban growth created jobs in construction and transportation; urban wealth generated employment in domestic service; urban density created the need for public services ranging from waste disposal to policemen and postal workers. Luccock, in his detailed description of the city in the 1810s, suggests that urbanization and the scarcity of labor raised wages in Rio "in an extravagant degree." One consequence of high wages manifested itself in the attraction of slaveholding. High wages and cheap slaves "gave rise to a new class in society, composed of persons, who purchased slaves for the express purpose of having them instructed in some useful art or calling, and then selling them for an advanced price, or hiring out their talents and labor."[35] In terms of the division of labor and social mobility, the urban environment favored the expansion of a large class of middling slaveholders who took advantage of low slave prices and a robust labor market to climb the social ladder.

By the same token, there appear to have been clear diminishing returns to slaveholding above a certain level in the urban environment. The only slaveholders in our sample with more than twenty slaves were all clearly identified with rural landownership. This state of affairs is really not so surprising if we account for the fact that the urban environment was dense and expensive, which made finding a place for dozens of slaves to live difficult, and that the problem of monitoring the location and activity of urban slaves was far greater than in the countryside. Indeed, middling slave owners who happened to be artisans often worked side by side with their slaves and dealt with the monitoring problem directly.

Work

Although much research has been done on the working conditions of slaves in Rio de Janeiro circa 1820, much less is known about free labor.[36] To a certain extent this is less of a problem than it appears: slave and free labor was largely interchangeable at lower income and skill levels. Construction contracts, for instance, often refer to the hiring of slave and wageworkers at roughly the same daily rate.[37] Slaves worked in all the trades, so the history of their labor covers much of the ground that a history of free labor would be required to account for. Nevertheless, there are obvious differences between free and slave labor that merit further elucidation.

Foremost, there is the distinction between coercion and the free choice of one's work. Slaves did not have the option of substituting leisure for work; at least, not in the same degree as did free workers. Yet even on this point, which seems such an obvious difference, we must be careful to qualify our claim. Since we know that many slaves purchased their freedom, we also know that many slaves must have opted for more work and less leisure in order to save money. Along these lines, following Marx, we are right to be skeptical of the extent to which free workers labored free of dull economic compulsion. In other words, there is a continuum between the raw coercion imposed on some slaves to force them to do work they would otherwise not do, running through a whole series of intermediate steps, to the opposite end where hunger rather than the whip compels people to do jobs they would otherwise avoid.[38]

This is not to suggest that a Panglossian interpretation of slavery is in order. Granting that slavery was so deeply ingrained in Brazilian society that freed slaves thought nothing of purchasing their former comrades, and admitting that the working conditions of some slaves,

Illustration 4. *The whipping post provided visual confirmation of slaveholders' authority to the crowd. Slaves were whipped systematically, often for a fee, for their real or imagined transgressions.* (*Johann Moritz Rugendas*, Voyage Pittoresque dans le Brésil, par Maurice Rugendas, *Paris, 1835*).

for instance artisans, may have been on par with their free counterparts, there is no disputing that most slaves wished to be free and were willing to go to great lengths to mitigate the worst aspects of their condition and to leave it as soon as they could.[39] Moreover, coercion, through corporal punishment, was a staple of the slave system throughout Brazil. When owners could not or would not discipline them, slaves were whipped by authorities in the infamous Calabouço jail of Rio de Janeiro, and a fee was charged to their masters. Robert Conrad estimates that slaveholders paid 528$000 to the police for a total of 330,400 lashes administered on 1,652 occasions in the year 1826.[40] The threat of a trip to Calabouço must have weighed heavily on the minds of slaves in Rio de Janeiro, whatever their conditions of work and life.

Returning to the varied occupations of Rio's workers, travelers' accounts shed light on the composition and social stratification of the labor force. Luccock was struck by the large number of attorneys in the city and attributed their number to a litigious society. As for health workers, he noted a lack of professionals, in the European sense, and the important role barbers played as surgeons and healers.[41] The class of merchants and shop owners was divided into two basic groups: those who engaged in large-scale trade and had ties to distant markets and those who serviced the local consumer market. Both groups failed to impress the prejudiced eye of Luccock, who found the former wanting in sophistication and the latter wanting in the quality of their goods.[42] Nevertheless, merchants and retailers were of growing importance in Rio as the city expanded in size and amplified its marketing area within Brazil.[43]

One of the most important sectors of the economy was services, which made up a large portion of the small businesses in the city. Taverns, barbershops, cobblers, and tailors, the integument of any urban milieu, proliferated throughout Rio and provided a living for thousands of families and their slaves. The barber-surgeon business, in particular, was the province of freedmen and slaves. According to Tânia Salgado Pimenta's analysis of petitions to perform the art of *sangrador* (bleeder) in Brazil during the period 1808–28, eighty five percent of requests were lodged by freedmen or slaves.[44] Dutra did not come upon his trade accidentally.

As for manual labor, slaves and free workers toiled in the same lines. Carpenters, masons, and mechanics stood at the top of the scale and earned good wages. According to the traveler Eschwege, skilled urban *escravos de ganho* were rented out for between $900 and 1$200 per day circa 1811.[45] This translates to roughly 200$000 per year, assuming about two hundred days worked. Below this stratum, many more semiskilled workers earned their daily bread, and, if they were slaves, some of their masters, by hiring themselves out as day workers.

An example of wages for unskilled urban labor is found in the inheritance record of José Sebastião de Castro, resident on Rua São Clemente on the Caminho da Lagoa. The owner of one slave, he rented his twenty-four-year-old male escravo de ganho (valued at 160$000) for $320 per day in 1818—roughly the same amount that Eschwege reported circa 1811 for unskilled labor.[46] At this rate, his slave probably earned between 50$000 and 70$000 per year, perhaps keeping half to feed and clothe himself, and giving half to José Sebastião.

Of course, not all escravos de ganho were manual laborers. We have already mentioned barbers and other service providers. Many slaves, and also a good portion of the free-colored population, worked as street vendors. Common items for sale included fruits and vegetables and sweets. Indeed, the confection and sale of sweets was the job of one of Dutra's female slaves.[47]

Illustration 5. *Free and slave alike provided services in the streets of Rio de Janeiro. Here, slave barbers attend to their brethren near the National Palace. Street barbers served the needs of urban slaves who, in many cases, earned their own wages and could pay for such services. (Jean Baptiste Debret,* Voyage Pittoresque et Historique au Brésil, *3 volumes, Paris, 1834–1839).*

At the bottom of the hierarchy of labor were slave porters (especially those associated with carrying water and refuse) and beggars, not always distinguishable one from the other, who earned what they could.[48] The porters, according to Luccock, struck foreigners with their unusual dress (many retained African elements) and the songs they sang as they carried their loads through the city's narrow streets.[49] Even at this level, however, distinctions were made. Slave porters working at the docks could, according to one observer, earn high salaries and purchase their freedom in a short period of time.[50]

From the lower reaches of the "respectable" classes on up, the aim of life was to avoid manual labor and to accrue and maintain a sufficient fortune to provide for one's family. Thus, the greatest distinction in Brazil with regard to work was between those who toiled with their hands and those who did not.[51] This is not to say that Portuguese culture or the Brazilian environment was inherently biased against manual labor. Anywhere in the Western world, circa 1820, one is likely to find the same sentiments and the same division of labor. The status accorded by work reinforced and overlapped other social categories based on race, gender, and location of residence.

Illustration 6. *Many of the free colored population worked as street vendors in Rio de Janeiro's bustling downtown district. This scene depicts free colored women selling fruit and flowers.* (Jean Baptiste Debret, Voyage Pittoresque et Historique au Brésil, *3 volumes, Paris, 1834–1839*).

Social Categories

Brazil developed an intricate mosaic of social categories over the course of the colonial era. On the eve of independence, in Rio de Janeiro, the two sharpest social distinctions were drawn along the lines of slavery and gender. At the most basic level, there were two major classes of people for whom many rights were restricted or denied: slaves, obviously, were denied many rights and were listed in estate inventories along with cattle and other self-moving property; women, for their part, occupied a range of subordinated positions.

To begin with, single women and widows enjoyed a fuller set of rights than did their married sisters. All women could own property, but married women's property fell under the "stewardship" of their husbands. This did not mean that husbands could sell or otherwise alienate their wives property at will. To the contrary, there were strict limits on what husbands could do, and wives could appeal to the courts if they felt their rights were being violated.[52] Nevertheless, so far as the law was concerned, the husband spoke for the wife in all

Illustration 7. *Slave porters carried, pulled, and pushed the bulk of goods throughout the city during the first half of the nineteenth century. European travelers often commented on their ubiquity, strange costumes, and songs.* (Jean Baptiste Debret, Voyage Pittoresque et Historique au Brésil, *3 volumes, Paris, 1834–1839*).

matters, including the household economy.[53] Single women enjoyed the most freedom with regard to their legal status. Widows gained control of a portion of their household wealth—if there were children, widows retained half of the estate, if there were none, and depending on whether there was a will, a widow could end up with between two-thirds or all of the estate.

Although they were not prevented from controlling property, and, indeed, held far more wealth than their counterparts in North America around the same time, women had no political rights whatsoever. Thus, in the nineteenth century, the two groups that could not hope to cast votes in elections were women and slaves. A key difference, ironically, was in the fact that a freed male slave, provided he was a native Brazilian or naturalized, could in fact obtain the right to vote (for electors in the first stage of elections), as the only barrier to voting at this stage, beyond sex, citizenship, and a minimum age requirement, was a property qualification.[54]

Social divisions based on slave status and gender were accompanied by a great number of subtle and not-so-subtle distinctions based on race and national origin. Unlike the United States, where the "one-drop" rule predominated, Brazilians accepted a continuum from black to white.[55] This does not mean that a fictional white purity at the top of the social structure was not maintained by members of the elite. Rather, it meant that in the lower and middle sectors of society there was a great deal of crosscutting of social categories: higher-status work accorded a "lighter" racial characterization; the work associated with slaves accorded a "darker" classification.

Along these lines the consumption patterns and housing arrangements of different social groups were intended to signal a firm position in what was really an ambiguous middle ground comprised of Rio de Janeiro's majority population—caught between the abject status of the slave and the exalted social heights. Here, in this middle ground, small gestures meant everything—literacy, owning musical instruments and books, living in the right neighborhood, obtaining the right furnishings—all contributed to the process of fixing a family's social location. The central aim of this book is to describe the conditions of this middle ground and to explain its relative rise and fall over the first decades of Brazilian independence.

Location and Neighborhoods

Rio de Janeiro, circa 1820, was still a small city in comparison to what it would become over the next half century. Three decades removed from the arrival of the railroad era in Brazil, the streets of Rio were narrow and transport was largely on foot. Carriages conveyed the wealthy to and fro, although there is some doubt as to the comfort of riding on Rio's cobbled streets. Mules and slaves carried heavy items throughout the city. Most of the population lived close to the bay and, for many, life revolved in some way around the port.

The literature often notes the fact that rich and poor lived cheek-by-jowl in nineteenth-century Brazil, especially in the beginning of the century when there were no railroads or trams and the concept of urban renewal and residential segregation was little developed.[56] It is true enough that levels of residential segregation were low compared to what would later obtain in Brazil; however, archival evidence regarding housing prices clearly indicates that some neighborhoods were more expensive than others and that a degree of residential segregation existed even in the 1810s and 1820s. Later, in the 1850s and beyond, the divisions become much clearer—by the

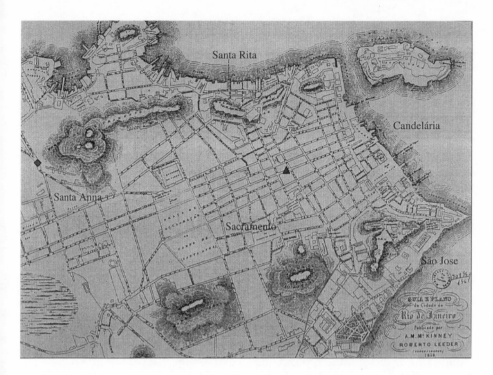

◆ Approximate Location of Dutra's Residences   ▲ Approximate Location of Dutra's Barbershop

Map 1. *The City of Rio de Janeiro and its Parishes.*

◈◆◈◆◈

census of 1872, neighborhoods are easily distinguished one from the other on the basis of occupational patterns.[57] One of the arguments explored in this book centers on this process of polarization during the first fifty years of Brazilian independence. In essence, I argue that social structures followed a U-shaped curve, trending toward greater equality and mobility through the 1840s and then shifting toward greater inequality and hardening social distinctions in the 1850s.

The central neighborhoods of Rio, which were known as *freguesias* (formal parishes with legal status) were comprised of Candelária, Sacramento, Santa Anna, Santa Rita, and São José, circa 1820. What might be termed suburbs included Engenho Velho, Lagoa, and Glória. According to the census taken in 1821, there were 86,323 souls resident in greater Rio; of these, 40,376 were slaves. All told, this population was divided among 10,943 households.[58] Slaves were distributed throughout the neighborhoods of the city, with the highest concentration per household in the central neighborhood of Candelária (4.91 per household) and the lowest concentration in the outlying neighborhood of Santa Anna (2.92 per household). Overall, there were 3.56 slaves per household in the city center and 5.3 per household in the more rural suburbs. Given that about one-third of all households owned slaves, the actual concentration of slaves per household was considerably higher than these figures indicate.[59] Evidence from inheritance records indicates that the mean number of slaves per slaveholding household was 8.3—implying that about 43 percent of all households owned slaves if the estate inventories are roughly representative of the distribution of slaves in general.[60]

Returning to the question of residential differentiation, an analysis of a limited number of properties indicates a clear relationship between total price and price per square meter: the costlier the dwelling, the higher the value per square meter. In other words, there was a premium to be paid to live in the better neighborhoods.

Large homes housed the wealthier residents of the city, who, in turn, lived in the same streets. For instance, João Gomes Barbosa resided at Rua da Candelária, number 2, on the corner of Rua dos Ferreiros near the city center. His residence measured 26 by 75 palmos (5.72 by 16.5 meters) and was valued at 3:200$000 (33$910 per square meter)—a considerable fortune in itself at a time when the same fortune could purchase more than twenty slaves. The interior was divided into two *quartos*, a living room, a kitchen, and an alcove for sleeping; no mention of a bathroom is made. Upstairs, were an unspecified number of additional bedrooms.[61] Compare this value, then, to that of Joanna Apolinaria, resident of Rua Nova do Livramento, in the neighborhood of Gamboa on the northeastern outskirts of the city, whose residence measured 5.5 by 14.3 meters and was valued at a mere 700$000 in 1819—8$900 per square meter.[62] Residences on the urban periphery, in semirural suburbs such as Iraja and Engenho Novo were worth even less on this basis. The home of Claudio Gabriel and Victoria Joanna Perpetua, in Engenho Novo, was appraised at just 50$000, with an added 4$000 in the value of the property's slave quarters (*senzala*).[63] This couple typifies the poverty of the outskirts of the city in the 1820s, particularly in the realm of housing values. Even a better-off couple like Rita Joaquina do Espirito Santo and her husband Captain Alexandre José Reis, owned a very modest home in Iraja appraised at 161$000 out of a total estate of 3:035$000.[64]

Thus, a resident's relationship to the urban core of Rio determined, to a certain extent, the value of his or her property as well as the relative cost per square meter. Along these lines, if someone said they owned a home in one of Rio's central streets, it was a fair assumption that they were reasonably well off. Nearly all the residences listed in

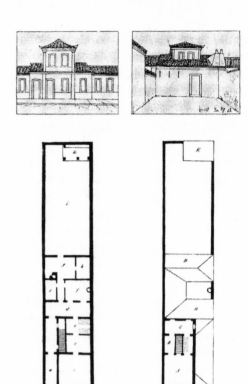

Illustration 8. *Floor plan of a small house in Rio de Janeiro during the first half of the nineteenth century, indicating the division of space. The largest rectangle at the back of the house (top of the plan) represents its walled garden, where slaves sometimes slept. The kitchen and slave quarters are at the back of the main structure. The square room in the front of the house (bottom of plan) is the visiting room, where middling owners of such homes could greet guests. The home depicted in this plan is slightly larger than the median home found in my estate inventory samples. (Jean Baptiste Debret,* Voyage Pittoresque et Historique au Brésil, *3 volumes, Paris, 1834–1839).*

◊◈◊◈◊

the central part of Rio were worth more than 1 conto circa 1820—representing the value of seven slaves or about five times per head income in Brazil at the time. Even so, there were often wide variations in the value of properties on the same street, as evidence from the 1840s will make clear in a subsequent chapter. Moreover, families were sometimes forced to rent out part of their residence, an upper story for instance, in order to make ends meet. In these cases, it is possible that families that could not otherwise afford to live in certain streets were able to do so.

The nomenclature of the rooms in nineteenth-century Rio de Janeiro can be a bit misleading. Although a quarto could refer to a

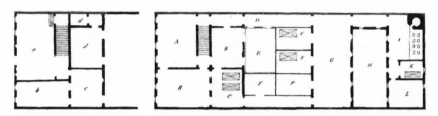

Illustration 9. *Floor plan of a larger house in Rio de Janeiro. This house includes a garage for a carriage at the front (far left side of the plan), as well as stables, storerooms, and slave quarters on the ground floor. The right side of the plan depicts the upstairs rooms where the family slept, ate its meals, and received guests. This plan depicts a house with four bedrooms, about twice the mean for houses at this time. (Jean Baptiste Debret*, Voyage Pittoresque et Historique au Brésil, *3 volumes, Paris, 1834–1839).*

bedroom, it also referred to living space in general, and the actual sleeping area was also referred to as an alcove (*alcova*). In single-story houses, the entryway opened to a living room (*sala*) behind which alcoves and the kitchen were placed in the back of the house. Wealthier residents lived upstairs; with the lower floor dedicated to the kitchen, servants quarters, and providing ingress and egress for the family's horse. For foreigners unaccustomed to such rusticity, the smell of the kitchen and stables below proved nearly intolerable.[65]

Many houses doubled as shops and businesses of various types. Given the high rents and property values in Rio de Janeiro, it made sense for poorer entrepreneurs to live and work in the same location. The accommodations, in these instances, were decidedly Spartan. In most cases, the upper floor was occupied by a wealthier resident who rented the lower to the shopkeeper who, in turn, shared his small space with servants and slaves. A small alcove sufficed for the shopkeeper, whereas his slaves slept on the counter or the floor.[66]

Interiors were a combination of whitewashed plaster and brightly painted cornices and baseboards. Ceilings, in the better homes, were divided in compartments and painted in the same bright hues. The colorful borders and ceilings contrasted with the meanness of the

Illustration 10. *Middling wealthholdlers and their rich cousins lived in relative comfort, served by slaves and surrounded by family and sometimes pets (note the monkey to the left). In this scene, a woman of middling wealth is accompanied by two adult slaves, an adolescent, and two babies, as well as by her own child. At her side, a whip represents a constant threat of punishment for her slaves.* (Jean Baptiste Debret, Voyage Pittoresque et Historique au Brésil, *3 volumes, Paris, 1834–1839*).

furnishings, even in the wealthier houses. Although a few rich dece-dents in this period reported sumptuous furnishings, paintings, and books, most owned only rudimentary furniture. Men sat on sofas, chairs, and improvised benches, while the women and slaves often sat on the floor. Tables were relatively uncommon. Wealthier houses had a dinner table, china, and linens, but the majority made due with some planks balanced on trestles or barrels. Kitchens were similarly rustic, containing an open chimney, a long hearth, and very few cook-ing implements.[67]

The Spartan nature of domestic life in early nineteenth-century Rio is a clear indication of a general lack of consumer culture in most households. What money there was to spend went to food, rent, and other necessities. Anything left over tended to be invested in slaves, real estate, and business ventures. Given the choice of purchasing more comfortable furnishings and an additional slave, most households appear to have chosen the latter course. Rita Mathildes do Sacramento, resident in the neighborhood of Gamboa, invested in ten slaves worth

Illustration 11. *The interiors of poorer and middling households were simple affairs. Note the lack of furniture and the presence of a hammock for sleeping. This scene depicts a poor widow with her child and lone slave, on whose labor we can presume the family subsisted.* (*Jean Baptiste Debret,* Voyage Pittoresque et Historique au Brésil, *3 volumes, Paris, 1834–1839*).

1:747$000; in contrast, her house was appraised at 250$000 and her furniture at 36$000. Perhaps out of vanity, the rustic nature of her domicile was livened up by a large and costly wardrobe.[68]

In the ensuing decades, this pattern persisted. The mean value of furnishings and all other personal items (omitting gold and other precious items) among decedents in the 1820s was 683$000. Discounting the very rich, this value fell to 458$000 (4 percent of the mean value of an estate). Three decades later, in the 1850s, the value of personal items was essentially unchanged. In spite of major changes in the size of the city, its trade and financial sophistication, and a rise in wealth and incomes, the demand for the basic comforts of life remained flat. It follows that the claim that the imitative consumption of European luxury goods by the middle and upper classes in Rio somehow undermined the domestic production of substitutes is more myth than reality: although consumption of European goods was common, the value of such goods was small relative to other kinds of consumption or investment.[69] The middle and upper groups spent their money on slaves and houses, building the urban environment, rather than spending heavily on European baubles and fashions, although European fashions and products were increasingly important markers of social distinction for the upper class, especially from the 1850s onward.

As Jeffrey Needell points out in his study of consumption patterns in Rio de Janeiro in the nineteenth century, especially prior to the 1870s, the main consumers of European luxury goods were already members of the economic and social elite. Such consumption did not signify the aspirations of a rising middle class; rather, luxury goods were important to the self-conception of the elite as "European" and endowed with superior taste.[70] This does not mean that there was not a middling group of wealthholders who might potentially have sought to imitate European fashions—it means that these middling wealthholders focused their consumption and investment in other areas.

Social Structures, a Quantitative Portrait

With the exception of my discussion of residential patterns and prices, little of the material covered thus far represents new information. In order to delve more deeply into the social structure of Rio de Janeiro in the early nineteenth century, I turn now to an analysis of a new dataset constructed from postmortem inheritance records.

Rio de Janeiro's structure of wealthholding can be retraced on the basis of estate inventories. The collection of these inventories, for the purpose of this analysis, was based on sampling. We selected one out of every three inventories in the National Archive for the periods of time comprised by the study (with the exception of the 1815–25 period, in which the paucity of cases led us to select every other inventory). Our aim was to yield a minimum of twenty observations per year within our periods, with a preferred outcome of thirty or more cases per annum.

One fact that became immediately apparent was that many records were incomplete or missing. Some contained evaluations of property values but no formal reckoning and division of property (*formal de partilha*); others contained the *partilha* but no evaluations; still others were missing pages.[71] On top of this, many inventories presented multiple evaluations or reckonings, some undertaken decades after the death of the subject. Overall, it took us an average of approximately three requests to yield two complete records. In the end, we collected 898 inventories with complete information (detailed reckoning of property values) for Rio de Janeiro during the period of the empire.[72]

The greatest challenge in using estate inventories as a proxy for wealth distribution in society as a whole resides in rendering the data consonant with the wealth of the living. The inventoried population is older than the population as a whole. It is also quite likely that the poorer the decedent, the more likely he or she would fail to be inventoried.[73] With regard to the censoring problem, there were no major institutional changes that would have made declaring wealth in estate inventories more or less likely. The fact that the minimum observed values of low-value categories of wealth do not change significantly over the periods is also strong evidence against censoring owing to changing thresholds at which wealth was declared.[74]

Because estate inventories in Brazil do not provide information on the age of decedents on a widespread basis prior to the 1880s, we cannot be certain as to the effect of age bias on our results. We are also unable to say for certain how many people were inventoried as a percentage of all decedents in a given year, although a best guess would place this figure at 8 to 11 percent of the decedent population that was likely to be inventoried (adults and heads of households and their spouses respectively).[75] These figures represent minimum values, however, because there is every reason to suspect that many inventories have been lost, destroyed, or have yet to be cataloged. Moreover, not all wealthholders who died were required to be inventoried. Indeed, most inventories derive from cases of decedents with minor children, falling under the jurisdiction of the orphans' court.[76] Those who died without minor children and having written wills were not required to be inventoried barring some other complication.

Although I argue that the inventory samples are large enough and do not appear to suffer from *major* problems of censoring or to be driven by outliers, we must underscore that the margin for error in these estimates is probably fairly large. Nevertheless, the results of the estimates are consistent with what we would predict based on independent information regarding the mean number of slaves per household, but slaves are a limited predictor of overall wealth. They are also consistent with what we know about incomes in nineteenth-century Brazil.

Forms of Wealth

Residential real estate made up the single most important category of wealth for the denizens of greater Rio de Janeiro in the early nineteenth century. Roughly 60 percent of wealthholders owned at least one residence; 29 percent of all wealth was tied up in such properties.

Table 1

Wealth in Rio de Janeiro: 1815–1825

	N obs.	Urban Real Estate	Slaves	Rural Property	Cash and Bank Deposits	Stocks and Bonds	Business Assets	Debts	Credits	Furn. and Precious Metals	Other	Total
Total	176	910,176	386,980	328,722	260,171	43,473	135,503	-197,535	551,244	168,836	109,254	2,696,824
Mean		5,171	2,199	1,868	1,478	247	770	-1,122	3,132	959	621	15,323
% of Total		33.7	14.3	12.2	9.6	1.6	5	-7.3	20.4	6.3	4.1	100

Source: Estate Inventories, Rio de Janeiro, AN. Please see Appendix for details of the sampling procedure.
Note: Values reported in constant 1850 mil-réis deflated by weighted index composed of .55 Lobo index and .45 pound sterling to mil-réis exchange rate. Lobo index derived from *História do Rio de Janeiro* (1978), 748–750, using her 1919 series. Please see Appendix for a discussion of inflation in Brazil.

Slaves, by contrast, accounted for just over 14 percent of all wealth. In this regard, Rio de Janeiro differed from the smaller towns and hamlets of the interior of the Southeast, where slave wealth often outweighed residential real estate by a significant margin. Yet, by the same token, 88 percent of wealthholders owned slaves in Rio de Janeiro, according to inheritance records. Slavery was truly ubiquitous in Brazilian life in the early nineteenth century: slaves made up nearly half of Rio's population, and nearly all wealthholders participated in slaveholding.

After housing, informal credit instruments (*dívidas ativas*) were the second most important form of wealth. Net of debts, they were worth slightly less to the wealthholders of Rio than slaves, but in themselves they constituted more than 20 percent of total wealth. It is important to note the salience of these credits for the following reasons. First, even though the economy of Rio de Janeiro was cash poor in the 1820s, this did not prevent the wheels of commerce from turning. Cash and bank deposits made up less than 10 percent of total wealth. Credit, however, was issued to all levels of society in the merchant houses, taverns, and bodegas of the city. Second, these credit instruments were widespread in Rio society, unlike stocks and bonds, which were concentrated in a few hands. A small shopkeeper, like Manoel de Oliveira Machado, had 1:200$000 in credits outstanding at the time of his death in 1819. Owner of a tool shop, his wealth in credit amounted to over half his entire estate.[77] Meanwhile, the poor couple of Claudio Gabriel and Victoria Perpetua, resident in Engenho Novo, had access to credit to the tune of debts worth 62$000 out of a final estate valued at 227$000.[78] Middling and poor residents, in both urban and rural zones of Rio de Janeiro, extended and received credit.

In keeping with Rio's connection to the rural hinterland, ownership of land also constituted an important form of wealth for a minority of wealthholders. There were two main types of landowners in Rio circa 1820. First, wealthy city dwellers sometimes maintained a rural presence as well. Maria de Oliveira Gonçalves and her husband, Lieutenant General José Barbosa, owned a block of small houses on Rua das Marrecas, just outside the Passeio Público. In addition to this, they lived in a *casa de sobrado* (traditional two-story house) on the same street. The total value of their urban real estate came to 51 contos, to which they added rural land and improvements worth 6:436$000. Against these real estate values, their extensive slaveholdings amounted to 5:450$000. Along with their houses, lands, and slaves, the couple owned an extensive library and a large store of gold and silver. Even more rooted in the countryside, the widow Eugenia Thereza Filgueiras de Barbosa Ribeiro left an estate in which rural assets predominated, although she owned many houses in the city itself. To wit: she owned urban residences worth 11:890$000 and rural properties (sugar plantations) worth just over 25:858$000. Her slave-holding accounted for a relatively small part of her total wealth (7:142$000) but included no fewer than 61 slaves.[79] The elite of the 1820s often had one foot in the city and the other in the country.

A second group comprised rural landowners with minimal connections to the city. These individuals marketed their goods in town but were otherwise rooted in the rural districts surrounding Rio de Janeiro. The neighborhoods of Engenho Novo, Guaratiba, Inhauma, and Iguape all appear in the sample with poor, small-time farmers, most of whom owned fewer than half a dozen slaves. For example, Josefa Maria da Conceição and her husband owned a house worth 50$000, a rancho worth 70$000, and land and improvements worth 251$000 in the rural district of Inhauma, about ten kilometers from the city center. Their six slaves, by far the most important source of wealth for the couple, were appraised at 530$000. Although the inventory does not specify where the couple sold their corn, it is likely that they were drawn into the marketing area of the city.[80]

A closer look at the distribution of wealth in the middle 60 percent of estates, representing Rio de Janeiro's diverse middle groups, illuminates the key differences between middling wealth and the estates of the rich. Slavery was far more important for middling wealth-holders than for their wealthy counterparts. The richest 20 percent of decedents owned 52.1 percent of all slave wealth. On the face of it, this is evidence of significant concentration. Yet, this same segment of Rio society owned 78.2 percent of housing wealth and controlled 86.7 percent of the outstanding credit (dívidas ativas). Slave wealth, therefore, was the most evenly distributed and most common of all major forms of wealth in the 1820s.

The middle 60 percent of wealthholders, meanwhile, accounted for 44.9 percent of slave wealth, but just 21.8 percent of houses and 12.9 percent of dívidas ativas. On the whole, this group held 21 percent of total net wealth, whereas the rich accounted for nearly all of the rest. The relative importance of slaves to middling and poor wealthholders is graphically presented in Figure 1. Here, all estates are ranked from largest to smallest, with the ratio of slave wealth to net wealth plotted on the graph. Note that the ratio can exceed 100 percent owing to cases in which decedents' debts lower their net estate below the value of their slaveholdings.

Figure 1

Slave Wealth as a Percentage of Total Wealth by Size of Estate:
Rio de Janeiro, c. 1820

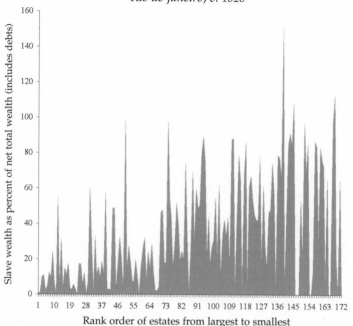

Source: Inventories, Rio de Janeiro, AN.

Two factors may have been at work in creating this pattern of slaveholding. First, there is the cultural argument, set forth by Mary Karasch among many others, which asserts all potential wealthhold-ers strove to purchase at least one slave.[81] Given that 154 of 176 estates list at least one slave, it does seem that slaveholding was nearly ubiquitous. Another factor, when Dutra's pathway to wealth is explored, is that slaves were the cheapest and most widely available income-earning asset available to middling and poor wealthholders. Houses were expensive and in short supply; credit was mainly the province of the well-to-do. Slaves, by contrast, were easily obtained and profitable investments. I have estimated that the ratio of slave prices to house prices was about five-to-one in the 1820s.[82] It would take five times as long for a middling or poor wealthholder to save up the purchase price. Meanwhile, his or her opportunity cost in lost returns to slaveholding would have been quite significant. No wonder, then, that the traveler Schlichthorst suggested that skilled laborers from Europe could immigrate to Brazil and become wealthy through slave purchases, not real estate investments.[83]

Slaves were the most evenly distributed form of wealth, and the most important for the middle sectors of Rio de Janeiro's social hierarchy. This finding comports with what we now know about slavery in Brazil as a whole during the first half of the nineteenth century. According to Laird Bergad's meticulous analysis of slaveholding in neighboring Minas Gerais, slaves were far more evenly distributed than other forms of wealth such as land. Among slave owners in Minas during the period 1800 to 1850, the Gini coefficient of inequality (measured from 0 to 1, with values closer to 1 indicating higher inequality; a reasonable guide to the interpretation of this index would suggest that values below 0.5 represent low inequality, between 0.5 and 0.7 represent moderate inequality, and above 0.7 represent high inequality) ranged from 0.52 to 0.54; the coefficients for landholding, during roughly the same period, ranged from 0.71 to 0.77.[84]

Turning to Rio de Janeiro, we find similar measures of inequality in terms of land and slaves. Among slave owners, the Gini coefficient in Rio de Janeiro was 0.57 circa 1820 and 0.63 circa 1855. Meanwhile, the coefficients for owners of urban residential property, a more useful metric in the case of the city than rural land, were 0.72 circa 1820 and 0.70 circa 1855. Perhaps more usefully, we can calculate the Gini coefficient for each category of wealth among all wealthholders—that is, including zero cases. In this rendering, levels of inequality outside of slaveholding rise commensurately, owing to the lower incidence of other forms of wealth in the estate inventory sample. The Gini coefficient among all wealthholders for slave wealth, by this reckoning, rises to 0.63 and 0.71 in the two periods in question, whereas the coefficient for urban real estate rises to 0.83 and 0.82 respectively. Overall, counting total physical wealth (omitting debts and credits that cancel out in society at large) the Gini coefficient among wealthholders in Rio de Janeiro was 0.70 circa 1820 and 0.72 circa 1855. These estimates must be viewed as rough and provisional. As I discuss at length in the appendix to this volume, there are many complicating factors in the use of estate inventories to derive estimates of wealth distribution.

Slave wealth remained relatively evenly distributed compared to other major forms of wealth throughout the period covered by this book. Over time, however, rising slave prices and the expansion of alternative investment opportunities meant that slaves would become less equally distributed and inequality would rise. Along these lines, middling wealthholders like Antonio Dutra would find their avenue to social mobility constricted, especially after 1850 when slave prices rose dramatically and the export-based economy picked up steam, shifting the balance of the economy toward the well-to-do residents of Rio de Janeiro with strong ties to the Atlantic economy and formal financial wealth.

3

DUTRA'S WORLD, CIRCA 1849

The city of Rio de Janeiro was substantially transformed during the period 1820 to 1850. Rising exports and rapid urban growth combined to make it a wealthier, more cosmopolitan place. According to the census of 1849, the city was home to 205,906 residents—more than double its population in 1821.[1] This chapter focuses attention on the social structures and economy in which Antonio Dutra, former slave, barber, and bandleader, came to fortune. In particular, close attention is paid to the status of Rio's middling wealthholders as they enjoyed a period of unprecedented prosperity and relative status.

The Economy

By the 1840s, Brazil had become more integrated into the Atlantic economy, with nationwide exports more than doubling to 55,032 contos in the fiscal year 1849–50. Yet, with the devaluation of the milréis, the value of exports per head in pounds sterling actually declined slightly from 1 to 0.8.[2] In other words, Brazil as a whole had yet to enter its most dynamic phase of export growth, although the center of gravity in the economy was shifting from the sugar-producing regions of northeastern Brazil toward the Southeast, and Rio de Janeiro in particular.

The regional differentiation of Brazil's exports helps explain how Rio de Janeiro captured more than its share of export-oriented growth over this period. In 1821, Brazil exported 704,000 pounds sterling worth of coffee, mostly from the port of Rio; by 1849–50, this value had nearly quadrupled to 2,462,000 pounds sterling—again, mostly shipped through the capital.[3] As coffee became king, especially in the Paraíba Valley of Rio Province, the city reaped vast rewards from funding coffee planters, shipping coffee, and providing planters with ever more slaves. Slave imports into Rio rose dramatically in the 1840s, averaging about 36,125 per annum between 1844 and 1850, with many destined for the interior of the province or for neighboring states such as Minas Gerais and São Paulo.[4] At the same time, a great number of slaves remained in the city itself. Although the urban slave population did not grow as quickly as the free, it nearly doubled from 40,376 in 1821 to 78,855 in 1849.[5]

Work

The types of jobs and the social groups that worked them changed little from the 1820s through the 1840s. What did change, however, was the expansion of the urban milieu and with it the employment opportunities for Rio's middle groups. According to the census of 1834, midway between our two periods, there were 789 tavern keepers in the city—nearly a tavern for every one hundred residents. Merchants, agents, and clerks proliferated, as did employment in the manual trades. Free men of color, of which Antonio Dutra was one in 1834, found work at all levels, accounting for 22 percent of employed males enumerated in the census.[6]

As for the occupations of urban slaves, evidence from newspaper advertisements indicates a two-tier system in which domestic slaves were generally hired by the month and others, such as artisans and day laborers, were contracted on shorter, less formal terms.[7] Among domestics, female slaves predominated, with most advertisements offering washerwomen, cooks, and the like. In a minority of cases, these domestics were advertised with the stipulation that they restrict their labor to the household, perhaps reflecting their owner's concern that they not be allowed to run free in the streets. Male domestics were almost always advertised as cooks. The nature of domestic work appears to have lent itself to monthly contracts: the labor was continuous and not aimed at the completion of discrete projects.

In order to better understand the labor market for slaves in Rio de Janeiro in Dutra's time, I analyzed rental and sale data from the *Jornal do Commercio*, the leading paper in the capital in the years 1840 and 1850. The 1840 sample, culled from the months of January and July, reveals a complex rental and sale market. Owners of urban slaves needed to match their slaves with prospective renters or buyers, and they turned to newspaper advertisements to accomplish this. According to Carvalho de Mello's research, focusing on the 1870s, the cost of advertising amounted to about 7.5 percent of the gross earnings of slaves.[8] Because advertising was relatively expensive, few owners placed advertisements for short-term rentals. Day labor, performed by skilled or unskilled slaves, most of whom were male, was not generally advertised. Instead, the rental market revealed in the newspaper advertisements was tilted toward female slaves and male slaves performing tasks on a monthly basis.

The types of jobs performed by rental slaves (leaving aside day laborers) were quite varied according to the samples for 1840 and 1850. Male slaves were most often advertised as cooks and less frequently in many other occupations; female slaves worked predominantly as laundresses, cooks, wet nurses, and general domestics. On the whole, male slaves had a more varied run of occupations whereas female slaves tended to be advertised with more than one occupation specified. Detailed samples analyzed by Kari Zimmerman for 1850 show that only 3 percent of male slaves were advertised with three or more occupations whereas 33 percent of female slaves were so advertised.[9] In effect, female slaves were expected to work as general domestics, washing, cooking, and cleaning, while their male counterparts tended to specialize.

The scale of the slave rental market in Rio de Janeiro must have been large. The samples employed in this analysis were drawn from just one newspaper, yet an average of twenty-five rental notices were published each Sunday throughout the year. The same slaves may have been advertised more than once. Yet, by the same token, other slaves were advertised in competing papers, and still more were rented through commission houses and personal contacts without recourse to the ad pages. In the end, thousands of slaves were actively cycled through the rental market in a given year.

From a cultural perspective, the existence of a rental market for domestic slaves provides powerful indirect evidence of the pervasiveness of the idea that the economies of middling households required certain tasks to be performed by servants. Although we lack specific information on the status of renters, we can be relatively certain that, in the case of domestic slave rentals, they were not generally themselves, slaveholders. Otherwise, they would own their own domestic and dispense with the cost of renting. For these renters, the cultural commitment to obtaining servants ran against their own long-run economic interests. The yearly rental rate for a cook cum washerwoman was roughly one-third of the purchase price of the same; doing one's own wash for three years would suffice to save to purchase a domestic servant outright. Now, many slaveholders must have rented additional slaves as the need arose: a cook could fall ill or die and, as a short-term solution, a replacement could be hired.

From newspaper advertisements, there is no evidence of large-scale slave rental operations. At most, two or three slaves were offered for rent at one time (sales were another matter, and entire lots of slaves were sometimes auctioned off).[10] Indeed, this finding is in keeping with observed numbers of slaves per owner in the urban environment. During the period 1845–49 the mean number of slaves held by fully urban—defined as not owning rural property—slaveholders was just over seven.[11] The residences of advertisers, likewise, were distributed throughout the urban center of the city—although a few streets appear to have been particularly important for the rental market.[12]

Turning to the market for slave sales, day laborers and skilled manual workers were advertised with much less frequency. When they appeared, they were more likely to be offered for sale than for rent.[13] Although the information at hand does not allow us to reach any definitive conclusions, it appears that the rental market for day labor operated on an informal and ad hoc basis: slaves were hired for discrete projects as needed, and there was no need for monthly contracts or newspaper advertisements. Those slaves who were sold through newspaper advertisements were, for the most part, similar to those rented out—with the exception that more skilled male slaves were offered for sale than for rent and few wet nurses were offered for sale. We have already speculated that skilled male slaves were rented on an ad hoc basis for short-term work as carpenters and masons owing to the discrete nature of their tasks. It made no sense to rent a carpenter on a monthly basis (and the vast majority of advertisements are monthly) when a job could be done in a week. The logic behind the prevalence of rental rather than sale among wet nurses is similar, if the other side of the coin. Renting a wet nurse made sense because, although the period of performance was finite, it was quite long enough to justify monthly rentals. However, purchasing a wet nurse made less sense, given that demand for her labor did not extend long enough to justify a full purchase price.

Both rental and sale notices reveal something about the mentality of slaveholders and prospective renters and buyers. In the short space allotted them, advertisers took care to portray their slaves in the best possible light. Slaves in these moments are referred to in glowing terms. Gentle, caring, reliable, intelligent, and morally upstanding are just some of the attributes listed alongside occupations and rental rates. These positive attributes, in a sense, are one side of the Janus-faced system of slavery in nineteenth-century Brazil. Slaves were and could be all of these things—sometimes genuinely, sometimes out of calculated self-interest. When presenting their slaves to prospective buyers and renters, slaveholders' self-interest led them to refer to their slaves in glowing terms. We will never know how sincere any of these declarations of esteem were, and we are right to doubt them. Yet they are there, in the record, where at the very least they illuminate for us some of the rhetoric of slavery in urban Brazil.

Perhaps more indicative of slaveholders' true feelings are the many advertisements for runaways, printed alongside their upbeat assessments of their slaves for sale. The language used in these advertisements produces the opposite picture of owners' feelings about their slaves. In these instances, slaves are referred to as ugly, deformed, calculating, and dishonest. Runaway advertisements, as Gilberto Freyre noticed, are rife with detailed physical descriptions of slaves.[14] For example, the runaway Alexandrina is described in the following, almost clinical detail, in an advertisement from January 3, 1870:

> The slave Alexandrina continues to be a fugitive, [her] face is long, thin, and ugly, with dark circles under her eyes, and an upturned nose, [she] lacks some teeth, has high curly hair, is taller than average, with a strong body, and walks upright with a languid pace, [she] is 36 to 40 years old, was reported seen in Nictheroy (Niterói, capital of Rio Province) with cut hair, wearing shoes, and claiming she is manumitted.[15]

Not all advertisements for runaways were this detailed, but nearly all of them gave a combination of physical descriptions and psychological profiles.

It is impossible to miss the tone of outrage mixed with disdain in these advertisements. By running away, slaves undercut the carefully balanced market for slave rentals and sales in the city. In the aggregate, most slaves did not run away, and many probably conformed, at least superficially, to the glowing stereotypes printed in the rental and sale advertisements; yet, for an individual owner, a runaway was a social and financial disaster, especially among poorer slaveholders who relied entirely on income from their slaves to sustain themselves and their families.

Social Categories

An equally important phenomenon in relation to slavery, for our purposes, was the rise of the population of freed persons in Rio de Janeiro. Although we lack specific data for 1821, by 1849, there were 10,732 freedmen and -women resident in the city—about 5 percent of the total population.[16] Prior to his death, Antonio José Dutra was one of them.

The social status of freed persons was complicated by several factors. Although they were not constrained from owning property and participating at some level in civil society, they were also discriminated against in some mutual aid societies dominated by the free (such as the Santa Casa) and relegated to a few stereotypical occupations. Barbering, as we have noted, was the preserve of freedmen and slaves.[17] In fact, barbering and music went hand in hand in nineteenth-century Brazil, and barber's bands played popular tunes throughout the country.[18]

The foreign-born free population was also rising, although it was far from reaching the levels it would in the 1870s and beyond. In 1849, there were 36,320 free foreigners resident in the city, of which 28,936 were male. The sex ratio for the foreign-born free population was actually higher than for the foreign-born slave population—making Rio de Janeiro a male-dominated city in demographic as well as social and cultural terms. Foreigners predominated in petty commerce, as clerks, and played a major role in the business elite.[19] The locally born predominated at the top of public administration and property ownership, and they held a slight edge in absolute terms in commerce.[20]

As the nineteenth century wore on, the social categories of Rio de Janeiro became increasingly identified by explicit markers. Where one lived and what one wore became more important; social status became increasingly legible and constrained. Proper clothing, for the elite, became a barometer of civilization and social status in spite of the fact that "proper" meant layers of undergarments and heavy topcoats of wool, singularly unsuited for the climate.[21] Perhaps the most significant manifestation of the rising differentiation of social groups in Rio de Janeiro is found in the shifting urban milieu. By the time of Dutra's death, the city had already become a wealthier, more urbane, and stratified place, where the gap between the middle groups and the elite was widening. In the ensuing decades this process would accelerate.

Location: The Expanded Urban Milieu

Rapid population growth and the physical expansion of the city into previously rural zones continued the process of residential differentiation observed in the 1820s. Differentiation on the basis of price and along the lines of racial and occupational categories emerges clearly from census and estate record data. The relative concentration of slaves varied significantly by neighborhood and the price per square meter of housing depended greatly on location.

Table 2

Freedpersons and Residential Segregation in Rio de Janeiro, c. 1849

Neighborhood	Freedpersons resident	Freedpersons as percent of free	Slaves per household
Candelaria	194	2	4.68
Engenho Velho	1,367	12	4.09
Gloria	723	8	4.64
Lagoa	504	7	4.14
Sacramento	2,206	8	2.81
Santa Anna	2,687	10	2.95
Santa Rita	1,413	7	4.15
São José	1,638	10	3.88

Source: Karasch, *Slave Life*, p. 66, Table 3.6, drawn from the Census of 1849.

◈◈◈◈

Of the eight districts in Rio de Janeiro, Candelária, in the center, retained its relatively expensive character in the 1840s—although it was losing its place as a residential neighborhood for the elite and its large, two-storied sobrados were being converted into businesses, with shops on the ground floor and offices or lodgings above.[22] One measure of exclusivity is the proportion of freed persons resident in a district relative to its free and slave populations. In Candelária, there were a mere 194 freed persons in a sea of 9,949 free persons and 8,450 slaves. Expressed as a percentage of the total free population, freed persons made up a mere 2 percent. In contrast, freed persons accounted for 10 percent or more of the free population of the districts of Engenho Velho, Santa Anna, and São José.

The lessons to be drawn from this analysis are mixed. First, although it is clear that the wealthier (or at least more expensive) neighborhoods, such as Candelária and Glória, had relatively fewer freed persons as residents and a relatively high ratio of slaves to total households, it is also evident that the institution of slavery itself was rather homogeneous throughout the city. There was differentiation on the basis of class and property values, but even the poorer districts exhibit a fairly high ratio of slaves to households. Only the poorer neighborhoods of Sacramento and Santa Anna come in with a ratio below three-to-one in slaves to total households. Slavery permeated all sectors of society and all neighborhoods of Rio de Janeiro in Dutra's time.

As was the case in the 1820s, the rural periphery remained far cheaper, on the whole, than the central neighborhoods, although new

Illustration 12. *The population of the interior regions surrounding the urban core of Rio de Janeiro often lived in very humble abodes. Their wealth was often concentrated less in housing and real estate and more in slaves. (Jean Baptiste Debret,* Voyage Pittoresque et Historique au Brésil, *3 volumes, Paris, 1834–1839).*

neighborhoods to the South, such as Botafogo, took on an aristocratic cast from the 1820s onward as the elite of the city began to build a new style of urban abode (often known as *solares*) in what became "residential" neighborhoods.[23] A study of the 175 addresses listed in the estate sample for 1845–49, helps clarify the structure of Rio's expanded urban milieu. The analysis moves inward, from rural, to transitional, to historically urban districts.

Housing values in rural districts still averaged less than 1:000$000. Houses in Iraja could be bought for 750$000 to 940$000; other rural properties could be found for as little as 400$000. Nevertheless, districts like Engenho Novo appear to have been the sites of significant appreciation. Houses as cheap as 800$000 could still be found there, on the edge of Rio's urban core, but other houses were listed at 3:550$000. One property, in Engenho Velho, was appraised at 9:000$000.[24]

In the intermediate neighborhoods, which had been mainly rural in the 1820s but had now taken on an urban cast, prices were still significantly lower than in the city center. Antonio Dutra's two houses on Rua do Saco do Alferes, in the somewhat dodgy neighborhood of Gamboa, were worth 1:800$000 and 3:000$000 respectively. Nineteen small houses on Rua São Cristovão, not far from Dutra's, averaged

1:268 mil-réis each. Although these prices, nearer to the city center, were too high for the poorest workers to purchase a home, the rents were probably within reach of even unskilled urban laborers.[25]

Prices in the core neighborhoods of Candelária, Santa Anna, Sacramento, São José, and Gloria all saw considerable increase from the 1820s to the 1840s. A casa de sobrado in Candelária could go for as much as 20 contos, and houses in the newly settled neighborhood of Botafogo, along the beach to the South of the city center, ranged from 6 to 50 contos. Buildings on the venerable Rua da Alfândega went for 5 to 12 contos.[26] Not all residences in the city center were so expensive, however, and many others were subdivided and rented out to multiple families or were multiple-use buildings with shops on the ground floor and residences above.

In general terms, if the rural and semirural bands around the outskirts of the city are expressed in terms of kilometers from the urban core, residential prices seem to fall into the following three categories: rural-low (ten or more kilometers from center, ranging from 400–1:000$000); semirural-medium (ten to two kilometers from the center, ranging from 800–4:000$000); urban-high (within about two kilometers of the bay in the business district, extending south to the neighborhoods of Botafogo and Glória, costing 3–4:000$000 up to 20:000$000 or more).

Rio de Janeiro's businesses were distributed throughout the city in differentiated, yet mixed, fashion, just as were its residential neighborhoods. An analysis of 2,230 business establishments listed in the 1845 *Almanak administrativo [Laemmert]* (a nineteenth-century city directory) clearly indicates clusters of enterprises by neighborhood and street. General stores, selling *secos e molhados* (dry and fresh foods), were concentrated along Rua do Rosario in the old city center; businessmen, listed as *negociantes*, clustered on Rua Direita; many doctors and lawyers based themselves on Rua do Cano; and the city's central shopping street was, by the 1840s, Rua do Ouvidor, where the middle and upper classes shopped for clothing and fancy European baubles.[27]

Notwithstanding these clusters along certain streets, the impression of commerce in Rio de Janeiro in Dutra's time mirrors residential patterns: clusters of certain enterprises, like clusters of wealth, remained embedded in a broader urban fabric that mixed rich and poor, slave and free, lawyers and shopkeepers in the hustle and bustle of the city center. Few streets in the old center went wanting at least one lawyer and doctor; most were also home to a variety of shops and service establishments. Indeed, many of the large old sobrados in the old center were home to multiple businesses and residences. For example, Rua Direita, number 65, was home to four different businesses, including a shipping company, a metal dealer, and two brokers.[28] Multiple tenants were the norm in the larger buildings near the city center.

Class Structure in the 1840s

Dutra's world, circa 1849, was one of modest but quickening economic growth. This growth fueled the rise of entrepreneurs like Dutra and gave them the wherewithal to purchase slaves. Slavery permeated all of Rio de Janeiro; there was no neighborhood in which slaves were largely absent and no social group with a minimum of buying power that did not seek to acquire slaves. Moreover, freedmen like Dutra were scattered throughout the city, many with slaves of their own.

From the 1820s through the 1840s, Brazil suffered through a series of inflationary cycles. The mil-réis, which traded at 4.898 to the pound sterling in 1822, had fallen to 9.275 to the pound in 1849, with the bulk of the deterioration coming in the 1820s.[29] The exchange rate remained fairly stable and even strengthened during the 1830s, whereas it depreciated at very moderate pace for much of the 1840s. Prices for food and housing rose even faster than the mil-réis fell over the course of this period.[30] In this context, it is hard to say that real economic improvement was felt by the greater part of the population of the city. Mean real wealth per decedent was higher in 1849, but not dramatically so, than it had been circa 1820.

Yet, a series of factors converged to make the 1830s and 1840s a particularly good period for middling wealthholders. First, inflation, which had run very high in the late 1820s, proceeded at a slower pace.[31] Second, real wages for skilled urban workers appear to have risen slightly over the same period.[32] Third, wealthholders who had entered the game in the 1830s or before faced a buoyant market in urban property and slaves. This cut both ways, however, as rising house and slave prices raised the barrier to entry to aspiring wealthholders in the course of the decade. Notwithstanding this last factor, the economic and social environment of the 1830s and 1840s favored the expansion of the middle groups in Rio de Janeiro. The tipping point, which would begin to reverse these gains and place the city on a trajectory toward greater inequality and social polarization, was yet to come in the 1850s.

If the aggregate figures showed little improvement, Antonio Dutra's finances probably never looked better than in 1849 when he sat down to dictate his last will and testament. He was the owner of thirteen slaves when the median urban-type owner in Rio owned five; he owned two urban residences; and he was the father of a growing family on which his property would settle. Here, Dutra's wealth is placed in the context of wealthholding in the late 1840s. The aim of this analysis, beyond placing Dutra in his milieu, is to set the stage for subsequent chapters wherein Dutra's world is shown to have disappeared in the decade following his death, replaced by a social and economic structure in Rio de Janeiro that will be familiar, in many respects, to the version depicted in the standard literature.

Postmortem estate inventories are the richest source of information on material conditions and social structures in nineteenth-century Brazil. The same caveats regarding the use of these documents apply here, and interested readers are encouraged to dip into the appendix should they desire further detail on the construction of the samples and their reliability and interpretation.[33] Briefly here, to reiterate, these records are not perfectly representative of all wealthholders, although they are fairly close. Many households owned no wealth to speak of, and we can only make an educated guess as to the proportion of wealthholders to impoverished residents of Rio. The age of the decedents in the estate inventories cannot be assumed to be representative of the age of the potential wealthholding population at large. Finally, high outliers (the very rich) have a tendency to skew the results of estate inventory analysis. Notwithstanding these limitations, estate inventories provide excellent coverage of a full range of social groups, including Dutra's own.

In the context of wealthholding in his time, Dutra was well-to-do. His net estate was appraised at 13:187$280, whereas the value of the mean estate in the period was 19:450$000 (all values expressed in constant 1850 mil-réis).[34] Owing to the concentration of wealth in Rio at the time, his total estate placed him above the 30th percentile of wealthholders. When we account for the many potential wealthholders with minimal possessions who were not inventoried, Dutra's social position would rise further to the 15th percentile or higher, assuming, in this case, that 50 percent of households held no wealth. Looking deeper, it is evident that Dutra's wealth represented the fortunes of Rio de Janeiro's middle sector at the time of his death.

Urban real estate made up the preponderance of wealth in Rio de Janeiro in the late 1840s, with 47 percent of the total—although this figure may be a bit out of line owing to the smaller size of the estate sample for this period; for Dutra, residential property accounted for nearly 40 percent of his wealth. Of all forms of wealth, housing was one of the most unevenly distributed: 67 percent of wealthholders

Table 3

Wealth in Rio de Janeiro: 1845–1849

	N obs.	N Slaves	Urban Real Estate	Slaves	Rural Property	Cash and Bank Deposits	Stocks and Bonds	Business Assets	Debts	Credits	Furn. and Precious Metals	Other	Total
Total	116	1,142	939,534	382,556	233,409	192,239	179,225	77,455	-326,261	441,326	92,868	43,851	2,256,202
Mean		9.8	8,099	3,298	2,012	1,657	1,545	668	-2,813	3,805	801	378	19,450
% of Total			42	17	10	9	8	3	-14	20	4	2	100

Source: Estate Inventories, Arquivo Nacional, Rio de Janeiro.
Note: Values reported in constant (see Table 1) 1850 mil-réis.

owned urban residences, yet the wealthiest owner's houses were worth 157:000$000, and the poorest owner's domicile was worth just 189$000. The coefficient of variation of housing wealth was higher than all other forms of wealth save business assets and credits (*dívidas ativas*). Ownership of real estate, not slaves or rural property, formed the basis of the city's great fortunes. Indeed, this had been the case from the very beginning, as João Fragoso's analysis of notarial records from Rio de Janeiro in the early years of the nineteenth century makes clear. During the years 1800–16, notarized sales of urban buildings outweighed rural transactions by a ratio of two-to-one; and nearly half of all purchasers in this sample already owned at least one property.[35] Having said this, the 1840s marked the high point for middling homeowners relative to their wealthy counterparts. Whereas the top 20 percent of estates controlled 78 percent of urban real estate in the 1820s, this had fallen to 67 percent in the late 1840s—although the smaller 1840s sample precludes us from drawing any firm conclusions from this apparent swing.

Wealth in the form of slaves was more evenly distributed than any other category. Eighty percent of wealthholders owned at least one slave, and slaves made up 17 percent of total wealth—a proportion that was to represent the high point over the period 1815–60. Slavery tended to equalize wealthholding among the free population, whereas financial assets (and to a lesser degree housing) tended to worsen the distribution. The higher prices of slaves in the 1830s and 1840s, however, apparently dampened the incidence of ownership, as the percentage of slaveholders among all decedents fell from 88 to 80 percent. This ratio was to fall even further in the 1850s, when slave prices more than doubled. The middle 60 percent of the distribution lost a little ground in terms of slave wealth relative to the top 20 percent. In the 1820s, the middle groups held 44.9 percent of all slave wealth, whereas they held 39.9 percent in the late 1840s. This dip proved short-lived, as their share rose back to 44 percent of total slave wealth in the 1850s. All in all, these fluctuations are too small to reach any definitive conclusions about the function of slave wealth in shifting the status of middling wealthholders. The constant fact was that slaves, more than any other form of wealth, were broadly distributed throughout the upper and middle reaches of Carioca society from the 1820s through the 1850s.

Two findings derived from the data presented thus far are particularly salient for understanding the context in which Antonio Dutra and others of his social level built their fortunes. First, it is clear that growth was tepid over the first decades of the empire, but owners of slaves and residences, who made up the majority of wealthholders, saw substantial gains as Rio de Janeiro urbanized and began to participate more fully in the Atlantic economy. Second, the cost of entry into wealthholding was substantially lower circa 1820 than in the late 1840s. The prices of slaves and houses were relatively low in 1820, and inflation had yet to erode the purchasing power of the middle sectors. If we assume that Dutra began to accumulate wealth in this lower-cost environment, it is easier to credit his subsequent rise to relative wealth at the time of his death. Likewise, had he obtained his freedom in 1849, he would have faced far higher prices and much greater difficulty in building his estate, as we shall see in the analysis of wealth in the 1850s presented in Chapter 4.[36]

The middling wealthholders of Rio de Janeiro are, with Antonio Dutra, the core subjects of this book. How had the fortunes of this group changed over the first decades of the empire, and what are some of the chief characteristics of wealthholding at this level? The analysis proceeds along three lines. First, general comparisons are made between the periods 1815–25 and 1845–49, highlighting the changing components of middle-sector wealth over time. Second, nominal characteristics, such as civil status and place of residence are accounted for in both periods. Third, and last, detailed case studies are presented to form a typology of middling wealth during the first decades of the empire.

The rise in value of certain forms of wealth, such as urban residences and slaves, was marked over the first decades of the empire by whatever measure. The mean slaveholder saw an increase of 32 percent; meanwhile, homeowners' mean wealth in residences grew 9 percent. In the middle 60 percent of the distribution of wealthholders, the rise in these categories was 33 and 110 percent respectively. Mean wealth overall grew 27 percent, whereas the mean holdings of the middle 60 percent grew 39 percent. The performance of slave and residential assets over the period 1820 to 1850 was remarkable, and wealthholders in the middle 60 percent of the distribution benefited disproportionately from the run up in asset prices. This seemingly minor shifting of wealth from the top to the middle of the distribution nevertheless indicates an important aspect of economy and society in Rio de Janeiro during the period 1820 to 1850—its relatively greater openness and social mobility compared to the period that came before and the period that began in 1850 with the definitive suppression of the slave trade.

The middle sector was far more dependent on slaveholding than were the wealthy. This fact is crucial to understanding social structure

Table 4

Housing Wealth by Class of Wealthholder, Rio de Janeiro, 1840s

	Wealthy	Upper middling	Lower middling
Total Value (mil-réis)	697,050	97,803	26,686
Mean House Value	4,944	5,148	1,779
Median House Value	3,000	3,500	1,800
N Houses	141	19	15
N Houses per Owner	7	1.3	1.15

Source: Estate Inventories, Rio de Janeiro, AN.
Definitions: Wealthy = top quintile of wealthholders; Upper Middling = second
    quintile; Lower Middling = third quintile
Note: Values expressed in current mil-réis.

in mid-nineteenth-century Brazil and the context within which Dutra lived and prospered. For the very wealthy, slaves were overshadowed by two other forms of wealth: urban residences and financial assets. Rich residents of Rio de Janeiro generally owned more than one house, and often owned dozens.

Because housing prices were high and much of the market was already controlled by the very wealthy, the middle sector invested more heavily in slaves than did their wealthier counterparts. Houses provided a similar return compared to slaves over the long run, but slaves were available in great quantities and much lower prices during the 1820s and 1830s, and even 1840s, when the wealth of the 1840s was being accumulated. This is not to say that middling wealthholders did not invest in real property. In the top third of the middle sector, wealth in houses grew dramatically. All told, however, slaves were about twice as important for middling wealthholders in terms of the composition of their estates as for the rich. Note, along these lines, that the poorest 20 percent of wealthholders depended enormously on slaves for wealth—slaves were really the only productive assets they could afford, as a second house for rental purposes or sophisticated financial assets were beyond their purchasing power.

Slavery and Middling Wealth:
The Logic of Dutra's World

The attraction of slaves as investments for middling wealthholders becomes clearer when we consider the rate of return on slave rentals.

Throughout Brazil, researchers have provided estimates of rates of return ranging from 10 to 20 percent. Calculating the rate of return is complicated by the fact that urban slaves earned wages and remitted only part of what they received to their owners, who, in turn, picked up some but not all of the costs of their maintenance as well as advertising and commission fees. Bergad's estimate of a rate of return of about 20 percent for Minas Gerais circa 1844 may be too high, given that it is unclear how he has accounted for the division of wages between slaves and masters.[37] Carvalho de Mello's estimates of returns on coffee plantations in Rio de Janeiro suffer from a different possible defect: he calculates the return on the most expensive class of slaves—males aged twenty to twenty-nine—and reports returns ranging from 11.5 to 15 percent per annum.[38] Naturally, as Bergad points out, had Carvalho de Mello included cheaper slaves in the slightly younger and older age bands (that is, the fifteen to forty age group), he would have found a higher rate of return.[39] Then again, playing this game, one could include all slaves and get a lower rate of return owing to the net losses associated with children, the lame, and the elderly. In both instances, the authors do not explicitly distinguish between the hire rate and the actual remittances to owners, although Carvalho de Mello does provide detailed information on the number of days worked and the cost of clothing, food, medical care, and housing for slaves.[40]

In an example from 1818, where we have information on the hire rate and price of a slave in Rio de Janeiro, the return, calculated along the same lines as in Bergad, accounting for wage retention/upkeep costs on the part of slaves, was about 20 percent per annum—assuming the slave in this case, appraised at 160$000, worked 250 days at $320, paid for his own upkeep from half of his earnings, and remitted the rest (minus tax, commission, and advertising fees).[41]

Additional information on hire rates is available in newspaper advertisements. A small sample (N=12) of hire rates for domestic slaves culled from the *Jornal do Commercio* in 1849 yields a mean monthly hire rate of 12$250 for cooks, laundresses, and washerwomen.[42] These advertisements do not provide the price or age of the slaves in question, so we can only approximate the implicit rate of return on these rentals. Nevertheless, knowing that the mean price of an adult slave circa 1849 was about 400$000, we can calculate a rough "guesstimate" return of 147$000 per year, resulting in "profits" of 58$800 (15 percent) to the owner net of retained wages on the part of the slave assuming that 60 percent of all earnings go to maintenance and retained wages of the slaves.

To be sure, this figure in many ways represents the best-case scenario from the point of view of both parties. The slave might have kept a smaller portion of her wages or been forced by circumstance to pay a higher price for food or lodging; the owner, by definition as an advertiser, probably could not expect to rent out his or her slave for a full twelve months, and would have to pay advertising costs. On top of this, the slave could fall ill or the renter could fail to pay (although this problem was often resolved at the outset by demanding payment in advance). Even so, a lot would have to go wrong in a given year for the rate of return to fall below that of the next-best alternative.[43]

Given what we know about returns to other assets, slave owners earned a significant premium over alternative investments during the years in which their slaves were at their peak earning potential. A small sample of rental properties in Rio de Janeiro in 1855, drawn from a single estate inventory, yields an average return of 7 percent per annum in rents.[44] The selection of this case was determined by the fact that *all* the decedent's properties were accounted for, allowing us to estimate the overall rate of return on residential property for an owner with a diversified portfolio of real estate investments. Other estate inventories provide information about rents for some but not all of their properties, rendering an estimate of the overall return problematic.

As the analysis of the rental data makes clear, the return varied greatly from property to property, depending, in some cases, on the physical condition of the home. In addition, there is little evidence, at least in this case, for higher returns based on more desirable properties (measured in terms of mil-réis per square palmo)—in fact, the highest returns were attained from the two least expensive properties, located in the Ladeira do Livramento, in a working-class district; the third-highest return was found in Rua do Saco do Alferes (today Rua América), Antonio Dutra's own street. The more expensive homes, in Rua da Imperatriz, returned less. A corollary to this, on which we can only speculate given the data at hand, is that poorer residents of Rio de Janeiro probably paid more, per square meter, for inferior housing. Of course, the calculations presented above do not include the capital gains that homeowners saw with rapidly appreciating real estate values. Yet, the rate of increase in the value of housing and slaves was virtually identical over the period in question, so we can be relatively certain that, on the whole, slaves returned more than houses over the medium term.

In the long run, slaves "depreciated" substantially in value, ending up at zero and wiping out the capital gains obtained, on paper, during their more productive years in times of rapidly rising slave prices. Over the course of *many* years, houses were probably as good or better investments than slaves. Nevertheless, it would seem that most investors, if given the choice between earning 15 percent with slaves and 7 percent with real estate, would choose the former. Why, then, do we not see estates of urban slave owners with scores of slaves?

Essentially, two factors determined the size of slaveholding relative to other forms of wealth: accessibility and the optimal size of holdings in an urban environment. First, slaves were cheaper and hence more accessible than urban real estate, the other leading form of wealth. Thus, more wealthholders owned slaves than houses, and more poor and middling wealthholders depended on slaves for the bulk of their estates. Because slaves yielded such high returns at least through the 1870s, nearly all wealthholders, richer and poorer alike, owned slaves and benefited from their exploitation.

The second factor determining the size and prevalence of slaveholding, after accessibility, was the optimal scale of slaveholding in an urban environment. In this regard, three factors account for the prevalence of medium-sized holdings over the long run: housing costs, slave agency, and slave frailty. Clearly, in an expensive city like Rio de Janeiro, there were limits to how many slaves an owner could possess based on the size of his or her property and the availability of alternative space in the rental market. Although it would technically be possible for an owner to place scores of slaves in rental housing, the monitoring costs associated with slave agency would have constrained this option.

Slave agency played a significant role in limiting the overall size of slaveholdings, placing a ceiling on how many slaves an individual or family could conceivably control and discipline. Even when slaves apparently "accommodated" their condition, their actions may have limited the scope of their master's authority.[45] Owners were restrained by slave's demands for relative autonomy to live and work in the urban environment. Keeping tabs on half-a-dozen slaves in the hurly burly of Rio de Janeiro's busy streets was a tall order; monitoring costs were simply too high for individual families to maintain control of scores of urban slaves.[46] The extent to which urban slaveholders depended on a repressive police force for enforcement of their property rights and assistance in monitoring their slaves testifies to the difficulty in maintaining social control.[47] Slave agency manifest itself in many ways, perhaps the most powerful of which was the choice by a significant number of slaves to opt out of the system by running away.[48]

Slave runaways were a fixture in newspaper advertisements in Rio de Janeiro. The rate at which slaves ran away is impossible to determine with precision, and the occupations and locations of residence of runaway slaves are also hard to pin down. Nevertheless, a sample of runaway-slave advertisements from Dutra's time, circa 1840, yields suggestive results regarding these questions. To begin with, slaves ran away at an alarming rate during the 1840s. In January alone, seventy-two runaways were advertised in the *Jornal do Commercio*. Caution must be taken when interpreting this figure, however, because a significant number of these slaves were runaways from small towns and plantations in the region surrounding Rio de Janeiro and beyond.[49] In any event, dozens of slaves in the city itself most likely ran away in the course of a given month.

Ideally, it would be possible to show that runaways were progressively more likely as the size of slaveholdings increased. This would confirm the hypothesis that slave agency in the form of flight (and shirking and stealing for that matter) limited the optimal size of slaveholdings in the city of Rio de Janeiro, given urban slaves greater mobility and their tendency to live and work out of the view of their owners for extended periods of time. Unfortunately, such information is lacking, and the hypothesis remains untested by data.

We do have information from runaway advertisements that allow for a rough description of the types of slaves that ran away. In the sample collected for 1840, most runaways were male, accounting for 105 out of 123 individuals; most were also of African birth, accounting for 53 out of the 75 instances in which race and place of birth could be reasonably ascertained. The average age of a runaway was just over twenty-two years old—precisely at the age when slaves were entering their peak earning years.[50] Faced with the loss of valuable slaves like these, owners often explicitly offered rewards for the capture and return of their bondsmen. In the 1840 sample, few advertisements stated the precise monetary reward, but those that did stipulated an average of about 40$000, or 11 percent of the average sale price of slaves advertised in the same year.[51]

If slave agency provided the ceiling, slave frailty provided the floor to the optimal size of holdings in Rio de Janeiro. Most owners sought to own more than one slave, not just because the returns were high, but also because the risk that went with high returns was also quite elevated. Over the course of a slave's lifetime, the risk of sickness or death loomed large. Many estate inventories list a substantial portion of their owner's slaves as sick or disabled.[52] Antonio Dutra's heirs, for instance, were saddled with extensive medical bills and lost income from sick days when their father's slaves fell ill in 1850.[53] Although the terminology of finance appears unseemly with regard to the institution of slavery, there is no doubt that slaveholders knew that their investments in individual slaves were risky and that they sought to "diversify" their investment with the purchase of other slaves. Once they had accumulated ten to twenty slaves, they then sought out other investments.

It also made sense to own more than one slave inasmuch as most owners expected to be served in their own home by a domestic cook and laundress. Indeed, as Lauderdale Graham points out, "The culturally preferred image of a household called for numerous servants."[54] To be sure, only the relatively well off could afford them, but middling wealthholders of the 1840s were, almost always, waited on by at least one slave in the home. For instance, Dutra owned, along with twelve income-generating slaves, one female domestic. In order to realize the high rates of return, an owner had to rent out or otherwise employ his or her slaves. By definition, a domestic serving the owner's own household would not be able to earn anything approaching rates of 10 to 20 percent, as his or her labor was restricted to the home and augmented, at best, by taking in some washing or other tasks from neighbors without slaves.

The value of domestic work for slave owners and renters of such services must have been high indeed. Domestic slaves toiled throughout the day, cleaning, lending a hand in cooking, washing clothes, and otherwise serving their masters. Lacking any of the modern conveniences of domestic life, this work must have been hard, dull, and tiresome. No "respectable" family in the city wanted to see its own members doing this sort of work, so we must take care to recognize the economic value of this generally unremunerated work.

Overall, these findings regarding the size of slaveholdings make sense inasmuch as slaveholders faced greater risks. Urban real estate, for example, could burn down or fall apart without proper maintenance; but, on the whole, it was a much more secure investment. It could not run away, abscond with its wages, fall sick, or die. Slaves were popular investments, particularly among middling wealthholders, because they were relatively cheap and provided a relatively high return in compensation for greater risk. Higher up the social scale, wealthholders substituted more secure and equally attractive, over the long run, real estate assets rather than continue to invest in slaves. This helps explain the equilibrium attained between these two asset classes over time: otherwise, if slaves really did return anything on the order of 15 percent, we would have to conclude that Rio's wealthiest residents were irrational investors in low-yield real estate.

This analysis also helps explain the difference between middling and rich estates in terms of the ratio of slave wealth to other components. On average, a family pursued a strategy of accumulating slaves up to the optimal size of holdings in Rio de Janeiro: slaves were accessible and yielded the highest return. Richer wealthholders doubtlessly would have liked to increase the high-yielding slave component of their estate but were prevented from doing so by the monitoring costs and negative scale economies in the urban milieu. To the extent that the very wealthy invested in slaves above and beyond the optimal scale for the urban environment, they located these slaves in rural plantation settings where monitoring and discipline were easier and scores of slaves could be exploited.

The primary distinctions between rich and middling wealthholders turned not on the ownership of slaves, which they both owned in roughly equal numbers, but, rather, on the ownership of residential rental property and financial assets. To illustrate this difference, consider the cases of Gregorio José de Abreu and Ignacio Caetano de Araujo, two wealthy men in our sample. Gregorio's net estate was valued at 149 contos, of which houses accounted for 134 contos or 90 percent; meanwhile, the total value of his slaves came to 6 contos. Gregorio's primary residence, on Rua Areal (canto da Rua Formosa, Campo d'Acclamação), was worth 28 contos. Along with his primary residence, he owned fifteen other houses throughout the city— including houses in the center of the city and in the beach neighborhoods of Botafogo and Flamengo.[55] Gregorio's estate exemplifies the wealth of the traditional property-owning elite as it developed in the *first half* of the nineteenth century: the vast bulk of his estate was in urban real estate, he had relatively little of his wealth tied up in slaves, and he held no financial instruments in the form of stocks and bonds. In keeping with his status as one of the wealthiest residents in the city, Gregorio's primary residence was very well furnished with many imported items and luxury goods. He kept a carriage and a horse, was married with three children, and died knowing that his family would be well taken care of in his absence.

Ignacio Caetano de Araujo, lower on the social scale than Gregorio, but still wealthy, died with an estate of 29:413$000 in 1849. Of this, 26:400$000 were accounted for by his urban real estate—distributed in a total of nine houses. His slaves, numbering six and averaging fifty-nine years of age (indicating a very old group of slaves, probably most having served him for many decades) were worth just

1:130$000. Ignacio's postmortem income, from his rentals, was 1:692$000 over ten months—implying a return of about 8 percent on his real estate assets without accounting for depreciation. Again, like Gregorio, Ignacio held no sophisticated forms of financial wealth in stocks or bonds. Unlike Gregorio, Ignacio really could not be sure about the status of his children after his passing. His wealth, once divided among his heirs, was not sufficient to guarantee them a life of ease. However, Ignacio's children were the illegitimate offspring of a union with one of his slaves, so the fact that they had their freedom and a substantial legacy settled on them by their father was no doubt considered a great boon.[56]

Turning to the upper reaches of middling wealthholding, we begin with the case of Antonio José Dutra himself. Unlike the wealthy landlords described above, Dutra's estate was weighted much more heavily toward slaves, who made up 55 percent of its value. Urban real estate, by contrast, comprised 36 percent of his wealth. Dutra owned no stocks or bonds and did not appear to have a bank account.[57] In this, he was like many middling wealthholders whose estates mainly comprised slaves and urban property, with an emphasis on the former. Dutra's estate, as extraordinary as it was for a man of his background, was far from sufficient to maintain his many offspring at the same standard of living they had enjoyed during the latter years of his life.

Lower yet on the social scale were middling wealthholders with fortunes in the range of 5 to 10 contos. One such person was Cantilda Carlota Pereira do Lago, deceased in 1847. As with Dutra, Cantilda depended on the labor of slaves for her income and the value of slaves for the bulk of her estate. Her slaves accounted for 3:950$000 of an estate worth 6:068$000. In addition, her estate, upon settlement, was owed 1:476$000 in rental income from the labor of her slaves.[58] All told, then, slaves and their labor made up nearly all of Cantilda's wealth. This was commonly the case among the lower-middle groups—those with enough wealth to afford a few slaves but little else.

Paradoxically, middling wealthholders who happened to own real estate prior to the 1840s both benefited from rising residential real estate values and suffered from it. Whereas this component of their wealth grew faster than any other, they were severely limited in their ability to acquire additional rental properties. A one-time windfall proved hard to sustain in the ensuing decade, when the value of houses continued to skyrocket but middling estates fell behind in this category of wealth. By the 1850s, the middle 60 percent of wealthholders owned a smaller percentage of all urban real estate wealth than they had in the 1820s.

Speculations on an Ephemeral World

In a sense, the relatively strong performance of the middling sector in the 1840s marked the culmination of two decades of favorable economic and social conditions. Rio de Janeiro, in the late 1840s, was truly a world built by slaves; patterns of wealth, too, were deeply influenced by the institution of slavery. Slave ownership was the first rung on the ladder of social mobility. If the middle sectors came to profit from the urban real estate boom, they would never have amassed the wealth needed to buy their homes without the profits from their slaves.

Rapid urbanization also contributed to bettering the fortunes of middling wealthholders. To the extent that they were able to enter the real estate market in the 1820s and 1830s, the decedents of the 1840s reaped a windfall in rising property values. In the 1850s, the number of estates reporting real estate remained unchanged; what changed was the number of and quality of homes owned by the wealthy. Middling wealthholders failed to keep pace in this market and continued to rely on slaves to form the income-generating portion of their wealth.

A further change in the social structure of the city was associated with shifting patterns of immigration. Dutra's world was characterized by high levels of forced immigration in the slave trade and moderate levels of free immigration from Europe. The majority of European immigrants worked in commerce, bringing with them skills and capital from the mother country. Meanwhile, labor remained scarce in the manual trades and wages were fairly high, notwithstanding the long-held misconception that slavery lowered wages. Free workers, in the first decades of the nineteenth century, faced a favorable environment, especially if they were skilled in a trade.[59] Likewise, skilled slaves were able to earn their way to freedom more quickly.

The end of the slave trade and the increasing immigration of workers rather than traders and petty businessmen from Europe tipped the scales against the working class in Rio in two ways. For Brazilian workers, this meant greater competition from skilled white male immigrants. For slaves, this meant that the price of freedom was radically revised upward as their price doubled and their earning power was put under strain from added competition from free labor. In a sense, the parameters of social mobility shifted toward skilled immigrants and those with the education and capital to make their way in an increasingly sophisticated and costly market economy. Whereas the native-born dominated the manual trades by a margin of nearly three to one in the census of 1834, by the census of 1872, when the process set in motion in the 1850s was almost complete, foreign-born manual workers equaled or exceeded their native counterparts in many districts of the city.[60]

In the neighborhood of Santa Anna, once a bastion of the population of freedmen, foreign-born carpenters outnumbered natives by a margin of 3:2. Among stonemasons and cobblers, the foreign-native ratio was even higher at 2:1.[61] Foreign day laborers, in turn, outnumbered the native-born by a wide margin. Yet, for all this, the native population outnumbered the immigrant by more than two to one. The same pattern of increasing immigrant pressure on working-class jobs is repeated throughout the city.

Dutra's world, in which a paradox of high wages and relatively cheap slaves existed side by side, was doomed for three reasons. First, the slave trade could not last forever. Pressure mounted against the trade from the early nineteenth century onward. The definitive suppression in 1850 was only a matter of time, and the trade had been technically illegal since 1831. Low-cost slaves were a temporary phenomenon that greatly abetted social mobility for middling wealth-holders who were able to extract high returns from the labor of their slaves. Second, standard economic theory explains why a high-wage, relatively mobile social environment drew increasing numbers of immigrants to Rio de Janeiro, as well as the effect this demographic shift had on the city. As the foreigners continued to flood Rio, downward pressure was placed on wages and upward pressure was placed on property values as the profile of immigrants shifted from owners and employers to workers. The so-called wage-rental ratio fell as a result.[62] Third, and last, the development of the Atlantic economy over the second half of the nineteenth century brought with it enormous changes in the economy, transportation network, and social structure of southeastern Brazil.

4

JOCIAL JTRUCTURE IN RIO DE JANEIRO, 1850J AND BEYOND

The literature on Brazilian social and economic history tends to begin or end with this critical period. In 1850, the British (with help from a grudgingly acquiescent Brazilian state) definitively suppressed the Atlantic slave trade.[1] What had been a river of sorrow binding Africa and Brazil dried up within the course of a year. In a related move, the Brazilian government began in earnest to shore up property rights institutions by passing a new land law that same year.[2] Along similar lines, a new commercial code was adopted, with important provisions regarding the formation of joint-stock companies.[3] Improved institutions, regarding land and commerce, set the stage for changes in the rate of economic growth and the shape of social structures in Rio de Janeiro.

In addition to these institutional changes, Brazil's economy was boosted by the explosion of the coffee cycle in the Paraíba Valley of Rio de Janeiro Province and beyond. Although exports and the coffee economy had been growing throughout the 1830s and 1840s, the rate of expansion attained in the 1850s was of greater magnitude. This period of economic growth, concentrated in the Southeast, brought with it Brazil's first railways and an expansion of capital, cash, and financial institutions. According to William Summerhill, the construction of railroads and concomitant savings in transport costs (which also amplified marketing regions and the domestic economy) raised Brazilian GDP by about one-fifth above where it would have been without rail transport between 1854 and 1913.[4] Most of the railroad network, and most of the gains, were concentrated in and around Rio de Janeiro, São Paulo, and Minas Gerais.

In short, the 1850s remade Brazil by setting it on a different trajectory, especially in the booming southeastern region in which Rio de Janeiro held a dominant position. The social structures and gradual economic growth of the first half of the nineteenth century gave way to a new world of wealthholding.[5] Dutra's world was shrinking; middling wealthholders, in particular slaveholders, faced a different environment in the 1850s. Dutra's children, who during the last years of their father's life must have enjoyed a reasonable standard of living and good life prospects with prosperity underwritten by the barbershop and band, faced a much bleaker future in the 1850s and beyond.

Yet, with all this change, there was much continuity in Carioca social structure. The orders of magnitude may have shifted, and middling wealthholders may have found their way of life and social mobility constrained, yet they continued to share many characteristics that distinguished them from their wealthy and poor counterparts alike.

From Bureaucratic-Commercial City to Financial and Export Center

The rapid rise of Brazil as an exporter is evident in its summary trade statistics. From 1821, when it exported a total of 4,324,000 pounds sterling worth of goods, exports had risen gradually to 5,932,000 in the 1849–50 fiscal year. In less than a decade's time, the value of Brazil's exports jumped to 13,150,000 pounds sterling at their peak in the 1850s.[6]

The source of most of this growth was concentrated in the southeastern part of Brazil, particularly in the interior of Rio de Janeiro Province. Coffee exports, which had been second to sugar in 1821, surged ahead by the 1840s, when they accounted for 42 percent of all shipments by value. The next decade saw coffee exports more than double in value, accounting for 47 percent of all exports.[7] Most of the coffee produced in Brazil in the 1840s and 1850s was grown in Rio Province, and an even greater proportion was shipped through the port of Rio de Janeiro. In fact, the port of Rio de Janeiro handled about half of all Brazil's foreign exports.[8] Money poured into the city like never before.

Among the many changes begat by coffee, railroad construction began in earnest in Brazil during the 1850s. Although the length of track laid was not itself expressive, rising from a mere 14.5 kilometers in the city and suburbs of Rio in 1854 to 222.7 kilometers in all of Brazil in 1860, the arrival of the railroad age soon transformed the urban landscape of Rio de Janeiro as well as the economy and property relations of the countryside.[9]

Railroads and export growth were accompanied by a dramatic expansion of the money supply. Export earnings allowed Brazil to print paper currency at an unprecedented rate without seriously undermining the rate of exchange between the mil-réis and the pound. Over the course of time, the emission of paper currency led to inflation and a falling exchange rate; yet, in the 1850s, the mil-réis showed remarkable stability versus the pound sterling. On a per-head basis, the expansion of the money supply was significant, raising the level from 3$800 per head in 1830 to 6$400 in 1850, 8$100 in 1854, and 12$290 at the peak in 1859.[10] More money meant more commerce, particularly in Rio de Janeiro's complex and growing urban economy.

Institutions, Economic Growth, and Social Structure

Estate inventory data provides strong evidence that wealth grew at a fairly strong clip over the period 1815 to 1860, with especially fast growth in the 1850s. Mean wealth, sans debts and credits, grew in real terms at an annual rate of between 1.6 and 2.1 percent during the period 1820 to 1855.[11] This result is not driven by outliers and is robust to different methods of calculating the total value of estates. Given the strength of these findings, there is simply no way to view the first three decades of Brazilian independence as economically stagnant, at least for Rio de Janeiro.[12] More to the point, measures of mean wealth rose substantially between the 1845–49 sample and the 1850–60 sample. In the late 1840s, around the time of Dutra's death, real mean wealth was 19:450$000, whereas the average wealthholder accounted for 27:577$000 during the 1850s—the pace of growth in wealth picked up in step with economic and institutional changes.

This finding of growth in wealthholding is accompanied by limited evidence of similar increases in urban wages over the long run. Unskilled day labor earned between $300 and $320 per day circa 1820; by 1860 unskilled labor's wages were four times higher in nominal terms, at about 1$200 per day. The average monthly rental price of a slave, likewise, rose from 11$110 circa 1840 to 24$000 circa 1860.[13] Inflation was substantial in the 1850s, so the real gains in wages or increases in rental rates were much lower than these figures suggest. Nevertheless, wages were increasing in real terms—converted using Buescu's price index, rental values were 11$527 in 1840 and 16$531 in 1860.[14]

Three major forces were at work raising the level of wealth in this part of Brazil. First, continuing a trend begun in the early 1800s, internal growth occurred as southeastern Brazil underwent an "industrious revolution." Responding to market opportunities and limited international trading stimuli, households allocated their assets more efficiently and exploited the labor of more of their members.[15]

Table 5

Wealth in Rio de Janeiro: 1850–1860

	N obs.	Urban Real Estate	Slaves	Rural Property	Cash and Bank Deposits	Stocks and Bonds	Business Assets	Debts	Credits	Furn. and Precious Metals	Other	Total
Total	363	4,394,678	1,419,651	879,400	1,061,345	885,417	787,627	-1,043,873	998,468	335,659	291,944	10,010,318
Mean		12,107	3,911	2,423	2,924	2,439	2,170	-2,876	2,751	925	804	27,577
% of Total		43.9	14.2	8.8	10.6	8.8	7.9	-10.4	10.0	3.4	2.9	100.00

Source: Estate Inventories, Rio de Janeiro, AN.
Note: Values reported in constant 1850 mil-réis.

Markets mattered, even in the absence of technological change or major social savings in transport costs (railroads, with one small exception, were entirely absent during the period under review), because they gave households, investors, and entrepreneurs new incentives to raise productivity. Moreover, the rise of major urban centers such as Rio de Janeiro created much larger zones of market activity, as demand in the cities expanded into the countryside.[16] Urban growth also fed into this process, as the expansion of cities such as Rio de Janeiro led to rising property values and rents—thereby providing stronger incentives for more residents to enter the workforce.

The second major factor raising real wealth in Brazil during the 1850s was institutional change. One of the most important consequences of the suppression of the Atlantic slave trade was the stunning rise in the value of slaves in Brazil. Another consequence was that the population of slaves began to decline in absolute and relative terms owing to the fact that slaves did not reproduce naturally in Brazil as a whole. Internal institutional change, in the form of the new commercial code, led to an expansion in chartering of companies and other forms of financial wealth. Finally, the factor that usually gets the most attention, but really deserves to be bracketed by the others outlined here, was the rapid expansion of the export-oriented economy from the late 1840s onward.[17]

These factors—made up of a combination of internal and external institutional changes regarding property rights, expanding urban markets, and growing exports—explain Rio de Janeiro's especially rapid growth experience in the 1850s. Elsewhere in Brazil, the first factor, internal growth, was often lacking and real wealth did not grow significantly over the same period. Katia Mattoso's data for Salvador, the capital of the large northeastern province of Bahia, help place Rio's growth in national perspective. For Salvador, growth was much slower, perhaps even negative when inflation is accounted for. The mean value of wealthholding in Salvador, again assuming my calculations based on Mattoso's data are correct, rose from about 10:000$000 current mil-réis in the period 1801–21 to 20:000$000 current mil-réis in the period 1845–60. Assuming that the price level doubled over this span of time, there was no growth in real wealth in Bahia according to Mattoso's figures.[18] It should be noted that the long-term growth rate estimated for Rio de Janeiro compares favorably with the rate reported for the United States over roughly the same span of time.[19] From the data presented here, we can assert, at least provisionally, that parts of Brazil saw rates of wealth creation nearly on par with the United States.[20]

Perhaps surprisingly, not only did wealth grow at a healthy rate, inequality appears to have remained remarkably stable in Rio de Janeiro over the first half of the nineteenth century. Rising values of widely held assets—especially slaves—dampened the wealth-concentrating effects of the rise of export growth and financial capitalism in Brazil during the first half of the nineteenth century, at least in Rio de Janeiro. This fact holds significance well beyond the study of economic growth and wealth distribution. If slaves were relatively equally distributed in Brazil's metropolitan center, and if the returns to slave ownership rose over the period 1815–60, we can predict, at least in economic terms, that the political will to abrogate or abolish the institution will be lacking. Slavery meant the most to people of middling wealth; it was the backbone of Brazil's nineteenth-century "middle class." Of course, the overall effect of slavery on wealth distribution and social structure was to increase inequality among all persons when slaves are counted as potential wealthholders.

If the shifting institutional environment and economic context favored growth in wealth in southeastern Brazil in general and Rio de Janeiro in particular, was this growth also reflected in rising wages and living standards? Along these lines, did the institutional changes that impelled slave prices higher result in lower returns to slave-holding? Evidence from newspaper advertisements for slave rentals can help resolve these questions.

The suppression of the Atlantic slave trade ramified broadly in Rio de Janeiro's economy and society. Higher priced slaves meant that avenues to social mobility were constricted for those still on the outside looking in on the institution as well as for slaves themselves confronted suddenly with the need to save up twice as much to secure their freedom. Beyond this, it is possible that the growth in slave prices and wealth more broadly was not accompanied by higher real wages in Rio de Janeiro, in which case it would be better to speak of an asset bubble than of economic growth.

To illustrate, if slave prices doubled and wages remained the same, the rate of return on slaves, ceteris paribus, would have been cut in half. Yet, according to data on slave rental rates in the late 1850s, "wages" had increased almost as quickly as slave prices. In 1849–50, the mean price of a prime female slave, aged fifteen–forty, in our inventory sample (N=62) was 425$000; at the same time, the rental rate for a female cook or laundress was 12$250 per month—yielding about 14 percent retained by her owner under a typical arrangement. In 1859–60, the mean price of a similar slave (N=67) was 997$000 and the average rental rate was 24$000 per month—yielding 29 percent gross, and approximately 12 percent to her owner.[21] The suppression of the slave trade was the main reason slave prices doubled. Rapid urbanization, economic growth, and labor scarcity helped wages rise in roughly similar fashion. Consequently, the abolition of the trade did not lead to a significant diminution of returns to slaveholders in the form of rents and, at the same time, contributed to a major windfall.

Rather than cut into slaveholder's returns, the rise in slave prices set the table for a dramatically different environment for social mobility after 1850. For example, the average number of slaves held by non-landowning, urban-type wealthholders fell from 7.1 in the late 1840s to 5.75 in the 1850s. Increasingly cut off from access to highly profitable slaves, Rio de Janeiro's middle groups began to lose ground; at the same time, the economic expansion that had begun with higher prices for houses and slaves as the city urbanized over the first decades of the nineteenth century shifted perceptibly toward an economy driven by much more concentrated forms of financial wealth.

The Problem of Inequality

Brazil's capital began the national period marked by high levels of wealth inequality. The top decile of wealthholders (counting only the decedents in the inventory sample) in Rio held approximately 57 percent of wealth sans credits and debits circa 1820.[22] During the heyday of Dutra's world of middling wealth, in the late 1840s, the top decile's share of wealth had fallen slightly to 54 percent. In the decade following Dutra's death, the top decile's share rose again to 61 percent of all wealth. It should be noted that these figures refer to the distribution of wealth among inventoried decedents. Clearly, the distribution of wealth among all potential wealthholders, including slaves themselves, would be much more concentrated. It remains noteworthy that inequality apparently fell slightly from the 1820s through the 1840s, only to rise again by the 1850s. The margin for error in these calculations is too large to sustain definitive claims about the evolution of inequality in Rio de Janeiro, but the direction of change in underlying forms of wealth is consistent with a story of falling, then rising, inequality.

Put in slightly more precise terms, using the Gini coefficient, wealth distribution appears to have been highly unequal in Rio de Janeiro throughout the period under review. If we assume, for the sake of argument, that 50 percent of all households held no wealth whatsoever, and that the distribution among inventoried decedents represents the distribution of wealth among the remaining 50 percent of households, the Gini coefficient for Rio circa 1820 is 0.84, rising slightly to 0.85 circa 1855.[23] These coefficients would rise even higher if slaves were considered potential heads of households. In other words, it is very important to underscore in our discussion here about the relative movement of inequality measures and the relatively dispersed nature of slaveholding that the society we are describing is one of great overall inequality.

Although its effects varied over time and by region, the widespread holding of slaves put downward pressure on the degree of inequality *among wealthholders* in Brazil over the first half of the nineteenth century. To be sure, slavery increased inequality among all persons living in Brazil, as slaves themselves were effectively barred from wealthholding and yet were considered part of the wealth of others. Slaves were widely held assets in Brazil. Measures of concentration typically indicate that slave wealth was much better distributed than wealth in land—at least prior to the 1870s.[24] For instance, the Gini coefficient of concentration among slaveholders ranged from 0.46 to 0.60 in Minas Gerais between 1831 and 1840.[25] The Gini coefficient for landholding was higher, ranging from 0.71 to 0.75 throughout Minas Gerais in the 1850s.[26] This dispersion of wealth in the form of slaves meant that when the British definitively cut off the flow of slaves from Africa, the boom in slave values was felt throughout Brazilian society.

Because slaves were better distributed than other forms of wealth, the suppression of the trade and the inflation of slave prices had little *immediate* effect on social structures. In fact, in a counterfactual world without slavery in the period 1850–60, wealth inequality in Rio de Janeiro would have *increased* by about 7 percent.[27] Over time, however, the higher prices for slaves raised barriers to entry at the first rung on the ladder of social mobility. Likewise, as the institution of slavery eroded over the ensuing three decades, inequality among wealthholders rose as the other components of wealthholding, particularly financial assets, were more unequally distributed.

Patterns of Slaveholding: The Long View

Slaves were more equally distributed than any other major category of wealth during the period 1815 to 1860. Moreover, when the rural component of Rio de Janeiro's urban residents' slaveholdings is discounted, the continuity of relatively small and equally distributed slaves is further highlighted as is the effect of the suppression of the

Figure 2

Slave Wealth as a Percentage of Total Wealth by Size of Estate, Rio de Janeiro, 1850s

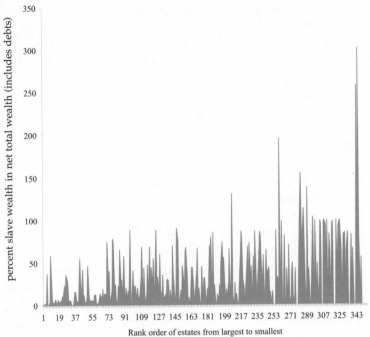

Source: Inventories, Rio de Janeiro, AN.

Atlantic trade in 1850–51. The mean number of slaves owned by wealthholders reporting no rural property, as an imperfect but convenient proxy for purely urban slaveholdings, ranged from 5.74 in the period 1815–25, to a peak of 7.09 in the period 1845–49, to 5.75 in the period 1850–1860. The suppression of the slave trade raised prices and restricted access to new slaves; the mean urban holding fell as a result.

These findings regarding the mean size of urban slaveholding lend further credence to the argument regarding the determinants of the optimal range for the size of slaveholdings in the urban milieu—that is, slave agency, monitoring costs, and the risk-aversion of slaveholders embodied in their propensity to diversify their holdings. The mean size of holdings appears somewhat sensitive to radical changes in the price of slaves; also sensitive was the overall proportion of slaveholders among wealthholders, which tended to decline in secular fashion as rising slave prices raised barriers to entry.[28]

Housing

Yet, before we jump to the conclusion that social change was limited over the period 1815–60, it is necessary to examine the categories of wealthholding in greater detail. Just as with urbanization and rising rents, the most profound force of change in social structure in Rio de Janeiro was neither slavery nor commerce nor finance, but residential real estate. In the early 1800s, housing made up 29 percent of wealth; by the 1840s this had risen to 47 percent. Throughout the 1850s, housing remained steady at more than 40 percent of total wealth, even with the stupendous increase in the value of slaves after 1850. All told, from 1815–25 to 1850–60, the mean value of housing in the estates of the decedents in our sample rose at a faster real rate than did the mean value of slaves.

Housing, whether measured by the mean or median, started the period under review significantly more expensive than slaves, and it ended it even more expensive. This fact has far-reaching consequences for understanding social structure in Rio de Janeiro. Contrary to the widespread notion that wealth was equated with slaves, it appears that it was really measured in houses. The rich were far more likely to own multiple houses and to depend on rents from real estate rather than slaves for their income. Consequently, whereas many scholars have tried to deduce social structures from lists of slaveholding (perhaps, in part, because such lists are more readily obtained), the proper place to begin the discussion is with real estate. In the city of Rio de Janeiro, this essentially means residential property—very few wealthholders indicate ownership of commercial property, and most businesses rented their premises. Of course someone had to own the commercial property in the city, and they must have been a very small and rich group indeed. Lacking sufficient data on this group, and more interested in the middling wealthholders that are at the center of this book, let us turn to a closer examination of the housing market over the long term.

If we compare the percentages of wealthholders reporting urban real estate over an extended period of time, it becomes apparent that the proportion of urban property holders remains fairly steady at more than 60 percent. Only slaves and personal items were more widely held categories of wealth among decedents in the samples. The importance of real estate to the fortunes of middling wealthholders was also relatively stable during the period 1815 to 1860.

Rapid urban growth is often associated with degradation of housing quality, as more people are packed into smaller spaces. Although there is no doubt that density was high, limited data (forty-nine obser-vations) on the size of houses during the period 1815–60 show a slight increase in the mean size of housing.[29] Likewise, the number of rooms per house shows a small rise, mainly in the form of a second living room (sala). One element that would have contributed to better qual-ity of housing was bathrooms (perhaps more precisely, water closets), which did not generally exist.

Bearing in mind that these figures derive from a small sample of houses, the price of housing per square palmo (0.0484 meters) rose from $620 réis circa 1820 to 1$980 circa 1855.[30] Contrary to the expec-tation that the highest prices per square palmo would be found in wealthy neighborhoods like Botafogo, the costliest residences by this metric remained concentrated in the old city center. The most expen-sive residences in terms of appraised value were found in the wealthy newer neighborhoods, but these were large homes. In addition, there was great diversity in price in the same streets, sometimes in the same blocks, depending on the quality of the building and its upkeep.[31]

As for crowding, the housing data indicate a stable median of 2 bedrooms per house over the whole period, with a mean of 2.5. Given the large number of people per household throughout the period, and especially given the fact that many slaveholders lived in houses with just two bedrooms, it is clear that many people had nowhere in particular to sleep. The mean number of people per household reported in the 1821 census, in the urban center of Rio, was just under eight; by the census of 1849, the mean had risen above ten people per household.[32] Greater crowding does seem to have occurred, although the total area of houses also increased slightly in compensation. Slaves slept on the floor, in the street or yard, or rented their own housing—although this last option was discouraged (inef-fectively) by the authorities after the passage of a regulation 1842.[33] Most houses had two bedrooms, so presumably the majority of households with minor children divided sleeping space between the parents and their brood. Nearly every home had a room denomi-nated as a kitchen, and many had yards of varying size (quintais) from which a family could provide itself with greens and fresh eggs (if there was a galinheiro). The quintal also afforded extra space for slaves to sleep.

To this picture, we must add, by the 1850s, the appearance of large tenement dwellings, known in the nineteenth century as cortiços. Although such dwellings no doubt existed before this period, public authorities (the police in particular) began to count the number of cor-tiços in earnest during the 1850s. According to one such count, taken in 1856, there were 114 cortiços with 4,003 inhabitants in the city of Rio de Janeiro. By 1867, there were reportedly 502 cortiços with 15,054 inhabitants, mostly concentrated near the older core of the city. Public officials lamented that high rents allowed only the well-off to afford decent accommodations.[34] It is fairly clear from this information that rising housing prices and the booming economy in Rio de Janeiro bred tenement slums to house the city's growing working class. In addition, it is likely that the growing concentration of poverty in the old city center contributed to a sharpening of residential segregation. Wealthy residents moved farther out from the core, to the South and Southwest, where they could ride the newly constructed streetcar lines to the business and retail district.[35]

A last consideration regarding housing regards the rental rate. There are essentially two key issues involved here. First, how many households owned their domicile and how many rented? Second, what was the behavior of rents over time? The rate of homeownership and the costs of renting are both critical to understanding the social fabric of the city.

We have not been able to access urban property tax lists for this period (they exist, but we could not obtain access to them), with which a calculation of the ratio of owners to renters could be derived. Instead, we must rely on our estate inventories once more. The procedure adopted is simple: the number of houses was divided by the number of owners. This calculation will not yield a definitive owner/rental ratio because many households fell in between these categories—sons and daughters living rent-free in the houses of their parents. Nevertheless, a simple calculation suffices to provide a best guess as to the ratio of owner-occupied to rented domiciles. A sample of forty-eight homeowners culled from the period 1845–49 yields a total of 175 separate domiciles (see Table 4). By definition, 127 of these homes were not owner occupied. It follows, then, that about 28 percent of homes were occupied by owners and 72 percent by renters or those living rent-free at the pleasure of their owners. This figure probably overstates the number of renters inasmuch as the sample was drawn from the top 60 percent of the wealth distribution. Projecting a similar number of homeowners down into the lower deciles would adjust the owner/rental ratio closer to 1:3. A similar ratio of owner-occupied to rental housing is found in São Paulo, circa 1888, when that city had attained a degree of urbanization and wealth similar to Rio in the first half of the nineteenth century.[36]

For the majority who evidently had to rent their homes, the costs were high and rising in pace with the rapid appreciation of residential property values. Rents averaged between 7 and 10 percent of the appraised value of the home throughout the period 1815–60, with significant variation depending on the location and quality of the property. Anna Theodora Mascarenhas de Barros, a major property holder at her death in 1855, owned five properties on Rua da Imperatriz. Of these, one was under construction and rented at a steep discount of 3 percent per year; another two were combinations of residences and small storefronts that rented at 7 percent per year; a fourth was in need of repair and rented at a rate of 8 per year. Anna Theodora also owned low-cost housing on Ladeira do Livramento valued at 1:000$000 and renting for 100$000 per year. It is worth noting that, at this rate, a skilled artisan, such as a carpenter, would have spent more than one-third of his income on housing of the cheapest sort: living in a one-room house measuring 16 by 26 palmos (approximately 20 square meters).[37] Poorer residents of the city had to make do with renting rooms or building their own shacks on unclaimed land.[38] According to contemporary reports by travelers, these rented rooms were often filled with as many as ten or twelve people (although this was probably an exaggeration) in areas no larger than about 150 square feet.[39] Although slightly removed from our time period, Carvalho de Mello reports that a *shared* tenement room could be rented by a slave during the 1870s for 41$000 per year.[40] Projecting this value backward into the 1850s and accounting for inflation, such Spartan accommodations probably went for between 25 and 30 mil-réis on an annual basis.

Financial Wealth

Another category of wealth that was exploding in value during the first half of the nineteenth century was formal financial wealth—the key difference being that this form of wealth was far from well distributed in the population of wealth holders at large. Whereas informal credit instruments predominated in Rio prior to independence, by the 1840s and 1850s, the metropolis was beginning to be transformed by financial wealth held in the form of cash, stocks, and, most importantly, bonds. The commercial code of 1850 added to this legacy by creating laws allowing the formation of joint-stock companies, although it must be remembered that these companies were few and trading activity in stocks was low prior to the 1880s.[41] Over time, these changes in property rights institutions shifted investment away from slaves toward real estate, businesses, and financial instruments.[42]

The 1850s were also a period of change and expansion in the banking system. A look at the balance sheets of Brazil's major banks (with the right to print currency) for the period 1839 to 1854 highlights the growth in this sector. Deposits in the Banco Commercial do Rio de Janeiro rose from 424:237$000 to 1,372:520$000 from 1839 to 1853, while its capital more than doubled and loans quadrupled. The Banco do Brasil (second) entered operation in earnest in 1854 with a capital of 8,000 contos.[43]

Railroad construction and the expansion of the state apparatus in Brazil were expensive projects. Funding the state and its bureaucracy and building railroads required more formal forms of credit. Railroads and the government proceeded to issue bonds. A rise is registered in the value of bonds in the estates of Rio's wealth holders. For the entire period 1815–25, just three decedents indicated ownership of *apólices* (bonds) worth an average of 1:098$000. By the middle part of the nineteenth century, twenty-six decedents reported owning an average of 11:230$000 worth of bonds. Ownership of *ações* (stocks) increased as well, from seven observations averaging 5:740$000 in the first period to twenty-nine observations averaging 7:755$000 in the 1850s. The real value of bonds, in particular, rose faster than any other major category of wealth.

The salience of informal credit instruments (*dívidas ativas*) as a form of wealth varied considerably over time. The proportion of wealth in this category fell dramatically between the 1840s and 1850s, only to rise again in the 1870s and 1880s. Perhaps more importantly, the tide of credit represented by these diverse transactions (store credit, short-term loans, larger advances over months or years) added up to more, in percentage terms, than bank deposits, stocks and bonds, cash, and business inventories and equity in every sample period save the 1880s. Throughout the century, large commercial houses expanded their operations, granting credit throughout the city and beyond. When the banking house of A. J. A. Souto and Co. failed in 1864, it owed various creditors a whopping 41,187:911$000. All told, the crisis of 1864 resulted in the destruction of about 70,000:000$000, which, put in perspective, indicates the vast scale of the lending operations of commercial houses in the city.[44] Turning to the estate inventory sample for the period, the six wealthiest creditors held dívidas ativas worth an average of 78:624$000. For the small fraction of Rio de Janeiro's residents with capital to lend, the informal credit market could be a lucrative business.

Middling Wealth: Change and Continuity

The consequences of economic growth and social transformation in Rio de Janeiro played themselves out among the city's middling wealthholders in a way that undermined Dutra's world. From the 1820s through the 1840s, the middle 60 percent of wealthholders saw their relative share of wealth increase in Rio's fluid, service-based economy. As an indicator of this process, mean wealth held by the middle 60 percent as a ratio of mean wealth in the full sample rose from 35 percent circa 1820 to 44 percent in the late 1840s. Average wealthholding among the middle 60 percent rose nearly 60 percent during the same period in real terms, whereas mean wealth in the full sample rose just 27 percent. The socioeconomic landscape in which Dutra made his way to fortune was distinctly different from what came before, at the end of the colonial era, and what was to come in the 1850s and beyond.

Although middling wealthholders saw their mean wealth rise at a good clip during the period 1845–1860, rising from 8:618 to 10:561$000, this rise was not accompanied by a continued increase in the ratio of middling wealth to the entire sample. In fact, the ratio of the middle 60 percent to the entire sample mean fell back to 38 percent—close to the level of the late colonial period. The 1850s were a period of wealth concentration after a prolonged period of equalization. The sources of this change have already been outlined: rising financial wealth and the concentration of real estate in the hands of big landlords drove inequality higher, even as the relatively even distribution of slaves applied downward pressure on inequality.

Dependent on slavery for social advancement, the middling groups peaked in their reliance on slave wealth in the 1850s, when fully 27 percent of their assets were in slaves. Indeed, without the one-time windfall implied by the doubling of slave prices after the end of the slave trade, middling wealthholders in the 1850s would have seen almost no gains in the values of their estates over the decedents in the 1840s sample. Holding slave prices constant at 1840s levels, mean wealth for the middle 60 percent of the distribution would have been 9:139$000—a small increase over the previous period.

Along these lines, the barrier to entry to slaveholding was much higher in the 1850s than before. As a consequence, we can predict that the pace at which smallholders expanded their slaveholding would decline. Although we do not have direct evidence to this effect, we can test the hypothesis indirectly in the following way. The mean age of slaves held by different categories of owners gives us an idea of the

dynamism of each class of owner. A high mean age is evidence of stag-
nation or decline, as it indicates limited purchases of prime-age
slaves. The largest slaveholdings, however, will be predicted to
have a higher mean age owing to the survival of some small number
of slaves into old age. Thus, our hypothesis is that the smallest and
the largest holdings should have a higher age structure than holdings
in the medium range. Changes in these stated relationships, over
time, are *indirect evidence* of the effects of changing slave prices on different types of slave owners: if prices are high, owners will make do
with older slaves and postpone purchase of prime-age slaves
(fifteen–thirty years old).

The evidence for this effect is limited but points in the expected
direction. First, for the 1820s, the mean age of slaves in the top 10 percent of slaveholdings was 24.37 years compared with 31.33 years in
the smallest 10 percent of holdings. Smallholding meant fewer and
older slaves from the beginning of the period under review. An examination of the ages of 2,677 slaves between 1845 and 1860 reveals a
subtle shift in the status of different groups of slave owners. In the
1840s sample (N=1174), 95 owners each held an average of 12.36
slaves; in the 1850s (N=1503), 163 owners held an average of 9.22
slaves. The average age of slaves rose from the 1840s, when it was just
under 30 years, to 31.52 years in the 1850s.

This generalized shift toward smaller and older holdings was,
clearly, associated with the shutting off of the Atlantic trade and the
rapid rise in prices. Supply and demand met at a new equilibrium.
For the purpose of our argument, the critical question is how this shift
affected middling and small slaveholders. In both periods, the middling group with between 5 and 10 slaves owned the youngest slaves
on average: 27.68 years in the 1840s and 27.8 years in the 1850s. If an
owner already had five slaves before prices spiked up in the 1850s,
he or she could conceivably continue a strategy of accumulating more
slaves, or at least maintain the productive age structure necessary to
profit from their holding. The big losers in the new equilibrium were
very small holders, either of the incipient or the decadent type.
Among owners of fewer than five slaves, the mean age of slaves rose
from 31.66 years in the 1840s to 36.39 years in the 1850s. Put simply,
the only group that shows a major change in the mean age of their
slaves is this one. At the same time that the mean age of slaves held
by the smallest slaveholders rose dramatically, their proportion of all
slaveholders also rose from 32 percent in the 1840s, to 50 percent in
the 1850s. Essentially, the smallholders of the 1850s were not able to
promote themselves to the ranks of middling ownership at anywhere

near the rate they had prior to the end of the trade and the rise in prices. The ratio of owners with four or fewer slaves to owners with five to ten slaves was 1:1 in the 1840s; by the 1850s, this ratio had risen to 2:1.

The idea put forward here may turn out to be wrong, but it accords with the run of the facts: rising prices and limited supply began to cut smallholders out of slave ownership; the avenue of social mobility provided by cheap slaves began to close down in the 1850s, leading to an expansion of the poorest segment of slaveholders, but not the number of slaves held, and an ageing of their slaves.[45] Clearly, the middle groups were loosing traction in the new economy of the 1850s. The full consequences of the narrowing of avenues of social mobility would not be felt immediately. In order to trace the arc of social change initiated in the great transformation of the 1850s, we must look ahead to the last years of slavery and empire in Brazil.

Coda: Wealth in the Waning Years of Slavery

The transformation of Rio de Janeiro from a smallish bureaucratic-commercial center to a financial metropolis was well underway in the 1850s. Dutra's world of middling wealth and relative social mobility narrowed with the rise of slave prices beyond the reach of aspiring wealthholders and the continued appreciation of urban real estate, which made the purchase of additional income-generating properties all but impossible for any but the rich. Financial capitalism, railroad construction, and export growth placed an ever-greater premium on financial sophistication and business skills that eluded the largely illiterate class from which Dutra rose. Finally, the suppression of the slave trade had the consequence of shifting the demographic balance in Rio over the ensuing decades toward whites—a process that picked up steam with European immigration. Portuguese and other European immigrants competed for work and fortune with Dutra's children, making their social ascent all the more unlikely.

Export growth and railroad construction remade southeastern Brazil by the 1870s. Whereas exports had averaged around 10,000,000 pounds sterling in the 1850s, they rose to more than 20,000,000 per year in the 1870s and 1880s. In per-head terms, this translated into 1.57 pounds sterling per head circa 1888, most of which flowed through the ports of Rio de Janeiro and Santos. More than half of Brazil's exports were now accounted for by coffee.[46] Meanwhile, the railroad network centered on the Provinces of Rio de Janeiro, São Paulo, and Minas Gerais expanded the marketing region of the city;

by the end of the empire, there were 9,321 kilometers of track in all of Brazil—nearly one hundred times the length in 1859. Major cities, led by Rio, sat at the center of a booming import-export nexus in the Southeast. Import-export houses based throughout the Southeast and beyond purchased their goods on consignment or obtained credit from Rio's leading merchant houses. Beyond goods, Rio de Janeiro exported services (credit and insurance, for example) to the rest of the country. Although its stock exchange and financial markets were incipient in the nineteenth century, the only real player in the game of high finance, with the partial exception of São Paulo after about 1880, was Rio de Janeiro. In sum, Rio's transformation in the 1850s and beyond led to its emergence as the central place in the Brazilian economy in the second half of the nineteenth century.

The change in the composition of wealth, identified in the 1850s, gained momentum over the next three decades. By the time Dutra's younger children were grown, the transformation was nearly complete. Whereas Dutra's world of the 1840s had seen the apogee of slavery in Rio de Janeiro, in terms of the value of slaves relative to other assets and in terms of the ratio of slaves to the free population, the 1870s saw the retreat and the 1880s witnessed the complete unraveling of the institution. In the early 1870s, slave wealth accounted for less than 10 percent of net wealth, down from a high of 17 percent in the late 1840s. By the late 1880s, slaves made up less than 1 percent of total wealth. The slaves that remained were likely to be owned by the wealthy, not the middle groups, and to labor in domestic service or reside outside of the city on a city dweller's rural estate.

Not only was slave wealth less pronounced in decedents' estates in the 1870s and 1880s, but its relative importance to the middle groups had also declined. Focusing on the middle 60 percent of wealthholders in the sample, the shift from the 1850s to the 1870s was already pronounced. Whereas 79 percent of this middle group of wealthholders owned at least one slave circa 1855, just 55 percent of the same group owned slaves circa 1870. Just as significantly, the relative importance of slave wealth to net wealth declined dramatically for middling wealthholders. In the 1850s, counting all wealthholders in the middle 60 percent of the distribution, slave wealth accounted for an average of 30 percent of net wealth; by the 1870s, this figure had declined to 13.5 percent.[47]

Finally, by the early 1870s, slavery was undergoing a process of ruralization in the region surrounding Rio de Janeiro. Whereas urban slaveholders, defined as not owning rural property, consistently held an average of about six slaves throughout the period 1815 to 1860, the

Table 6

Wealth in Rio de Janeiro by Category (percentages): 1868–1873 and 1885–1889

	N obs.	Urban Real Estate	Slaves	Rural Property	Cash and Bank Deposits	Stocks and Bonds	Business Assets	Debts	Credits	Furn. and Precious Metals	Other
1868–1873	87	39.4	9.7	5.9	5.4	11.5	14.4	-9.1	14.2	2.7	5.9
1885–1889	143	28.5	0.2	2.0	5.4	32.2	10.7	-3.7	20.4	2.3	2.0

Source: Estate Inventories, Rio de Janeiro, AN.

mean holding of slaveholders in Rio's urban milieu had fallen to 3.8 by the early 1870s. There were fewer slaveholders in the city, and these individuals owned fewer slaves. Meanwhile, the few large slave-holdings that remained were clearly associated with large-scale rural agricultural production. In the 1868–73 sample, two slaveholders with extensive rural landholdings accounted for 456 out of 621 slaves. All told, the ratio of urban to rural slaves in the estate inventories of Rio de Janeiro fell from 43 percent in the period surrounding Dutra's death (1845–55) to 24 percent in the early 1870s.[48]

Clearly, a form of wealth that had been widely distributed and especially salient in middling urban estates had undergone a profound transformation into a far less accessible and far more uncommon source of wealth in less than two decades. Dutra's sons could not have followed in his footsteps had they wanted to; the acquisition and exploitation of slaves on the part of the middle groups, on the scale achieved by Dutra and his contemporaries, was difficult by the 1870s and almost impossible by the 1880s. Worse yet, urban real estate all but priced them out of the market, and they were unlikely to have the skills, knowledge, and connections to benefit from Rio's mercantile growth.

An equally expressive indication of this consummation in the transformation of wealthholding in Rio is found in the category of stocks and bonds. Whereas a significant rise was seen in this category by the 1850s, this was just a hint of what was to come. Circa 1870, stocks and bonds accounted for 11.4 percent of net wealth. By the late 1880s, the wealthiest estates were, with few exceptions, dependent on this form of wealth, which now accounted for 32.2 percent of net wealth. Two of the wealthiest decedents in the 1885–89 sample held approximately half of their wealth in stocks and bonds. Maria do

Carmo Louzada Macedo, wife of Manoel José Fernandes de Macedo, died in 1885 with an estate (representing that of her husband as well) of 522:725$000. Of this, 254:740$000 were invested in stocks and bonds.[49] Francisco Belizário Soares de Souza was even more heavily invested in financial instruments. Of his 508:952$000, 323:287$000 were held in stocks and bonds.[50] Between them, these two wealthholders held nearly as much in stocks and bonds as the entire 363 decedent sample for the 1850s and more than ten times as much as the 176 decedents in the 1815–25 sample.

The couple of Maria do Carmo and José Fernandes also invested heavily in urban real estate, with fifty houses spread around the city. This concentration of real estate wealth was the other pincer, along with financial assets, that squeezed the middle groups over the last decades of the empire. The high cost of housing and the concentration of property in the hands of great landlords raised the barrier to entry into wealthholding; stocks and bonds, for their part, remained exclusive to the rich or educated.

Middling wealthholders presented a much different profile by the 1880s than in the middle of the century. Many were European immigrants. Francisco José da Cruz, native of Portugal, is representative.[51] Single, white, male, and engaged in small-scale commercial activity, he amassed a middling fortune in a relatively short time between his immigration and his death at age thirty-two in 1887. Without descendents, his fortune of 31:153$000 passed back up the family tree to his father (two-thirds) and laterally to his four brothers (one-third), all of whom resided in Portugal.

The transformation of wealthholding from a regime dominated by urban real estate and slaves was remarkably complete by the late 1880s. Bonds and stocks now accounted for more than 32 percent of total wealth, and such assets were concentrated in the hands of the few, with the top 20 percent of wealthholders accounting for more than 90 percent of the wealth in these categories. Meanwhile, slaves had ceased to figure in importance in all but a few estates. Even residential housing declined as a category of wealth as the rich and sophisticated wealthholders of the late empire invested heavily in railroad and government bonds. Business wealth and credit assets also grew. Informal credit and business assets, both closely associated with commercial and retail enterprises, accounted for more than 30 percent of total wealth by the 1880s.

The transformation of wealthholding over the course of the nineteenth century is graphically evident in Figure 3. Prior to the 1840s, stocks and bonds made up a small fraction of net wealth; by the end

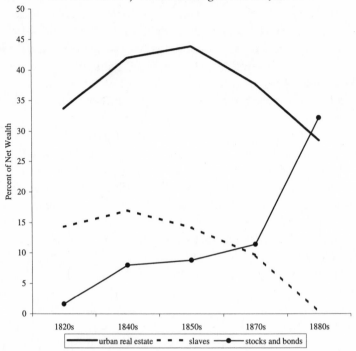

Figure 3
The Evolution of Wealthholding in Rio de Janeiro

Source: Inventories, Rio de Janeiro, AN.

of the empire, in the 1880s, such financial wealth made up nearly one-third of net wealth. Meanwhile, the rise and fall of slavery as an institution in the nineteenth century can be discerned in the curve traced out from the 1820s through the 1880s. Slaves as a form of wealth peaked in importance precisely during Dutra's adult years, in the 1840s. By the 1870s, without recourse to inexpensive new slaves from Africa, the importance of slavery was declining in the estate inventories of Rio de Janeiro. In the final years of the institution, slavery had all but ceased to figure in the estates of wealthholders in Brazil's capital.

Finally, along with the diminishing importance of slaves, the decline in the importance of identifiable rural wealth marked the latter 1880s. Rio de Janeiro was, by this point, a metropolis with a band of urbanized suburbs extending for ten kilometers or more from the old city center. On top of this, we must recognize that the older plantation zones in the province of Rio de Janeiro also underwent a prolonged phase of agricultural atrophy from the 1860s onward. Many coffee plantations in the Paraíba Valley, as Stanley Stein made so abundantly clear more than a generation ago, were in serious trouble by the 1860s and no longer provided the basis for major fortunes in Rio de Janeiro in the 1880s.[52] To be sure, some coffee entrepreneurs succeeded in transforming their operations in the city into commercial and banking enterprises; yet, our data support Stein's contention that much of the wealth in the Paraíba Valley was destroyed during the second half of the nineteenth century as many coffee fazendas fell into decadence and the coffee barons found themselves poorer and indebted.

The slaves and rural landholdings that composed some of the largest fortunes of Rio's wealthholders in the 1850s sample, and even into the 1870s, were gone by the late 1880s. In their place, a class of financiers and investors stood at the top of the city's social hierarchy. This fact, combined with the gradual disappearance of slaves from the estates of middling wealthholders, helps to explain why abolitionism gained traction in the 1880s. The social structures illuminated in the estate inventory analysis ventured in this book go further to explain why so many voters and intellectuals were amenable to abolition in the 1880s than do theories based on the supposed rise of a middle class ideologically opposed to slavery. On the contrary, the closing of the slave trade in 1850 spelled the gradual end to the middle groups' reliance on slaves as a form of social mobility, and the slow decline of the Paraíba Valley estates led to the erosion of large land-holding and slavery in Brazil's political heartland—although this latter process was gradual and the province of Rio de Janeiro remained a bastion of hard-core slaveholders to the bitter end.

The Social and Economic Map of Rio de Janeiro Redrawn

Immigrants poured into Rio de Janeiro in the 1880s, filling the ranks of the rich and poor alike. By 1890, there were reportedly 124,352 foreigners in a total population of 522,651.[53] European immigrants appear frequently in the estate inventory sample for the later 1880s. Although most were Portuguese, other middling wealthholders included a widow from Italy and a French carpenter.[54] The data do not provide a clear indication of the effects of immigration on the social mobility of Brazilian-born members of the lower and middle groups. Notwithstanding these limitations, it is reasonable to conclude that immigrants increased competition and cut away at the opportunities for poorer Brazilians, especially former slaves and people of mixed race.

One indication of the shifting social map of the city is the prevalence of foreigners by neighborhood. In the old central neighborhood of Candelária, the population had actually declined significantly between 1849 and 1890—mainly due to the disappearance of slaves from the area. Immigrants had always been important in the neighborhood because of its commercial character and the enduring role of the Portuguese in this branch of the economy; they constituted about half of the neighborhood's population throughout the period.[55] The pattern for immigrants was to settle in the old city center. Neighborhoods on what had been the semirural periphery were home to far fewer foreigners. In neighborhoods such as Iraja and Engenho Novo, the native-born population outnumbered foreigners by seven or eight to one.

Closer to the center, in the districts where Rio's freed persons were concentrated in 1849, the pressure of competition from immigrants is palpable in the census figures. The neighborhood of Santa Anna, for instance, saw a rise in the foreign population from 4,546 in 1849 to 18,880 in 1890.[56] This change fell particularly hard on freedmen and other free men of color who found themselves competing with an overwhelmingly male, working-age population—72 percent of immigrants were male.

Nevertheless, there remained plenty of homegrown Brazilians among the middle groups. Here again, however, their profile was changing. Although financial wealth was concentrated at the top of Rio's society, many wealthholders in the middle also reported owning stocks and bonds. In addition, with the near complete extinction of slavery, middling wealthholders had come to rely ever more heavily on real property to ground their estates. For the lowest members of the middle group, their homes often made up their entire fortune.[57] Many other middling wealthholders were small-business owners and entrepreneurs. In this regard, social mobility was still open to people with a little capital and business acumen. It is noteworthy, however, that so many of these small businesses were run by Portuguese immigrants. In some sense, Rio de Janeiro provided means of social ascent for the striving middle groups of Portugal!

What was true of the image of the 1880s was even more sharply etched in the social structures of the 1890s. Although there are many problems with using estate inventories from the 1890s for comparative purposes with earlier periods, including a very different institutional environment, radical demographic changes manifesting themselves after building for the previous three decades, and a stock market bubble, it is nonetheless worthwhile to venture a few simple comparisons. Changes that are evident in the 1890s can be explained as the result of either continuing trends from the post-1850 period, by unique circumstances of the era, or some combination thereof.

Slavery

First, and most importantly, Dutra would have looked in vain for his main source of wealth and income: his slaves. The abolition of slavery in 1888 was, according to the best of the recent literature, the result of several important developments and tendencies. Slave resistance raised the social and economic costs of the institution. International shame heaped on Brazil for its continued failure to abolish the institution galvanized some in the government against slavery. Rising middle groups composed of public servants and professionals increasingly turned against the institution.

As I argue in this book, the turning of the middle groups away from slavery had less to do with their ideology and more to do with their shifting material interests: slaves became scarce and expensive; they meant less to the middle sectors over time. Of course some opposed slavery out of deep principles, but my more pessimistic measure of human nature precludes me from believing that these were in the majority. Slavery was an incredibly callous institution, and Rio de Janeiro, at least through the 1870s, was a very callous place. In the end, the government (with the emperor's daughter Princess Isabel at the fore), the middle sectors, some "progressive" planters, the international community, and the slaves themselves brought an end to slavery in Brazil.

In the new environment that followed, Dutra would have had to work as a barber-surgeon and build a fortune on the basis of his own wages and savings. He would have labored a long time indeed to save up enough money to purchase a house (median price, 7:000$000, in 1890), much less start a business and band of his own. In fact, as the century wore on barber-surgeons lost some of their respectability as the medical profession attempted to formalize and regulate the provision of healthcare.[58] To make matters more difficult, the great era of the barber-musicians was also gradually drawing to a close.[59] The central irony of Dutra's world was that it was one where thrift and luck on the part of the few could be leveraged into a fortune on the backs of slaves. Even a former slave like Dutra could be thrifty and lucky in the 1830s and 1840s. By the 1890s this was no longer the case in Rio's urban milieu.

Immigration

Dutra's arrival in Brazil in the early nineteenth century was a teardrop in an ocean of sorrow. Tens of thousands of Africans were transported each year against their will to Rio de Janeiro during the first half of the century. These involuntary immigrants and their offspring largely built the Rio de Janeiro that would be so transformed at the end of the century. In Dutra's day, slaves made up nearly half of the city's population. They worked and lived in all parts of the city. Some, like Dutra, obtained their freedom. By the 1870s, owing to the end of the Atlantic trade, manumission, legal changes, and the efforts of slaves themselves, there were far fewer slaves in the city as a proportion of the total population. Still, at this late date, Dutra would have recognized a familiar world. Would he have opposed the Law of the Free Womb had he lived through 1871?

These forced immigrants and their children and grandchildren were swamped in the 1880s and beyond by an unprecedented wave of voluntary immigration to Brazil's capital. The demographic profile of the city looked very different in 1890 than it did in 1849. Brazil was "whitening" and aspirants to middling status from the population of former slaves and their offspring faced increased discrimination (obviously nothing new in kind, but new in degree).

Financial Wealth

Dutra and his ilk were accustomed to a simple world of wealth. Slaves, houses, and small businesses were the only major investments they understood or sought to make. This made perfect sense circa 1849, when the city of Rio was filled with small businesses and slaves and when urbanization made houses an attractive, if expensive, investment option. To the extent that credit played a role in their lives, it was through informal networks, store credit given or received, and notarized contracts with individual lenders. By the late 1880s, owing to major institutional reforms enacted at the end of the empire and the stunning growth of the railroad sector, financial wealth in the form of stocks and bonds exploded in value relative to other assets. Some middling wealthholders owned such instruments, but they tended to come from an educated, "white" segment of the population in the professions and public service.[60] Few freedmen or free colored were likely to have invested in stocks and bonds—which, after all, were just pieces of paper of new and dubious value.

Although informal credit in all its diverse guises was extremely important to Dutra's world and really throughout the empire, by the early 1890s this form of wealth was almost completely eclipsed in the city of Rio de Janeiro. Dutra would not have recognized this new world in which cash was plentiful (printing it in such quantities led to a massive devaluation of the mil-réis), banks were thick on the ground, and middling wealthholders put their money in bank accounts rather than under the mattress. In a sample of 219 decedents for the period 1890 to 1895, cash holdings made up 6.1 percent, bank deposits 12.9 percent, and stocks and bonds 16.1 percent of net wealth. Meanwhile, informal credit all but disappeared, accounting for 2 percent of net wealth in the period. Cash and bank deposits and loans took the place of informal credit networks to a great extent.

Three major transformations occurred after 1850, as Rio de Janeiro's economic and social structures shifted toward the "modern" forms they would take in the 1890s: the gradual decline and eventual abolition of slavery; the rise of free, European immigration; and the institutional transformation of Brazil's credit markets with the creation of a modern banking system and stock market. Clearly there were other important processes and developments during this time. Railroad construction, which was intimately tied to capital markets and institutions was one thing; the coffee boom increasingly centered in São Paulo was another. For Dutra, the enduring irony is that the inhumane and "backward" world of 1849 was better for him and his family than would be this new world of wealth and political change in the 1890s.

5

PATHWAYS TO WEALTH IN RIO DE JANEIRO, 1815–1860

There have always been two paths to wealthholding: saving and inheriting. In many cases these paths intertwine. A small inheritance, with thrift and luck, can result in a fortune. The likelihood of social mobility, in turn, depends on a broad set of contextual factors. Periods of rapid economic growth can generate conditions ripe for social ascent; likewise, relatively fluid social structures permit a wider range of people to enter into the ranks of wealthholders; finally, the institutions that define and protect property rights will influence the type of wealth people hold, whether they are able to accumulate substantial wealth over time, and the conditions under which their wealth is passed on to the next generation.

From a distance, it is hard to view Brazil's social structure in the early 1800s as particularly amenable to social mobility. After all, in Rio de Janeiro, roughly half of the population was enslaved. Institutionally, in addition to slavery, Brazil lacked banks and other sophisticated means of mobilizing and expanding capital.[1] Surely, then, we are looking at a rather closed social structure in which upward social mobility was the exception rather than the rule. Yet this portrait is misleading. Although the absolute majority of the population of the city, slave and free, labored with little prospect of upward mobility, a substantial minority experienced life differently. Rapid urbanization, increasing occupational specialization, and the creation of wider networks of marketing and service within the ambit of Rio de Janeiro all contributed to real growth and mobility.[2]

Slavery was obviously a barrier to social mobility for slaves themselves—and this is no small point—yet for many lower and middling wealthholders, slaves provided the primary means of social ascent.[3] Slaves were relatively inexpensive and accessible relative to other income-generating assets such as residential real estate. The barrier to entry to owning slaves was low well into the 1840s. In addition, if Brazil lacked formal financial institutions, it nevertheless compensated for this in part with an enormous informal credit network channeled through individual contracts between private parties (sometimes mediated through notaries).[4] Property rights were actually fairly well specified and protected in the city of Rio de Janeiro and people in Brazil's capital could generally look to the courts and the law for neutral third-party enforcement rather than invest in the private (violent) enforcement of their property rights.[5] The relatively peaceful transition from colony to independent nation also saved many Brazilians from the uncertainty and property loss associated with violent revolutions in other Latin American countries.[6] Under these conditions, the argument of this chapter, however ironic, is that slavery, entrepreneurship, and informal credit networks provided the ladder of social mobility for most lower and middling wealthholders in the first half of the nineteenth century.

Three Pathways to Wealth: A Theoretical Parenthesis

Before we attempt to explain how Antonio José Dutra accumulated his fortune, it is necessary to consider, in general terms, the conditions under which the wealth held by his contemporaries in the late 1840s was obtained. Inheritance no doubt played a major role, especially in the larger estates. Although it is possible that some wealthholders in the top 20 percent of the distribution earned their fortunes in their own lifetimes, inheritance doubtlessly played a large role in many great estates.[7] The middling wealthholders of Rio de Janeiro probably cobbled together their estates through a combination of inheritance and savings. Because we lack data on the age of the decedents in our sample prior to the 1880s, and because we neither know how much of their wealth was inherited nor when they began to accumulate their fortunes, we must turn to a proxy measure of the process of accumulation over time. No proxy will perfectly capture this process. Indeed, what follows, is, bluntly stated, theoretical speculation.

The number of slaves held by a particular wealthholder provides a clue to the possible trajectory of wealth accumulation. If we begin with a very simple assumption, that the person began with no slaves (no inheritance), we can model the possible rate of slave purchases over time and, in this way, estimate the time required to accumulate a certain number of slaves. In order to construct these estimates, we need three basic sources of information: the income and rate of saving on the part of the prospective slaveholder; the rate of return on slaves; and the rate of inflation in slave values.

From the rate of saving, we can estimate the amount of time it would take to save to purchase the first slave—assuming that the poorest prospective entrants into slaveholding did not have ready access to credit. For the sake of simplicity in this example, income and the saving rate are assumed to remain constant in real terms over the course of accumulation. Once the first slave is purchased, the rate of return on the slave is then plowed back into savings to buy the next slave. Again, for simplification, the rate of return is assumed to be constant in real terms relative to the mean price of slaves over time. Finally, inflation enters the model in the form of lagged savings and returns relative to the price of a new slave. Lacking, for the most part, financial institutions in which to place savings in between purchases, wealth accumulators faced the problem of seeing their savings and returns decline relative to the cost of new slaves.

Putting the model in motion, we draw on salary and price data and apply some reasonable assumptions about savings and rates of return. How long, for instance, would it take a skilled urban worker, such as a carpenter, to save enough money to buy his first slave? Table 7 explores this question by assuming the following stylized facts: savings per year are equal to 20 percent of the wage of a skilled urban tradesman; the rate of return on slaveholding is a constant 15 percent; and all savings and returns are reinvested in the purchase of additional slaves.[8]

Beginning in 1825, our hypothetical carpenter saved 20$000; at the time, he congratulated himself on being about one-seventh of the way toward purchasing his first slave.[9] Over the course of the next year, he was disappointed to see the price of a slave rise, putting off his future purchase. Further slave price increases followed, but our carpenter's wages and savings began to catch up. By 1832, after eight years of saving, he was able to purchase his first slave. With the income from his newly acquired property, the time required to buy his next slave was considerably shortened to a little over three years. A third slave followed after a little over two years, followed by additional slaves in increasingly rapid succession. Clearly, the greatest barrier to entry into the class of slaveholders was the time and expense required to purchase the first slave. Along these lines, rapid increases in slave prices could delay acquisition for several years, and the death, illness, or flight of a newly acquired first slave constituted a severe blow to a fledgling slave owner. It also follows that those who inherited several healthy slaves, even if just three or four in number, stood a good chance of reconstituting a sizeable estate.

Many other factors came into play in the real world outside our model. Slaves died; others gave birth. Carpenters lost their jobs; others supplemented their income from additional work. The cost of food

Table 7

A Simple Model of Accumulation:
Slave Purchases in Rio de Janeiro

Year	Slave price	Savings, 20% of Skilled Slaves Labor Income	Income from Slaves	N Slaves
1825	155[a]	25		
1826	175	25		
1827	175	25		
1828	200	30		
1829	250	35		
1830	250	35		
1831	250	40		
1832	250	40		
1833	250	40	38	1
1834	250	40	38	
1835	250	40	38	
1836	250	40	75	2
1837	250	40	75	
1838	300	40	135	3
1839	330	40	149	
1840	360[b]	45	226[c]	4
1841	360	45	226	
1842	360	45	282	5
1843	360	45	338	6
1844	360	45	395	7
1845	366	50	439	8

Sources: For slave prices, Estate Inventories, Rio de Janeiro, AN, and the
Jornal do Comercio. Values interpolated except in years in bold type.
Savings rate is set at roughly 20 percent of the skilled wage of a
manual laborer, e.g. a carpenter; wages estimated at roughly twice
the yearly rental for unskilled slave labor, some values interpolated.
All values in current mil-réis.

Notes: a) mean price of slaves aged 15–40, both genders, estate inventories,
N = 139; b) mean price of slaves aged 14–40, both genders, Jornal do
Comercio, N = 61; c) rate of return calculated from rental
advertisements in the *Jornal do Commercio,* following the cost
estimates in Carvalho de Mello (1992): expenditures = 60 percent of
gross income from slave rental; gross income = 141$600 per year;
return = 56$400, or 15.7 percent. The model also asssumes that the
second through eighth slaves can be purchased in the year in which
their added income would suffice to cover their purchase price
when added to accumulated savings.

Table 8

Pathways to Wealth: Urban Wages and Slave Purchases

Year	Slave Price (age 15-45)	Nominal Income, Unskilled Worker	Nominal Income/ Slave Price	Years to Purchase at 20% Savings
c. 1820–25	148	80	0.54	9
c. 1845–49	421	147	0.35	14
c. 1855–60	978	300	0.31	16
c. 1868–73	808	328	0.41	12

Sources: Slave prices from Inventories, Rio de Janeiro, AN; Nominal income is the unskilled wage, derived from slave rental rates, *Jornal do Commercio*, Rio de Janeiro, with the exception of c. 1820, which is from inventories.

Note: Slave price derived from mean values, age 15–40, both genders, minimum of 250 observations per period. Values expressed in current mil-réis.

and rent (if our carpenter did not own his home) went up and down and affected savings rates and returns on slaves. In this regard, the model presents the best-case scenario for a prospective slaveholder; most likely, baring inheritance or other windfall gains, it took longer to acquire slaves than indicated in Table 7. Nevertheless, from this simple exercise, we can see how it was possible, in an environment of relatively inexpensive slaves, for a former slave barber-surgeon like Dutra to accumulate thirteen slaves of his own by the time of his death.

Time to purchase was intimately connected to the context in which savings started. Table 8 provides rough estimates of the relationship between slave prices and per-head income, showing how, over time, the cost of slaves rose relative to income.

Slave prices rose radically after the British suppression of the Atlantic trade in 1850. Whereas the mean price of slaves was in the range of 300$000 to 400$000 in the 1840s, it rose to over 1:000$000 by the end of the 1850s.[10] Real per-head income did not rise at anywhere near this rate. In fact, according to Goldsmith's estimates, real GDP per head rose just 14 percent from 1850 to 1860 in Brazil as a whole.[11] Although real wages probably rose faster in Rio de Janeiro, the ability of workers to purchase slaves was diminished. Equally importantly, the ability of slaves to save up the cost of their freedom was undermined by rapidly rising slave prices. Imagine a slave having worked and saved assiduously for a decade or more only to find that the last 50 mil-réis to freedom had turned into 500.

More specifically, according to Lobo's data (which we must take with a grain of salt) a carpenter saw his nominal wage rise about 30 percent between the mid-1840s and mid-1850s.[12] Meanwhile, the average price of a slave between the ages of fifteen and forty doubled over the same span. Naively assuming constant wages and slave prices projected forward from any given year, Table 8 indicates the implicit number of years required for someone earning a skilled urban wage and saving 20 percent per year to purchase one slave. Granting there were many intervening variables, it appears that the time required for the purchase of a slave roughly doubled from the 1820s to the 1850s; if this was indeed the case, then slavery, especially after 1850, became a much more restricted, elite-oriented institution. However, there would also be a lag period in which those who accumulated slaves in the middling wealthholding group saw their property rise dramatically in value over a few short years.

Exploitation and Expropriation: Pathways to Wealth Turned Upside-Down

Just as we can assess the pathways to wealth of the likes of Dutra, we can estimate, in rough terms, the amount of exploitation that slaves experienced at the hands of their masters over their lives.[13] Now, to be clear, it is much easier to measure the rate of expropriation (economic exploitation) than it is to measure the degree to which physical, mental, and sexual abuse battered slaves. In what follows I concentrated on the appropriation of income and wealth from slaves to their masters.

In the simplest terms, slaves transferred wealth and income to their owners at a rate corresponding to their economic "return." That is, after food, clothing, retained wages, advertising, and insurance, what was left over represented the rate of return for the slaveholder on his or her investment. The rate of return on slaveholding in Brazil is generally accepted to have been between 10 and 20 percent of the mean price of an adult slave.[14] Of course, this rate could be affected by myriad intervening variables, including, but not limited to: loss through flight or death; loss through slave resistance in the form of shirking or stealing; sunk costs associated with raising slaves to income-earning age; gains associated with rising wages in the urban milieu; and gains or losses associated with shifting slave price/rental ratios.

Obviously, prior to the 1850s, Brazilian slaveholders partially overcame the problem of sunk costs in rearing slaves by importing many adult slaves directly from Africa. However, slaveholders could never completely dominate their slaves, so we must assume that there was "leakage" in the system and that the rate of expropriation was never as high as owners would have liked. These considerations should make it clear that any discussion of the rate of expropriation of slave labor and the net value of transfers from slaves to owners will, by necessity, be conducted on a general and somewhat speculative level. Notwithstanding these limitations, it is worth considering what the level of expropriation was and how much it contributed to levels of wealth observed among the free population in general and the estate inventory samples in particular.

To begin with, the rate of expropriation over a slave's lifecycle depends fundamentally on whether they were born in Brazil and brought up as a slave at the expense (nominally at least) of the owner, or they were transported to Brazil during the years of the Atlantic slave trade. In the former case, it is proper to deduct the cost of raising a slave to young adulthood; in the latter, the owner begins to receive his or her full income stream from the very beginning of the relationship. Yet, as we know from analysis of runaway-slave advertisements, the majority of runaways were of African birth, so the "benefit" of buying a young adult slave from the slave market in the Valongo was counterbalanced by the "cost" of his or her higher propensity to run away (and perhaps lower degree of human capital formation). On this basis alone, we would predict that Brazilian-born slaves of the same age would fetch higher prices, *ceteris paribus*, than their African-born counterparts. This is, in fact, precisely what Laird Bergad's massive study of slave prices in Minas Gerais shows.[15]

At this juncture, we simply do not have the necessary data to render conclusive estimates of the average rate of expropriation or the net transfer of income and wealth this entailed in Rio de Janeiro. Rather, what is ventured here is an educated guess as to the upper and lower bounds of these values. Let us begin with the average rate of expropriation circa 1849. If we assume for the sake of argument that costs associated with slave children and slave resistance (runaways, theft, and so on) cut into the real rate of return by 50 percent, and we assume, furthermore, that the rate of return absent these factors was 15 percent, we arrive at an annual figure of 7.5 percent of the mean slave price as the level of expropriation.[16] There were 78,855 slaves in Rio de Janeiro according to the census of 1849.[17] The average price of a working-age slave that year in the city was about 400$000.[18] Thus, the average working slave (deducting for child costs and resistance) transferred about 30$000 to his or her owner. To reiterate, these are very rough figures. Adding it all up, it appears, by this rough and conservative calculation, that slaves may have transferred something like 2,365:000$000 to their owners during 1849 alone.

In the course of a slave's life, or in the course of the decades for the population as a whole, the net transfer of wealth through expropriation of slave labor must have been truly staggering. On the basis of the foregoing, it is possible that the generation of slaves associated with Dutra's world transferred more than 20,000 contos to their owners during the decade leading up to Dutra's death in 1849. I estimate that mean wealth per head in Rio de Janeiro, circa 1849, was on the order of 800$000. Of this, about 17 percent was represented by the value of slaves. In a city of 205,000 people, this translates to 164,000 contos in total wealth: 27,880 contos in slaves, and 136,120 contos in nonhuman wealth. Put in this perspective, the truly colossal value of the expropriated labor of slaves is thrown into high relief.

For historians interested in counterfactual analysis, it would be worth exploring the implications for Brazilian social and economic structure had slavery been abolished in 1850 around the same time the Atlantic trade was ended. The stream of expropriated income that slaveholders continued to enjoy, on a large scale through the 1870s, would have been retained by the former slaves in this counterfactual world. At the rate of more than 2,000 contos per year, this would have given the former slaves of Rio de Janeiro resources to improve their housing, clothing, food, education, and health. Compounded over a generation, the retention of these expropriated resources could conceivably have lifted many Afro-Brazilians from poverty, increased their human capital endowment, and made for a more egalitarian society.[19]

However, back in the real world of Rio de Janeiro in the middle of the nineteenth century, middling wealthholders depended disproportionately on this expropriated wealth to build their own estates. Were there other ways for the striving middle groups to gain ground economically?

Alternative Pathways to Wealth

Discounting inheritance, which was perhaps the most important path to wealth, we can also ask whether middling wealthholders built up their estates without recourse to slavery. The answer, for the most part, seems to be negative—at least for the 1820s through the 1840s. First, what were the alternatives? Simple savings clearly would not suffice unless a prospective wealthholder's salary was very high indeed: inflation took a toll; banks were very little used; and stocks and bonds were almost entirely absent—even in the portfolios of the rich. Informal credit mechanisms were an option, but middling wealthholders did not have the capital to lend out large sums—indeed, they tended to owe rather than be owed.

Thus, the role of credit was not to enrich the middle sectors but to provide it with the capital needed to start and run small businesses, purchase slaves, and smooth income and expenses over the years. The richest 20 percent lent out 82 percent of all informal credit in the late 1840s and the middle 60 percent absorbed 67 percent of all debts in the same period. Clearly, the wealthy operated as informal credit providers for middling debtors in Rio de Janeiro. This arrangement benefited both parties on the whole. Lenders generally received a good rate of return on their loans, often in excess of 15 percent per year, which was competitive with the return on both slaves and real estate.[20]

Remarkably little work has been done to date regarding the functioning of the massive informal credit market in Rio de Janeiro (and elsewhere in Brazil). Most often, the literature simply ignores the matter completely; when credit is brought up at all, high interest rates tend to be emphasized much more than the ubiquity of such credit and its economic utility. There was a far wider range in rates than is commonly assumed; moreover, we would need to know much more about risk, transaction costs, and the opportunity cost of capital to come to any firm conclusion about where the rates were really "high" by the standards of their time and place. Is it true that the interest rates charged for credit in Rio de Janeiro were high by the standards of more mature credit markets in the United States at roughly the same time? Preliminary indications are that they were not. In what follows, I examine a particularly revealing case from 1855 to draw some preliminary conclusions about the risks and rewards of lending.

Upon his death in 1855, Domingos José da Costa Guimarães left his widow to deal with an unraveling business empire. His firm, Guimarães and Klett, was declared bankrupt by the commercial court, owing to financial malfeasance on the part of his associates to the tune of 500 contos. As a partner in the firm, Domingos and then his estate ended up owing 60 contos. His widow, Dona Rita, was able to pay this sum in four installments of 15 contos. But more was to come. She also ended up paying an additional 10:916$000 to individual creditors as well as 19:461$000 to one Gomes Braga with the proceeds from an insurance policy. At the end of the process, this once rich woman was left with 25:520$000, far less than the appraised value, 96:445$000, of her and her husband's property.[21]

Embedded in this case are key bits of information about credit and borrowing in mid-nineteenth-century Rio de Janeiro. First, it is clear from this record that not all debts were paid in full. We might have assumed this, but here we have direct evidence. Dona Rita paid something to all the estate's creditors, but many received partial payments, most of which were equivalent to one-half of their face value. Clearly, if a rich man like Domingos could end up a credit risk, loans to less well-to-do borrowers must also have carried substantial risk as well. Thus, an interest rate of 1.25 percent per month may not have been so high after all. This rate, in fact, corresponds approximately to the opportunity cost of lending money rather than investing in a prime rental slave. The rate charged in this case and its relationship to slave prices and returns is strikingly similar to that found in antebellum New Orleans. According to one estimate, the implicit rate of interest in slave sales in New Orleans in the period 1804–62 was 1.547 percent per month, or 18.56 percent per annum.[22] Longer-term credit in the U.S. South was lent at about 10 percent per year.[23] The common claim that credit was scarce and expensive in Brazil during much of the nineteenth century may require revision, at least in the case of Rio de Janeiro.

Beyond this, the case of Domingos and Dona Rita has implications for how we think about the use of credit in Rio de Janeiro's urban marketplace. Along with the loans taken out to pay the debts of the estate, the couple owed small and medium sums to a whole range of urban types, most of whom we must assume were far poorer than they. Why did they obtain services, such as construction work and repairs, on credit rather than paying cash? One tempting possibility is that some such services were not charged at interest. The artisan Antonio da Conceição Portugal probably did not charge interest for the debt owed him for a carved image of Jesus (and in the end only received half payment); likewise with the pastry shop, Castellões, and the barbershop Baumelly and Guinard. Wealthy and middling residents of the city could obtain services and goods on credit to be repaid on a convenient basis. The lender of a service or retail goods was not in as good a position to charge interest as the lender of cash or the equivalent in notes. The next-best option for the service provider, for instance the woodcarver Antonio, may have been to carve nothing and make no money at all; likewise, a shop owner could sell on credit or perhaps sell nothing at all. For the moneylender there was a definite opportunity cost associated with lending inasmuch as the money could be invested in alternatives, such as slaves, with high returns.

Illustration 13. *Bakeries and other retail establishments were thick on the ground in Rio de Janeiro, providing income and wealth to the city's entrepreneurs. In this scene, set in the morning, the bakery has just opened and a sale of flour has been made to a young slave boy sent on this errand by his owner. In the background, the establishment's slave workers begin their day preparing wheat for milling.* (Jean Baptiste Debret, Voyage Pittoresque et Historique au Brésil, *3 volumes, Paris, 1834–1839*).

Many small and medium businesses were both debtors and creditors. José Ferreira Maia Sobrinho, owner of a combination bakery and import-export business located on Rua da Saúde, was owed debts, mostly for small sums, by seventy individuals and companies; he also owed large amounts to his suppliers—some of which were based in Baltimore and New Orleans. His outstanding credits totaled 13:538$000 and his debts came to 73:086$000. The nature of his debt is instructive, inasmuch as he owed money to creditors of cash as well as supplies. Of the first, his debts cost him between 8 and 9 percent per year—perhaps because they were destined for the purchase of flour and other supplies for the store and bakery, the rate of interest on these loans (*letras*) was relatively low by any standard. Along these lines, the estate was able to save a little by paying some loans back early, indicating that good borrowers were sometimes rewarded by their creditors.[24]

Borrowers, large and small, benefited from these credit arrangements in a variety of ways. Purchases of goods on credit allowed them to maintain personal or business consumption at steady levels—many of the debts owed to the wealthy were for small amounts, often representing store credit in the cases of decedents with retail or wholesale establishments. For example, when the aforementioned bakery owner José Ferreira's inventory was settled in 1856, his debtors numbered seventy, with the vast majority owing less than 100 mil-réis. Along with these small loans, José Ferreira also lent money in larger amounts of 3:500$000 and 2:500$000, for which his estate received the principal and interest.[25] Borrowers with assets, such as slaves or houses, could obtain larger loans using their assets as collateral. This was precisely what Domingos José da Costa Guimarães's widow, Dona Rita, did in 1855 when she mortgaged her house and thirteen slaves for a loan of 25:862$000 (at 1.25 percent interest per month) for payment of debts associated with the settlement of her husband's estate.[26]

The alternatives to building an estate on the back of slave labor, leaving aside the remote possibility of a middling fortune being built on lending, were to build a small business, such as a barbershop or a tavern, to obtain a well-paid government position, or to become a landlord. In the first case, business owners almost always invested in slaves as well—so slavery remained at the heart of their enterprises. The last option, becoming a landlord, as attractive as it may have been, was uncommon among the middling wealthholders of Rio de Janeiro—recall that most middling wealthholders owned just one residence. Public employment, which may have functioned to a degree as a source of social mobility and means of entry into middling status, was, however, restricted in a variety of ways. Most positions required literacy, some degree of "whiteness," and social connections: a combination possessed by a small minority of potential wealthholders. Indeed, according to Mary Karasch's analysis of the 1834 census for Rio de Janeiro, white males outnumbered free men of color by nearly sixteen-to-one in public employment.[27] Thus, the two pathways to wealth that were least directly associated with slaveholding, property ownership and public service, were also the least accessible to the majority of aspiring wealthholders in Rio de Janeiro.

Given that housing prices increased more rapidly than any other asset in the first half of the nineteenth century, why did wealthholders of moderate means fail to enter the market on a larger scale? The answer, simply, is that they could not afford to. The mean price of a house in Rio de Janeiro before 1850 typically outweighed the mean price of a prime-age male slave by a factor of ten. Even if a prospective buyer wanted to enter at the bottom of the market, the price of houses in the bottom 20 percent of the distribution of values still cost roughly three times as much as a slave. A simple calculation along the lines suggested in Table 8 indicates that a skilled urban worker would have to toil for a lifetime just to buy a cheap house. Moreover, the rate of return (leaving aside capital gains) on residential real estate in Rio de Janeiro may have averaged about 7 percent, so the purchase of a third house with the accrued returns from the second would take twice as long as a similar operation with a slave earning 15 percent per annum. Houses were expensive in Rio de Janeiro and were not, therefore, a means of social mobility for the majority of poorer and middling wealthholders. At best, the capital gains accruing over time from home ownership sufficed to provide a larger estate for the heirs of middling decedents.

On the basis of the foregoing discussion, we hypothesize that middling wealthholders during the 1810s through the 1840s would typically invest much more in slaves, in quantity and some cases in value, than in houses. The data from our sample bear out this contention. Whereas the wealthy typically owned several homes, wealthholders in the middle range typically owned just one or, at most, two homes; at the same time, many of these same middling fortunes contained a relatively large number of slaves.[28] It was not that more homes, especially of lower quality, could not have been purchased by this group; rather, the opportunity cost of saving the equivalent of three to ten slaves rather than investing in slaves and reaping immediate rewards was too high. The wealthy, in contrast, derived sufficient income to purchase homes outright, or at least without having to save for several years. Thus, for this group, there was no need to forego present opportunities for the future returns of residential property ownership. It follows, along these lines, that the lack of more sophisticated financial institutions tended to force lower- and middle-wealth groups into investing in slaves—the only relatively low-cost, high-return investment available to them at the time. It also follows that once slave prices rose dramatically in the 1850s, the opportunity costs associated with shifting to alternative investments would be lower.

Dutra's Way: A Typology of Middling Wealth in Nineteenth-Century Rio de Janeiro

The premise of this book is that Antonio Dutra, in spite of his unusual background, can best be understood as a fairly representative middling wealthholder in 1840s Rio de Janeiro. Delving deeper into his estate inventory, we can reconstruct, with some imagination, his path

Illustration 14. *Dutra's barbershop may have looked something like this. The inscription over the door indicates that the shop engaged in a full range of services, including barbering, bleeding, tooth extraction, and the application of leeches.* (*Jean Baptiste Debret,* Voyage Pittoresque et Historique au Brésil, *3 volumes, Paris, 1834–1839*).

to wealth. Placed alongside a dozen other wealthholders of his stature, we better understand how the middle class in Rio de Janeiro was created over the first decades of the nineteenth century.

Dutra's total estate, as we have had occasion to note, amounted to 15:420$680, of which 13:187$280 were left after deducting funeral expenses and other costs associated with his death. He owned two urban residences, but lived in neither, electing, instead, to live in his rented barbershop—which, looked at from one angle, was a form of saving inasmuch as he could rent out both of his houses. In this, he was better off than the median wealthholder, who generally owned but one house. Dutra did not own the building in which his barbershop was located. As with a great many small entrepreneurs, he rented his space. Paying 24 mil-réis per month in rent, he occupied an advantageous location near the commercial heart of the city on Rua da Alfândega, number 163, surrounded by other small businesses including a cabinetmaker, a sculptor, a woodcarver, a saddle maker, and a wicker weaver.[29] Along with his houses on Rua do Saco do

Alferes in the north-central neighborhood of Gamboa, on the border between the parishes of Santa Anna and Santa Rita, Dutra owned thirteen slaves, eleven of whom were male, and almost all of whom were African-born. Slaves and residences made up the bulk of his estate; sundry items, cash, silver, inexpensive furnishings, and musical instruments for his band accounted for the rest.[30]

Although he does not say in his testament, and there is no direct evidence in the inventory, we can reconstruct the manner in which Dutra amassed his small fortune with a fair amount of confidence. First, we know that he had six children, the oldest of which was his daughter Ignacia, married to the alleged adulterer and spendthrift, João Baptista, a semiliterate *pedreiro* (stonemason).[31] We know, through the legal maneuverings of her estranged husband in the aftermath of Dutra's death, that Ignacia was baptized in Rio de Janeiro on September 2, 1822, in the parish of Sacramento, just five days before Brazil became an independent country.[32] Ignacia was about twenty-seven years old at the time of her father's death in 1849. If we assume Dutra was about twenty when his first daughter was born, we can estimate his age at somewhere between forty-five and fifty years old at the time of his death.[33]

Both Ignacia and her mother, Josefa Mina, were slaves at the time of his daughter's birth. We cannot be sure whether Dutra himself was still a slave when his daughter was born, but we can be reasonably sure that he was enjoying his freedom by 1827, when he paid 128$000 for Ignacia's freedom to her owner, Antonio José Rebello. Once freed, Ignacia was sent to live as an *aggregado* (nonkin resident) in the house of a certain Tenente Saturnino.[34] Noteworthy as well is the fact that no further mention is made of Josefa in the record, with the exception of a moment when Ignacia's estranged husband challenges her assertion to have been the daughter of Dutra's second lover, Hilaria. Whether she died in captivity or was subsequently freed, and what role if any Dutra played in this, we simply do not know. It is possible that Dutra and Josefa were, at one time, both slaves of Antonio José Rebello. Josefa is listed as such in the baptismal registry and Dutra's first two names correspond exactly to Rebello's. It was common for freed slaves to take on parts of their former master's names.

Following our model presented in Table 7, it is tempting to speculate that Domingos, aged forty-six, was Dutra's first slave purchase. Next would have been Joaquim, age forty. With these two slaves working side by side with him in his barbering business, Dutra would have been able to acquire his homes and his other slaves within a period of about twenty years. At the other end of the age spectrum, his younger slaves point to a high degree of prosperity attained late in life. All told, Dutra owned four slaves under age twenty and six slaves under twenty-two—nearly half of his workforce was made up of young, prime-age males. Dutra did not own older female slaves. Thus, even his Brazilian-born slave, aged eighteen, was probably purchased and not the result of a union of Dutra's slaves in the past. The only addition via natural increase was the two-year-old child of Carlota, his cook.[35] Given the age structure of Dutra's slaves, it is likely that he refrained from purchasing slaves younger than thirteen or fourteen. He also purchased few female slaves, as they did not fit in with his enterprises—neither acceptable as barbers nor as musicians. This strategy made double sense for Dutra. Not only did his focus on adolescent and adult male slaves fit with his business needs, it also meant that he rarely had to worry about the costs of caring for young slaves.

At Dutra's death, the Brazilian legal system required a strict accounting of the income generated from his estate. The orphans' judge, required in all cases in which there were heirs under the age of majority, and the court-sanctioned tutor of Dutra's children took pains to ensure that each child received proper care and that the inheritance of each was not wasted. According to his estate record, Dutra was making a very respectable living in the last months of his life. To wit: his barbershop had earned 530$000 over ten months, his rental property generated another 484$000 over eleven months, and his band of musicians made an impressive 1:036$000 over seven months.[36] In other words, his postmortem income was 245$000 per month, representing a return of 2:940$000 per year on income generating assets valued at 10:300$000. The costs of running the barbershop included rent, supplies, and payments to the slaves. All told, when the business was running well, these costs ate up less than half of the gross income from the shop and the band. Small business, at least in this case, paid handsomely; yet, entrepreneurs like Dutra walked a fine line between profitability and substantial losses with their reliance on slaves who could fall ill or run away.

The most interesting aspect of Dutra's business strategy was his decision to employ his slaves in multiple roles. Had he limited their work to the barbershop, his income would have fallen by more than half. José Ramos Tinhorão's research into the history of barber-musicians suggests that the combination of barbers and music went back at least to the late eighteenth century in Rio de Janeiro.[37] Dutra's band was, therefore, of a piece with general trends in urban popular culture in Brazil at the time. Tinhorão also suggests why it was that barbers, of all the professions, became identified with music: they had spare time to devote to learning to play musical instruments. Although it is hard to subscribe to Tinhorão's depiction of barber-surgeons as "liberal" professionals, his explanation for their proclivity to music has merit.[38] Clients came to Dutra's shop sporadically; in the intervening hours, the workers could practice their music. Moreover, because Dutra owned a critical mass of slaves, he was able to form a complete band in terms of the expectations of the day.

The most likely venues for the band's performances were festivals associated with the patron saints of various churches and brotherhoods in the city. Travelers' accounts mention barber bands playing in the doorways of churches during these festivals.[39] One memoir of the city, published in 1904 by Melo Moraes Filho, recounts the prominence of the barber-musicians in the street festival held in the parish of Glória during the middle of the nineteenth century. Included in this memoir is a tantalizing reference to "a certain Dutra, master barber on the Rua da Alfândega," whose band played in this festival and was known throughout the city.[40] Although Tinhorão suggests that this reference to Dutra must be from the 1860s, owing to Moraes Filho's probable age at the time, it seems equally possible that Moraes Filho was recounting the name of Dutra himself, who may have been the most successful barber-surgeon and band leader of his day.[41]

Although we do not have information regarding the length of time during which Dutra's band played, it appears that his band started with two or three clarinets and a trombone, to which he added trumpets, drums, and other simple percussion instruments. It is noteworthy that the youngest members of the band all played at least simple percussion: even at this level, Dutra found ways to maximize the skills of his slaves.[42] The fact that his oldest, perhaps first purchased, slave did not play in the band is also suggestive. Perhaps he focused his initial energy on building his barbering business, then branched into band leading once he had purchased enough slaves to form a group.

The listed skill levels of Dutra's slaves also go toward estimating their time of purchase. Of the six male slaves twenty-one years old or younger, all but one is listed as an apprentice barber. If we assume that the period of apprenticeship was less than five years, it follows that the slaves aged twenty-one and twenty were probably purchased during the mid-1840s—otherwise, had they been purchased earlier, they would have been listed as barbers and not apprentices.[43] Along these lines, it is likely that the other four adolescent male slaves were recent purchases: they did not play complicated musical instruments, and they were all listed as apprentice barbers. On this basis, it is tempting to speculate that six of Dutra's thirteen slaves were purchased in the last years of his life. This comports with the simple model proposed in Table 7, in which the rate of slave purchases rises dramatically after the purchase of the fifth slave, as well as with what we know about Dutra's approximate age and length of time lived as a liberto.

One final piece of the puzzle helps confirm this surmise. In his testament, Dutra freed only the five oldest male slaves in his barbershop. Along with these men, he freed his domestic, Carlota, and her infant son Alexandre.[44] These were the five men and one woman who helped him build his fortune; years of work together in the barbershop and in the band created personal bonds and led Dutra to free his most valuable—in terms of income generation—assets. The younger slaves, having been purchased recently with the proceeds from the labor of the others, were relegated to continued servitude.

Small Businesses of Rio

Dutra's estate was just one of many in Rio built on small business wealth. Another prosaic example of this form of wealthholding is found in the estate of José Joaquim Gaspar dos Reis, a *funileiro* (tinsmith or tinker) of middling wealth. José Joaquim's business sufficed to leave his heirs with a liquid estate of 6:632$000—about half the value of Dutra's barbershop and band.[45] The greater part of the estate was tied up in two urban properties and a shop on Rua de São Pedro in the poor suburb of Cidade Nova.[46]

Along with his real property, José Joaquim owned six slaves, one of which was a one-year-old baby girl. Two of his slaves, both African-born males aged eighteen, are listed as working in the shop; the other adult slaves, all African-born women, are listed as domestics. The age structure of José Joaquim's slaveholding indicates that he may have just begun to use slaves in his primary business (or he may have replaced older slaves in the same capacity). Two of his female slaves were older—aged fifty-six and sixty—and the other, aged thirty, was still a bit older than his male slaves. It therefore appears that this small businessman originally used slaves as domestics, perhaps renting them out on a monthly basis.

Like many people of middling wealth, José Joaquim owed a significant sum in debts. The source of the debts is not specified, but it is tempting to speculate that he accrued some of it in purchasing his two young, expensive African-born slaves or perhaps one of his residential properties. All told, his estate teetered on the verge—a couple of sick slaves from ruin, another few years of luck from glory.

A further window into the lives of the middle groups of Rio de Janeiro in the middle of the nineteenth century is opened when we examine the receipts appended to José Joaquim's inventory. Among the expenses paid during the last year of his life was the rental of a wet nurse. The aspirations of the middle sectors included music lessons and wet nurses. Middle-class appearances were constructed through a combination of visible markers: place of residence, ownership of slaves, consumption of culture or upper-class services, and an emphasis on a respectable table setting, and proper attire in public. As one contemporary observer noted:

> It is presumed that every respectable person will dress well, not only in fact but also in form. Hence, none are allowed to go into public offices, or into the National Museum or Library, who are not dressed in coats. A jacket is the special abhorrence of the Brazilian laws of etiquette . . . he that would be respectable must put on a coat whenever he goes out, and if he pleases, a tolerably heavy coat of cloth.[47]

In a city characterized by complex social hierarchies and a heterogeneous population, appearances could be everything. Slaves, for instance, were generally not allowed to go about wearing shoes—a clear and visible marker of their status.

Along with providing services like barbering, many middling wealthholders engaged in small-scale commerce. Joaquim José de Almeida Freitas, a native of Portugal like many other small-time merchants in Rio, died in 1845 with a net estate valued at 13 contos. Owner of a small general store selling secos e molhados, his estate comprised a house worth 3:500$000, two slaves in domestic service worth 330$000, business assets of 6:354$000 (mainly in the stock of the store), various furnishings and clothing worth 742$000, and 2:291$000 worth of dívidas ativas (outstanding credits owed for merchandise from the store).[48] Small businesses like Joaquim's were thick on the ground in Rio during the middle part of the nineteenth century. The Almanack [Laemmert] administrativo, the capital's most comprehensive business compendium, listed no fewer than 715 enterprises in the category of secos e molhados (dried and fresh foods) in the late 1840s.[49]

The presence of dívidas ativas was common among members of the merchant class, whether rich or middling in wealth. Indeed, with an absence of banks and a nascent money economy, such credits played a key role in lubricating the wheels of commerce in the mid-nineteenth century. Even the poorest entrepreneurs in the retail and restaurant/liquor business extended credit to their customers. José Francisco Silva, tavern owner and native of Portugal, died in 1847 with all of 1:857$000 to his name. Of his estate, 600$000 were accounted for by two slaves, another 1:017$000 in the value of his business, and the rest, 234$000, were in dívidas ativas—that is, in the names listed as bar tabs owed by his customers.[50]

Another middling wealthholder, at the bottom end of the spectrum, was Joaquina Roza da Silva Guimarães. Owner, with her husband, of a tavern in the front room of their house on Rua do Catete, in Rio's central-south district, her estate was valued at 2:497$000 at the time of her death in 1849. Nearly all this sum was tied up in the family domicile/business. Somewhat unusually, given that more than 80 percent of wealthholders in the sample owned slaves, the couple owned no bondsmen. Mother of five children, Joaquina and her husband had probably been in the tavern business for quite some time, and the rate of growth in their wealth looks to have been minimal from returns to the business. Indeed, if their home was inherited, the only conclusion to draw is that they just made enough from their tavern to get by—as their meager personal possessions came to just 108$000 in furnishings and sundries, with another 365$000 in working capital invested in the tavern (in the form of food and drink).[51]

Of all entrepreneurs, tavern keepers were probably the most numerous throughout the period under consideration. According to Lobo's analysis of contemporary reports, there were no fewer than 1,150 taverns (generally taken to mean simple dining and drinking establishments, most often little more than a small storefront and a couple of tables in what was also a private home) in the capital circa 1852.[52] If we assume each tavern was kept by the members of a single household, it appears that up to 5 percent of Rio de Janeiro's households anchored their fortunes in such enterprises (calculated with ten persons per household) although it is likely the mean household size of these tavern owners was smaller than the citywide mean.

More broadly, the number of small and medium businesses in Rio de Janeiro circa 1850 is truly astounding. In his report to the city council (camera municipal) in 1853, Candido Borges Monteiro listed no fewer than 3,882 commercial establishments, 419 fábricas (workshops and small factories) and 919 oficiais (artisans) located in Rio de Janeiro in 1852.[53] By 1861, according to the Almanack, there were 1,117 fábricas, 3,683 commercial establishments, and 1,022 service businesses in the city.[54] What is remarkable about these statistics is what little notice

Illustration 15. *A bootmaker punishes a slave in his shop. Although the slave system in Rio de Janeiro included many "positive" incentives for slaves to conform and obey, such as wages and, sometimes, the prospect of manumission, they continually faced the prospect of corporal punishment.* (Jean Baptiste Debret, Voyage Pittoresque et Historique au Brésil, 3 *volumes, Paris, 1834–1839*).

they have received in the historical literature. This is particularly troubling from the perspective of social history. Most of these businesses were run by poor and middling wealthholders; their widespread prevalence and potential role in social mobility and class formation beg much more detailed study.[55] Indeed, it strikes this author that the story of more than one thousand tavern keepers merits telling as much, or more so, as the story of the fifty-eight sugar *engenhos* located within the boundaries of Brazil's capital.[56] Yet, we know infinitely more about sugar and coffee barons than we do about small-time entrepreneurs.

It was possible for skilled urban workers, such as stonemasons and carpenters, to acquire substantial wealth with hard work and thrift. Consider, for example, Francisco José Gonçalves, native of Rio and son of a Portuguese, who died in 1848 with an estate worth 22:745$000. A master carpenter, Francisco's wealth was mainly tied up in real estate worth a total of 18:300$000. Along with his houses and urban lots, he also owned eight slaves worth 3:900$000. Of these eight, five worked as carpenters, presumably under the direction of Francisco himself.[57]

His real estate returned a healthy 780$000 in the year after his death, and his slaves earned 1:036$000 from their carpentry work. The gross return on his rental property was just under 10 percent, whereas his slaves returned 32 percent before deducting their wages and sustenance. The yearly rental value of a slave carpenter was therefore about 200$000. How much of this could Francisco have hoped to keep? In order to estimate this, we need to know more about the earnings of slaves themselves.

We know from Dutra's record and other sources that the yearly cost of sustenance was likely on the order of 40$000 to 50$000 circa 1849. This estimate is based on the reported expenditure of 7$000 per month for food and clothing for Dutra's eldest boys and assumes that a little over half of this went to food.[58] We also know that slaves expected to be paid for their work in urban settings. Slaves working in Dutra's barbershop earned between 5$000 and 10$000 per month for barbering and as much again for playing music.[59] All told, they could make between 100$000 and 200$000 per year, from which they were expected to pay for their food and clothing—keeping whatever remained for possible self-purchase in the future or other expenses. On one side of the ledger, then, well-employed slaves such as Dutra's could accumulate the necessary funds to purchase their freedom in five to ten years. Of course, their problem was that if the price of slaves rose radically, as it did in the early 1850s, they could see years added to the time required to purchase their freedom.

From these varied examples, a clearer picture of the source of middling wealthholding emerges. Leaving aside inherited wealth, there were three main pathways to wealth accumulation in Rio de Janeiro during Dutra's time. The first, followed by Dutra himself, was in the provision of services in the growing urban economy. Barbershops, taverns, and other services could provide the basis for a modest fortune. Construction and repair work, likewise, offered opportunities for skilled urban workers to build surprisingly large estates. The second pathway, most often associated in the literature with the middling groups in Brazil, was found in government employment. Finally, for a few middling wealthholders, rental income from urban residential property sufficed to build wealth. This last option was limited insofar as the cost of housing was persistently high throughout the period and barriers to entry were consequently high. The cheapest housing tended to be owned by wealthier landlords, who owned tenements known as *moradas de casas*. Indeed, of the 175 residential properties surveyed for the period 1845–49, nearly all the cheapest—costing less than 1:000$000—were in the hands of the wealthiest decedents in the sample.[60]

Among middling wealthholders, an important distinction must be drawn between those who depended largely on slaves for their income and those who did not. Although we lack sufficient observations to claim with certainty, it appears that slave-dependent decedents had better prospects for wealth accumulation over the course of their lives. If this was the case, it is easier to understand the pervasiveness of slavery at all levels of society in Rio during the first half of the nineteenth century. Skilled slaves returned as much as 15 percent per year on their value, and no other investment was as accessible to lower-wealth residents of the city.

Middling slaveholders built up their holdings in accordance with the prevailing gender distinctions associated with their chosen line of work. Dutra's barbershop employed only men. Francisco's carpentry business, likewise, was an all-male concern. In contrast, José Jordão da Costa, owner of a tailoring and seamstress business, employed roughly equal numbers of male and female slaves, although his female slaves were more important to his enterprise. Of his fourteen slaves, six were male and eight female. Age and gender mattered a great deal in this case, as two of his male slaves were quite old (both aged sixty) and incapacitated for work (one was sick, the other, reportedly, a drunk). Of the four able male slaves, one worked as a tailor and another as a carpenter (rented out, no doubt). José da Costa probably lost money on his male slaves. The female contingent of his workforce was more productive—although it appears that their health was even worse than the males. The oldest slave in his estate was a seventy-year-old female listed as handicapped. Two others, aged sixty and seventeen, died between the time his estate was appraised in 1847 and the time the assets were distributed to his heirs in 1848. The remaining five all worked as seamstresses.[61]

José's slaveholding was not, by this accounting, particularly remunerative. Between sick and dying slaves and the elderly and incapacitated, it appears that no more than half of his slaves were still productive at the time of his death. This should caution us against falling into the trap of assuming that slavery paid dependably and well for the middle groups. Indeed, José Jordão, like many middling wealthholders, had more than one source of income—in his case, beyond the tailoring and sewing business, he had worked as a scribe (escrivão) in the almoxarifado (depository) of Márumba. His retirement income from this job provided him with a substantial supplemental income—roughly the equivalent of what he might have made from the labor of several skilled slaves. Projecting this income backward, it appears that most of José's wealth was accumulated on the backs, or better from the hands, of his slaves.

José Jordão's inheritance record raises a final point of distinction within the universe of middling wealth. Educated professionals such as José are the only middling wealthholders that held sophisticated financial assets to any significant degree prior to the 1850s. Whereas Antonio Dutra accumulated a sufficient fortune with which to buy stocks and bonds, he owned none. Financial instruments of this kind were largely outside of Dutra's understanding, because he was probably illiterate. José, a professional scribe, had no such limitations and owned 9:976$000 worth of bonds at the time of his death. Another educated wealthholder of middling stature who held bonds was retired navy captain José Thomas Rodrigues, whose 7:184$000 estate included 3:150$000 worth of bonds.[62] All told, the vast majority of middling wealthholders in mid-nineteenth-century Rio held no such assets. Only the educated, and particularly government workers, had access to the information required to invest heavily in financial assets, which remained almost exclusively in the hands of the very wealthy.

Government employment, however, was no sure path to riches. Only the highest echelons of the state apparatus earned incomes substantial enough to build a fortune on. For instance, the civilian employees of the War Arsenal in Rio de Janeiro earned an average (N=40) of 585$000 per year in 1846–47. A doctor in the Military Hospital earned 840$000, and a *porteiro* (doorman) in the same establishment earned 300$000 plus a daily ration of food worth about 200$000 per year.[63] A highly paid government official, such as a department head, made 1:600$000.[64] Average earnings in government work appear to have been about half again as high as skilled manual labor. Yet, a crafty entrepreneur like Dutra was able to generate 2:000$000 per year or more in cash-flow through his barbering and band leading, and very few government officials earned as much in salary alone.

The portion of the middle sector derived from the ranks of government employees is difficult to estimate. Many estate inventories do not specify the profession of the decedent, and few inventories indicate government employment. Other sources of information include the *Almanak [Laemmert]*, census figures, and the estimates of travelers. According to the incomplete but instructive census of 1834, there were 1,182 public officials in Rio de Janeiro, along with another

2,076 military and naval officers of varying rank. Many of these men were of low status and pay. Workers in the National Mint earned a median salary under 400$000 per annum circa 1825, with low-status jobs paying 200$000 or less.[65] The mean salary among civilian employees of the Military Arsenal, circa 1846, was 585$000.[66] Even if we assume, generously, that 10 percent of government workers and military men earned more than 1:000$000 per year in salary, circa 1834, this would amount to a little over three hundred individuals—a small number relative to the thousands of shopkeepers, slaveholders, landlords, and skilled laborers in the city. To be sure, many public workers must have entered the ranks of middling wealth, but they probably did so with the aid of income from slave labor and rents and capital gains from property ownership.

The most common pathway to wealth among middling wealthholders lay through a combination of slaveholding and entrepreneurship, with a minority of the middle sector deriving its income and wealth from government employment and urban rental property. Unlike the very wealthy, for whom slaves made up a small portion of their estate and an even smaller portion of their income, the value of slaves and the importance of their income rose significantly relative to other assets in the middle of the distribution of wealthholders. Indeed, the analysis developed here highlights the way in which aggregate values of wealth in categories such as housing and slaves can mask important differences in the strategies of wealth accumulation at different levels of society. Slaves may have been twice as important in the estates of the middle 60 percent of wealthholders than in the fortunes of the rich, but they were arguably much more important than this in the process of wealth accumulation for middling slaveholders. Whereas the rich counted on rental income from multiple urban properties, few middling wealthholders had this luxury, and if the wealthy earned interest and dividends on stocks, bonds, and informal credit instruments, the middle sector depended overwhelmingly on income from their own labor and that of their slaves.

It is now well established in the literature that rural slavery was not dominated by large-scale plantation ownership; so too was the case in urban Rio de Janeiro. What is less well understood is the fact that not only were the numbers of slaves per owner relatively low in the cities, but that the kinds of people who owned them were a diverse and largely middling group. Although the literature on urban slavery in Brazil does not explicitly state it, the impression given is that slavery in the cities went hand in hand with extreme wealth concentration—forming a dividing line, as it were, between the wealthy few and the impoverished many. One of the central contentions of this book is that this portrait of slavery, rarely explicitly stated but generally held, requires substantial revision.

Slavery in Rio de Janeiro, and by extension throughout much of urban Brazil, was not a source of wealth concentration among wealth-holders—on the contrary, slaves were among the best distributed assets. Of course, slavery greatly inhibited wealthholding among slaves themselves, so the effect of the institution on wealth inequality depended very much on the category of persons contemplated in the calculation. Moreover, slavery provided the most common pathway to social ascent for middling wealthholders. To be clear, slaves themselves were terribly constrained, often mistreated, always exploited, and forever calculating the odds of their freedom. We do not wish, in any way, to glorify Rio's social structure in the first half of the nineteenth century. Nevertheless, if we can put aside our moral outrage and attempt to understand that structure on its own terms, a portrait of diversity and mobility emerges.

6

DEATH AND DYING

Notwithstanding Machado de Assis's lighthearted deconstruction of death in nineteenth-century Rio de Janeiro in his classic novel, *The Posthumous Memoirs of Brás Cubas,* dying was generally a painful, expensive process filled with innumerable complications before and after the fact.[1] The thousands who died unlamented (at the time) in pauper's graves took cold comfort in the fact that their deaths were simple and cheap. Yet, for the middling wealthholders of Rio de Janeiro, dying was an art form that demanded great attention to detail.[2] Perhaps we should not be so surprised. After all, the nineteenth century is not so very long ago; lawyers, judges, sanitary authorities, the church, and, most of all, family members had a stake in what was to become of the deceased's estate.[3] The basic data for this book is almost entirely culled from the testaments and postmortem inheritance records associated with the complicated ritual that surrounded death and dying in Brazil's capital.

Here, the analysis turns to the minutia of the legal, economic, and cultural practice of death and inheritance among the middle sectors of Rio de Janeiro. The practices of the rich and poor will also be touched on inasmuch as they are required to place the ways of the middle group in sharper relief. On the most formal level, in fact, there was really no distinction between rich and poor, and it is with the basic rules and rituals that all deaths entailed that we begin.

Rules and Rituals: The "Good Death"

If a person was conscientious and owned any property, he or she would want to consider writing or dictating a will when the time came to turn one's mind to such things—usually when one was sick in bed and close to death.[4] Another common reason to compose a will and testament was to acknowledge "natural" children born out of wedlock to unmarried parents. This was a particularly popular course of action when testators had no other direct heirs and wished to protect the interests of their children from other parties such as greedy uncles and the state.[5] For the most part, if these "natural" children were not conceived in adulterous unions, there was little social stigma attached to them, although testators often excoriated themselves for their lax morals.[6]

Another option, of which we have one clear example in the estate sample, was to get married on one's deathbed. This did not automatically legitimize one's offspring, but it might well save one's soul. Manoel Rodrigues dos Santos, a wealthy resident of the neighborhood of Botafogo, married his lover, Carolina dos Santos, in April 1854, just a month prior to his death. In the couples' marriage contract, along with stipulating that their union would not be one of common property, Manoel also alluded to his reasons for seeking marriage at this late stage in his life. Having lived for years in "secret and illicit love" with Carolina Maria da Conceição, with whom he'd had two children he now recognized, he sought to terminate this "illicit affair," which was "disgusting to the eyes of God and Man."[7]

The process of writing or dictating a testament was, itself, quite formal and ritualized, beginning with the language itself. Dutra's testament, for example, follows the same basic structure seen in countless thousands of testaments from the period:

> In the name of God, Amen. I, Antonio José Dutra, being sick in bed and possessed of all my mental faculties, and fearing death, which is inevitable to all, have resolved to make my testament in the following form: I am a Roman Catholic, native of the Kingdom of the Congo and baptized in the neighborhood of Our Lady of the Remedies in the City of Angola. I never knew my parents. I am the widower of Maria Roza de Jesus from which marriage no children issued, but I have six natural children.[8]

Continuing in this vein for two pages, Dutra specified the names of his children, the names of his chosen executors, and his wishes regarding his own burial and the disposition of his estate. This last set of directives was of great importance, not only to his heirs but also to his slaves, as some would be liberated and others condemned to toil on for the support of his six natural children.

Dutra's proclamation of his religious faith, coupled with his decision to free some of his slaves upon his death, exemplify common patterns among middling wealthholders in Rio de Janeiro. Dutra's estate included a shrine with three statues depicting Jesus, Our Lady of the

Conception, and Saint Anthony. He also owned a small painting of Saint Francis. Although the monetary value of these objects was small, amounting to just 11 mil-réis, their importance in Dutra's spiritual life should not be underestimated.[9] In spite of his origins as an African slave, Dutra appears to have embraced Catholicism quite profoundly. There is no mention in his inventory of items that could be easily identified with Candomblé (which was slow to develop in Rio before the 1850s) or other alternative religious practices. What is more, we have evidence that Dutra was a signatory to the *compromisso* (statutes) of a religious brotherhood, Nossa Senhora do Rosario e São Benedito, in 1831. As a member of this brotherhood, he was sworn to work toward the emancipation of slaves—even though, paradoxically, he was a slaveholder himself.[10]

Much of the literature on the spiritual lives of slaves and freedmen in Brazil focuses on their participation in lay brotherhoods and their continued connections to African beliefs and practices. In Dutra's case, although he appears for the most part to have been assimilated into the dominant religious culture, there remain tantalizing traces of what might have been African aspects of his spiritual life. Dutra was baptized in Africa and, perhaps, given his first religious instruction there (beyond the preemptory and superficial catechism and baptism prior to embarking on the slave ship that brought him to Brazil).[11] Among the saints in his shrine was an image of Saint Anthony. We do not know which Saint Anthony Dutra prayed to, but we do know that Anthony was an important saint in the Kongo and that Dutra's initiation into Catholicism may have included references to him. A powerful religious movement led by the Kongolese mystic, Dona Beatriz Kimpa Vita, swept through the Kingdom of Kongo during the early years of the eighteenth century. Residue of the Antonian movement may well have included a general veneration of Saint Anthony. Among the notable features of the movement was the veneration of Jesus, Mary, and Saint Francis—all represented symbolically in Dutra's shrine or in paintings on his walls.[12]

Alternatively, Dutra may have prayed to the black Saint Anthony of the Moraria, one of Rio de Janeiro's most popular saints, an image of which was located in the Rosario church, a few blocks from his barbershop and home.[13] Perhaps in the end he prayed to both. We will never know what Dutra truly believed or where he first obtained his faith. As a native of the Kingdom of Kongo, a Catholic country in more than just nominal terms, he may have been born and raised a Christian.[14] If so, his arrival in Rio de Janeiro and subsequent integration into the city's religious life, including membership in a lay religious brotherhood, is more readily understood. Yet, there are clues indicating another interpretation. In his testament, Dutra professes never to have known his parents, suggesting that he may have been enslaved as a young child. His life as a slave may have begun some time before his shipment to Brazil and it is possible that his baptism in Christianity came along with a branding iron and embarkation on a ship bound for Rio de Janeiro.[15]

In common with their wealthier counterparts, the middle groups also sought, in their testaments, to provide concrete manifestations of their religious faith. In nearly all cases, a number of masses were to be said in their parish church for the benefit of their souls as well as the souls of family, friends, and business associates. Such requests were usually accompanied with small donations to the church itself or to lay religious brotherhoods and sisterhoods.[16] If a person had been of sufficient stature, their family would place advertisements in the papers requesting the presence of family and friends at their funeral mass as well as the mass celebrated on the seventh day after their burial:

> Manoel José do Rosario and his children very much appreciate the friends who attended the funeral of their wife and mother, and they hope these same will show their friendship in attending the mass of the seventh day, which will take place on the fifth of the current month, at 7 o'clock in the morning in the Church of the Carmo.[17]

In spite of his problematic relationship with Ignacia, João Baptista placed an advertisement requesting the presence of his father's family and friends at his funeral the day after his father-in-law's death:

> João Baptista Moreira da Silva requests all friends and acquaintances of Antonio José Dutra, deceased yesterday, to attend today his burial, which will take place today in the church of the terçeiros de S. Domingos, at four o'clock in the afternoon.[18]

Although advertisements of this nature were not uncommon, neither were they especially numerous. Just one other death announcement vied with Dutra's for attention that day in July 1849. Instead, in keeping with the current flowing through Carioca society, the news of Dutra's death was surrounded by advertisements for slaves for sale or rent.

As to their funerals, the rhetoric of death required testators to ask that their internment proceed in a "dignified manner without pomp." Modesty, if not necessarily practiced, was de rigor in one's testamentary requests. Dignified and "modest" funerals followed, in most cases, with burial in the parish churchyard or in the cemetery of a lay religious group. Rich and middling wealthholders alike followed this pattern; this distinguished both groups from the death of the poor, who were buried in pauper's graves, mainly in the cemetery of the Santa Casa, at the expense of church institutions or lay brotherhoods.[19]

The class and racial distinctions that fractured Rio society came into play in determining where, precisely, one was buried. The discourse of death was the same for most wealthholders, but the location of their remains depended on their own location in the physical space of the city and in its social hierarchy. Slaves had their own graveyards tended by their own lay religious brotherhoods, and many others were sent to the pauper's cemetery at the Santa Casa da Misericórdia—the city's primary charitable institution and hospital; the rich could be buried within the walls of the principal churches; immigrants were buried together in separate graveyards.[20] In this regard, the geography of death overlay the social geography of the city. Because the location of burial depended on religious institutions, which in turn were segregated according to color and economic condition, the odds of rich and poor, or black and white coming to rest side by side were relatively low.[21] Yet, as with so much in Rio, there was great mixing and diversity of practice in daily life. The segregation afforded the bodies of the dead did not always extend to the living. On the contrary, slaves worshiped (in the back) of elite churches and whites sometimes frequented churches identified with black or mulatto brotherhoods.[22]

The funeral rites for the wealthy and middling residents of Rio de Janeiro scandalized some foreign travelers and were objects of great interest to painters throughout the nineteenth century. In Luccock's account of his years of residence in Rio de Janeiro, which must be taken with a grain of salt owing to its florid cast, the deceased were carried exposed on litters through the cobbled streets with "indecent hurry." The tropical heat slowed the process of rigor mortis, and corpses jiggled about on their litters with "a considerable degree of motion, which greatly resembles what might be expected from a living subject in the lowest state of debility." To add to the macabre aspect of such funeral processions, the deceased was "decked out in all the gaudy trappings of a gala day; the face painted, the hair powdered, the head adorned with a wreath of flowers or a metallic

Illustration 16. *Various biers and funeral garb are depicted in this illustration. Starting at the top left, these are described by Debret as pertaining to: 1) a simple bier for a child covered in white taffeta; 2) a large sumptuous closed bier (associated with the wealthy); 3) a smaller closed bier for a child; 4) a reclining figure of a young woman dressed as an angel; 5) at the far left, a man in a simple rented bier from the Santa Casa; 6) at the far right, a similar bier with a woman dressed in the manner of Saint Theresa; 7) below the central reclining figure, a view from above of a simple rented bier; and, finally, at the bottom, 8) representing a slave tied up in a burial sack, and 9) an impoverished slave wrapped in leaves tied together with string. (Jean Baptiste Debret,* Voyage Pittoresque et Historique au Brésil, *3 volumes, Paris, 1834–1839*).

crown."[23] For the residents of Rio de Janeiro, such processions were an important aspect of the good death. The choice of shroud (white, black, or colored) and bier (simple or ornate) constituted visual cues as to the status and religious faith of the deceased. There was clearly much theater involved in death, and many decedents doubtlessly were conveyed in pious processions and buried in solemn black shrouds even through their lives had been filled with sinful activity.

A good death required the combined efforts of the deceased and his or her family and community. As João Reis describes it, the decedent needed to make a last testament and therein atone for past sins and prepare for the afterlife, as well as transact the worldly business of dividing the estate. In the course of dying, physicians were usually called on and the whole family was expected to maintain a vigil at the deathbed.[24] Once death had come, the family decorated the house with symbols of mourning, including much black fabric and color-coded cloths hung in doorways to indicate the civil status and age of the decedent.[25] Native and foreign artists alike painted many scenes of caskets and bodies lying in them as well as of burial processions, indicating both their visual characteristics and their broad significance to Carioca society.

Given the nature of the institution of slavery, which treated human beings as things, the callous disposal of many dead slaves comes as little surprise. According to Luccock, slaves were trundled off to their graves in sacks tied to a pole and carried by two "unfeeling Sextons." Their graves were nothing more than a trench, six feet long and four feet deep, into which they were frequently deposited one on top of the other "so that the head of one lies on the feet of that immediately below it."[26] João José Reis's meticulous research on the subject of death and burials in nineteenth-century Bahia indicates that even slaveholders who sought to accord their bondspersons a better inter-ment were often opposed by family members and society at large; for most interested parties, and sometimes the courts, any expense beyond the minimum was anathema.[27] Notwithstanding these con-siderations, many slaves sought decent burials through networks of kin and, more especially, brotherhoods and sisterhoods.[28]

After discoursing about their Christian faith, origins, family, and burial requests, testators got down to business. What did they own? How was their estate to be disposed? At this point, the name of their executor (*inventariante*) was given, along with the names of two default executors in most cases. If the testator was married, the role of executor usually fell to his or her spouse; if a widower with adult children, the job fell to the eldest son or daughter (or her husband if she happened to be married). Testators with minor children, whether widowed or single, needed to appoint a tutor to be executor of their estate. In most cases this job fell to their spouse, or, if widowed, to a brother or uncle. Lacking a male family member, the job would then fall to a respected friend. Complications often arose when sons-in-law sought to take control of the estate, raising objections from children of the deceased (as was the case with Dutra's daughter Ignacia although she was married to the would-be "usurper").[29]

Another common problem was that of the "surprise heir." There are many cases in the estate samples used in this book in which the decedent elected to recognize "natural" children on his deathbed and to convey part of his estate to them.[30] Strict rules of accounting for

Illustration 17. *In this scene, a slave woman is buried. Note that instead of a wooden bier, she is carried to the church in a hammock supported by two men. She is accompanied by female family and friends and watched by various onlookers in the street. The church itself is associated with the Afro-Brazilian population of the city and is overseen by a black priest.* (Jean Baptiste Debret, Voyage Pittoresque et Historique au Brésil, 3 *volumes*, *Paris, 1834–1839*).

minor children meant that many estates remained active, in a legal sense, for decades after the death of the wealthholder. Indeed, the last registered event in Dutra's inventory took place in 1884 when one-fourth of one of his old houses was put up for sale.

After naming his or her executor, the deceased turned to the specific disposition of the estate. Portuguese inheritance law, as it developed in Brazil, determined the amount of freedom a testator had in dividing up their fortune. If the soon-to-be deceased had a spouse, he or she stood to retain half of the couple's community property, unless the couple married with a contract stipulating separation of property. On the whole, such contracts were rare, and most spouses received one-half of the value of the total household estate.[31] Any children would share equally in one-third of the total estate. Finally, the remaining sixth of the estate was discretionary (that is, the *terça* pertaining to the deceased). From this value, the testator could pay for masses, leave small sums to godchildren (*afilhados*), and share with other family members and associates, including, in many instances, their slaves.

Of course, not everyone was conscientious enough to make a will, and death could come unexpectedly. Therefore, many died intestate. In these cases, the law was simple: half to the surviving spouse and half to the children. When there was no surviving spouse, children shared in the estate equally. If neither spouse nor children survived, the estate could pass back up the family tree to the decedent's parents or skip a generation to grandchildren.

Returning to the testamentary process, the documents closed with the signature or mark of the testator and a notarial certification. For a will to have authority it had to be notarized. This may explain, in part, the large number of people who died without wills—as the process was time consuming and bureaucratic. Notaries were then called on to provide a copy of the will to the orphans' judge in cases involving minor children.

The Appraisal

In most cases, an appraisal of the decedent's estate was made within weeks of their death on the request of the executor identified in the will or determined by law in the event that the wealthholder died intestate. Dutra's estate was appraised shortly after his death, with an initial listing of his personal property in August 1849 and a full appraisal in December of the same year. The process of appraisal was taken extremely seriously in the nineteenth century: most inventories contain a minute evaluation of every object in the decedent's possession, down to soupspoons and broken chairs. Rigid rules governed how and by whom the appraisal was carried out. Rather than leave matters to family members, whose accuracy and honesty were always in doubt, the job fell to professional estate evaluators or respected third parties. For this reason, the values adduced in the inventories used in the sample upon which so much of this book depends tended to be quite accurate. Many inventories include subsequent notes regarding the prices fetched for slaves and other possessions at auction; most of these values are within 10 percent of the appraised value.

Appraisers (*avaliadores*) went from room to room in the decedent's house. If there were multiple properties, each was evaluated in turn and the values were kept in discrete sections. Wealthholding was recorded by type, with houses and land entering first as the *bens de raiz*. Following this, slaves and livestock were entered as *semoventes* (self-moving property). This categorization acknowledged the intermediate status of such assets: on the one hand, slaves were clearly not akin to real property; on the other hand, they were distinct from movable possessions per se. Financial assets, gold and silver, and credits and debts came next. Last, the personalty of the deceased was entered as *moveis*—sometimes further distinguished in categories such as clothing, utensils (*trastes*), and china (*louça*). At the end of the process, which could take several days, the appraisers (there were always more than one) signed off on their evaluation and forwarded their findings to the orphans' judge or other controlling legal authority.

The next step, known as the *partilha*, proceeded to divide the estate according to the will (if extant) and the laws of inheritance. In order for the division to take place, a second reckoning of the value of the estate was made on the basis of the original inventory with amendments made to incorporate postmortem income and the payment of debts and funeral expenses. Dividing property was complicated by many factors. If the decedent had just one or two main sources of wealth and had a large number of heirs, an auction would usually be held to raise funds to distribute among the heirs.[32] At times, however, if the property in question was real estate (houses or land), it could be divided in sections according to inheritance law. Thus, we find in our sample of estate inventories many cases in which the ownership of one-half, or less of a house is recorded. For the most part, the executor (presumably under the watchful eye of the judge) sought to divvy up the estate in an equitable manner. Further complications could arise from the existence of dowries (which were quite uncommon in Rio in the nineteenth century) and postmortem income. In many cases involving continuing income streams after death, or the subsequent death of an heir, a second division was necessary (*sobrepartilha*) in order to distribute postmortem wealth.

The Division of Antonio Dutra's Estate

Antonio José Dutra died on July 19, 1849; his estate was settled and parceled out on February 8, 1850. In the intervening months, a legal dispute raged between Ignacia de Jesus Dutra, Antonio's eldest daughter and her husband João Baptista Moreira da Silva.[33] Caught in-between was Antonio Fernandes da Silva, the default executor after Ignacia renounced her role—and, by extension, her husband's role in settling the estate. Antonio Fernandes was, like Dutra, a barber-surgeon. A perusal of the *Almanak [Laemmert]*, Rio's city directory, yields an Antonio Fernandes, barber-surgeon, from the

1850s through the 1870s.[34] Perhaps he was selected as an executor precisely for this reason, given that he stood to know the ins-and-outs of the barbering business. In any event, his ties to Dutra only grew after Dutra's death, as he baptized little Fructuosa months later—she was living in his house as a *criada*—and became his friend's posthumous compadre.

Disputes regarding the division of estates were, no doubt, fairly common. Few rose to the pitch of acrimony evident in this case. The basis of Ignacia's decision to renounce her duty as executor was her husband's purported womanizing and wasteful spending. In one pungent phrase in the document where she renounces her role as executor, she refers to her husband as a "spendthrift living the greater part of the time with a black concubine with whom he spends most of what he earns." Then, in a burst of vitriol, she goes on to suggest that, were it not for her father's allowing them to live in the house appended to the barbershop and providing them with a female slave to make and sell sweets, her husband João Baptista would not be able to survive, given that "he is not capable of doing anything." Further information regarding Ignacia's complaints is found in her disputes with João Baptista following their divorce. According to her husband, he "categorically denied the mistreatment and abortions" alleged by Ignacia, claiming, on the contrary that he "treated her well, provided her with decent clothing, gave her presents of silver and gold, [and] provided housing with decent furnishings . . . all this on his wage of 1$600 per day . . . and for this reason it was impossible to spend money on concubines."[35]

It is tempting to read Ignacia's maneuvers as those of a shrewd and calculating woman aware that her father's death has given her a chance to bolt to freedom from an unsatisfying marriage. Married ten years at the time of Dutra's death, Ignacia may have wished to leave João Baptista long before—the fact that the couple remained childless and that Ignacia suffered at least one "miscarriage" suggests that she may have practiced folk forms of birth control and even, perhaps, aborted an unwanted child.[36] Now, as Dutra's only adult child, she was automatically in line to serve as the executor of his estate. And there was the rub: as long as she remained married to João Baptista, he would effectively control her and the estate. By renouncing her position as executor, and passing the duties to Antonio Fernandes, she cleverly cut her husband out of the process.

Suing for ecclesiastical divorce, then, was probably the final element of a carefully wrought strategy to obtain her inheritance and escape from her marriage. We know that Ignacia's childhood had been unusual, given her slave origins, and this may help explain her audacious behavior. Upon freeing his daughter in 1827, Dutra sent her to live as an *aggregado* (nonkin resident treated as a member of the extended family) in the household of a certain Tenente Saturnino. There, she was instructed by Saturnino's daughter, Maria Saturnina do Loreto, to read, write, and play the piano. Such skills were unusual among freedwomen, and Ignacia's education and literacy doubtlessly helped her navigate her course against João Baptista. Indeed, when she signed some of the documents contained in her father's estate inventory, her signature was clear and neat, a strong indication of real literacy. João Baptista's signature, in contrast, was very shaky and unsure—he was probably far less literate than his estranged wife, perhaps only able to sign his name.[37]

With five minor children involved, it appears that the judge, Araujo Soares, took no chances with Ignacia's petition and delayed a decision on the estate until the family feud was resolved. Meanwhile, João Baptista was busy filing legal affidavits and hiring lawyers. A lot was at stake for him. Not only did he stand to lose control of a substantial estate, he was also being sued for ecclesiastical divorce (on grounds of moral turpitude and abandonment). In one legal salvo against his "traitorous" wife, he sought to disqualify her entirely from the proceedings on the grounds that, as a married woman, she had no legal personality. In order to make this claim stick, João Baptista also claimed that, on the night of her father's death, he had moved with her to Dutra's house (the barbershop on the Rua da Alfândega) and slept in her company—presumably an indication that the marriage was consummated and in good standing.[38]

João Baptista's lawyer also peppered the margins of the documents with aspersions regarding Ignacia's parentage and moral qualities. Drawing attention to her lie regarding her birth (to Josefa, a slave, and not Hilária, mother of her brothers) and calling her a "stinker," a "shame to women who call themselves married," and a "coquette" he lashed out at her "low" origins and "bad" character. Not content to strike out at Ignacia, João Baptista and his lawyer also aimed barbs at Antonio Fernandes, the new executor named in lieu of Ignacia. In one pungent phrase scribbled in the margin, Antonio Fernandes is accused of being a corruptor living in a "secret marriage" with Ignacia. Closing with a flourish, the marginal remarks end with Cicero's famous lament: *o tempora, o mores*, alas for the times and manners.[39] For his part, the tutor and executor Antonio sought and obtained monetary compensation for his efforts in this contested case.[40]

Illustration 18. *A sample from Antonio José Dutra's inventory (caixa 68, n. 171, Rio de Janeiro, AN). Note his daughter Ignacia's relatively neat signature. In the right margin, Antonio Fernandes da Silva is excoriated as a corruptor of morals and marriage.*

Apparently, Ignacia had wanted to leave João Baptista for some time. As soon as her father was dead, she filed for separation and took steps to prevent her erstwhile husband from insinuating himself in her family's finances. Although this is just one extraordinary case, it does suggest that women had more room to negotiate their social and civil status at certain key moments such as the death of a wealthy parent.[41] At least in this case, Ignacia got everything she wanted out of the judge: João Baptista was prevented from exercising his traditional (and legally stipulated) role in the partition of the estate and her separation was granted. Legal separations were rare, but possible, and bold women like Ignacia were not afraid to seek them.

All this legal controversy delayed the final appraisal of Dutra's estate until near the end of 1849, five months after his death. The appraisers got down to work on December 3, 1849, and the paperwork was notarized on December 11.[42] The resulting minute evaluation of Dutra's estate is reproduced here in its entirety. There is nothing unusual about this level of detail: nearly all appraisals are of similar thoroughness. On January 7, 1850, Antonio Fernandes da Silva abjured that the appraisal was accurate and that the estate was intact. A month later, after more paperwork, the division of the estate commenced. In order to begin, a reckoning of all the income and expenditure over the past seven months ensued. Both had been substantial.

Did Dutra's family abide by his deathbed wish for a modest and dignified burial? We will never know. The cost, however, does appear modest—393$000, or about 3 percent of his total wealth. Being ill had its price as well, with medical expenses subtracting another 119$000 from his estate. Other expenditure accrued in the maintenance of the

Table 9

Inventory of Antonio José Dutra's Real Estate and Slaves
Rio de Janeiro, 11 December 1849

HOUSES	Appraisal
Rua do Saco do Alferes, 75	1:800$
Rua do Saco do Alferes, 77	3:000$

SLAVES	
Joaquim Rebello, barber and clarinetist, age 40 *	500$
Joaquim Congo, barber and clarinetist, 30 *	500$
Domingos Moçambique, barber, 46 *	250$
Felipe Moçambique,tailor, trombonist, 30 *	600$
Antonio Quilimane, barber and clarinetist, 28 *	700$
Carlota Cabinda, cook, 25 & Alexandre, 17 months *	600$
José Benguela, barber's apprentice, tropa	500$
Martins Quilimane, barber's apprentice, clarinetist[a]	600$
Benedito Benguela, barber's apprentice, clarinetist	650$
Mathias Benguela, barber's apprentice, bombo[b]	650$
Francisco Cabinda, trumpeter, 18	650$
Antonio Quilimane, barber's apprentice, clarinetist	600$
Gertrudes Angola, domestic	500$

Source: estate inventory, Antonio Jose Dutra, 1849, cx. 68 n. 171, Rio de
    Janeiro, AN.
Notes: * freed by Antonio José Dutra in his testament. a) requinta, a type of
    clarinet. b) a type of drum.

family and the barbering business. Payroll in the barbershop came to
431$000; food for the family, another 516$000; and repairs to Dutra's
two residential properties added 310$000. All told, the partible value
of the estate came to 13:187$280, about 86 percent of the value of
Dutra's holdings before expenses.[43] This percentage would have been
higher had Antonio da Silva not demanded that postmortem income
accrue to him in compensation for this labors as executor.

The bureaucracy of death and dying had its costs as well. It is
sometimes claimed, usually by those with little experience working
with inventories, that these costs deterred families from conducting
a formal appraisal and division of property. This argument rests on
two fallacies: that the costs of the process were high; and that taxes
on estates were steep enough to encourage underreporting of values

Table 10

Inventory of Antonio José Dutra's Personal Property

Silver:		11 straw chairs	4$4
1 pair of candlesticks	58$	2 wooden chair arms	$80
1 pair of small candlesticks	48$2	3 as above, rasas?	$96
idem	28$8	2 old wooden tables	4$
1 tray	21$12	1 rosewood table	1$6
1 small tray	9$8	1 pine table	$5
toothpick case	14$6	2 grindstones	$6
ladle	9$8	1 metal mortar	2$
9 forks	21$76		
8 table spoons	21$28	*Clothing & Linens:total value*	20$
15 tea spoons	12$64	5 old barbering smocks; 3 towels; 1	
15 knives	22$	old red damask coverlet with ink	

Silver:

Furnishings:		
1 wardrobe	2$
rosewood dresser	8$
1 small dresser	6$
2 wall hangers	$4
used rosewood sofa	5$
1 cupboard	10$

1 shrine with Our Lord in the
   Cross, Our Lady of Conception

and St. Anthony	10$
1 mirror	2$
1 anvil and hammer	$8
2 boxes for grindstones	3$
1 grindstone	1$
6 big paintings	1$2
2 small paintings	$2

1 small painting depicting
   St. Francis   1$

1 wooden vessel	$32
3 chests for water	$4
2 glass chimney	4$
2 basins for shaving	$8
idem	$4
China	6$
Gonsalo Alves' old bed	2$
2 love seats	3$

Clothing & Linens:total value   20$

5 old barbering smocks; 3 towels; 1 old red damask coverlet with ink stains; 2 black silk waistcoats; 2 pairs of white pants; 2 pairs of woolen white pants; 1 pair of dark pants; 2 pairs of stripped cotton pants; 1 white waistcoat; 1 stripped waistcoat; 8 pairs of socks; 1 pair of black pants; 1 very used fine wool frockcoat; 1 silk handkerchief; 1 pillowcase; 3 shirts.

Several iron tools for
   tooth extraction   6$

Musical Instruments:	
1 bass drum	16$
1 small bass drum	8$
2 drums	8$
1 good cymbal and 1 broken	2$
3 trumpets	15$
1 large clarinet	8$
1 corneta de chaves	4$
piston	10$
2 drums	8$
1 clarinet	6$
broken French horns?	12$

Source: see Table 9.

or outright evasion. Neither of these assumptions is merited in the case of most estates. Clearly, some decedents and their families found the formal legal process too confusing or costly and elected to parcel out their wealth informally. Yet, for the most part, administrative costs were low and taxes even lower. In Dutra's case, the total costs associated with his inventory came to 120$000 out of an initial estate value of 15:421$000—that is, less than 1 percent. Taxes paid to the Fazenda Nacional came to a mere 16$000. What is more, of the inventory costs, 67$000 went to pay the professional appraisers. The larger the estate, the higher this cost. Other, more fixed costs, included 3$000 to the judge and 19$000 for the required stamps.[44] In Dutra's case, the cost of the inventory was also elevated by all the legal wrangling among Ignacia, João Baptista, and Antonio Fernandes. The cost of formality, for a small estate, was no more than 60$000. In order for this to be a deterrent, estates would have to be quite small indeed—perhaps under 1:000$000. For this reason, along with others, we expect some censoring of small estates in our sample.

In keeping with the wishes expressed in Dutra's will, six of the adult slaves were freed, including the best musicians and most capable barbers (with one exception). By freeing these slaves, Dutra significantly lowered the value of each of his children's inheritance. Although the literature on manumission shows clearly that women, especially the elderly, predominated among the manumitted, cases like Dutra's highlight the diversity of the manumitted population.[45] Dutra freed only one female slave (and her baby). He also freed the most valuable slaves in his possession.[46] On top of it all, as if to make his case the exact opposite of what the literature leads us to expect, nearly all of Dutra's freed slaves were African-born.

Although we cannot be certain, it may have been the case that Dutra's close contact with his barber/musician slaves over the years had created a personal bond strong enough for him to elect to free them rather than pass along a much more viable estate to his children. For a man with six children to provide for, this granting of freedom takes on an almost heroic appearance. Indirect evidence for this interpretation comes from an odd notice regarding one of Dutra's slaves who had run away following his death, refusing to work because "he ought not remain as a slave because his services (to Dutra) were the same as those who obtained their freedom."[47] José, the runaway, found himself in the Casa de Correcção; the nature of his argument for freedom bolsters the idea that it was based on an affinity derived from shared work in the barbershop and band. The alternative explanation, that Dutra freed his barbers because, as a former slave himself, he sympathized with their plight is belied by the fact that he left seven other slaves in bondage.

Dutra's largesse extended beyond freeing his six favored slaves. He also left small sums to his four godchildren, Firmina, Roza, Joaquim, and Quitério. A token 20$000 went to Roza Benguela (almost certainly a freed former slave, born in Africa), listed somewhat cryptically in his testament as "a black who lives in my company."[48] The remaining part of Dutra's discretionary estate (*terça*) came to 802$000, which was distributed among his heirs. It is worth paying closer attention to the mechanics of the division of Dutra's terça. According to inheritance law, he could dispose of one-third of his estate in the manner he saw fit. The remaining two-thirds then comprised the "necessary" portion destined to his heirs.

With a surplus of more than 800$000 in his discretionary estate, Dutra could conceivably have freed at least one more of his slaves or given more to his nonkin legatees. In particular, it is striking that Dutra failed to mention his lover Anna Maria Matildes, mother of three of his children. Had they broken up? The documents are mute on this question. We do know, however, that the three daughters born to Anna Maria did not live with her following Dutra's death. Instead, the two older daughters were taken in by a woman, Dona Antonia Maria da Conceição Fluminense, for 4 mil-réis per month (not including food and board, to be paid from the rental income of their house). Little Fructuosa moved in with her tutor, Antonio Fernandes. It seems odd that Dutra would not have considered his lover in his will, if not solely to ensure that she could care for his daughters; yet, middling wealth meant middling morality, and although it was perfectly acceptable to recognize "natural" children in one's testament it was not appropriate to recognize out-of-wedlock sexual relations with monetary compensation.[49]

All told, each of Dutra's minor children stood to inherit 1:732$000—a substantial sum considering that this represented about six-times the annual income of a skilled urban worker at the time. Each of Dutra's three minor daughters, children of his liaison with Anna Maria Mathildes, received a slave and one-third of his residential property on Rua do Saco do Alferes, number 77. The net value of their inheritances were discounted by the cost of their food and clothing. Two minor sons, born to another woman, Hilaria Maria do Rosario, earlier in Dutra's life, each received a slave and one-half of Dutra's other residential property, number 75 on the same street, which was rented out to the mother of the family doctor.[50] Like their younger sisters, they had their inheritance discounted by the cost of their upkeep over the seven months since their father's death.

Last, João Baptista Moreira da Silva, as head of the household, was to receive payment for his and Ignacia's portion of the estate. He never did. Although she was successful in preventing him from performing his duties as executor, Ignacia was not necessarily able to bend the law to her liking in this regard. On this point the law was clear: *married* women did not have a legal personality when it came to property ownership, although in the case of divorce matters were different. The law did stipulate that married women's property be conserved and protected, but it did not give them the right to control it themselves. Ignacia, therefore, took steps to insure that the inheritance remained in the hands of Antonio Fernandes, the tutor, by requesting that the orphans' judge block the transfer of the estate until her divorce was final and a division of property could be arranged.

The inheritance due to Ignacia and her estranged husband included two slaves, Dutra's musical instruments and furnishings, and 1:021$000 in cash. A larger inheritance, in this case, was attributable to expenses incurred by Ignacia in maintaining her siblings and paying for other expenses after her father's death. We can imagine, then, what difficulties lay ahead for the headstrong Ignacia. Having attacked her husband's character and sued for divorce, she remained uncomfortably constrained until her divorce was finally granted at the end of 1850. In fact, Ignacia played the game beautifully, entering a petition to block the transfer of her *legítima* (inheritance) on the grounds of her husband's alleged profligacy and tying this request into her ongoing divorce proceedings.[51] Thus, she was able to leave João Baptista, obtain a divorce, and prevent him from inheriting (at least right away) his portion of her father's estate.

Getting separated was not the end of the couple's troubles: the dissolution of a marriage called for a separation of property; and this process was not completed, if indeed it ever was, in this case until 1856. In other words, the couple continued to do battle for six years following the granting of their divorce (*divórcio perpétuo com separação de bens*). The legal separation of property (*partilha de divórcio*) finally took place on December 10, 1856—in the interim it is unclear what was done with the property. According to João Baptista, he never received any inheritance from Dutra's estate. In fact, according to his petition leading up to the partilha, he was owed six years, eight months, and fifteen days of income from the two slaves he and Ignacia had inherited from Dutra. By his reckoning, this amounted to 24$000 per month for Antonio Quilimane's barbering income and 12$000 per month for Gertrudes Angola's wages as a *quitandeira* (street vendor). Apparently, João Baptista did not take into account the retained wages or upkeep costs of these slaves in his calculation. Along with these wages, he sought a division of 1:040$000 (plus 6 percent annual interest) allegedly in Ignacia's possession at the time of her father's death and a long list of household items including a large bed in the French style with mattress and headboard, a piano, and a large clock.[52]

Ignacia fired back with her own version of things. According to her, João Baptista was making "extravagant" claims based on his "crazed imagination." She had, in her words, run out on João Baptista in June of 1849 in order to escape his abuse with little more than the clothes she was wearing. Her possessions amounted to no more than a couch, two vases, a broken table clock, and a few small pieces of wooden furniture.[53]

In an earlier dispute recorded in 1852, Ignacia charged her former husband with stinting on her maintenance payments, of which she claimed to be due 1$200 per day on the basis of João Baptista's daily wage of 2$400. Her former husband protested, claiming to the contrary that his income was uncertain, lower than Ignacia alleged (just 1$600 per day), and sufficient only to sustain himself and his mother. In his protest, he alleged again that Ignacia was an adulteress, implying that she was unworthy of support. The court, seeking to strike a balance, rendered a sentence requiring João Baptista to pay his former wife 200 réis per day—a minimal sum that nonetheless reiterated his obligation to support Ignacia after the divorce while the couple's property remained in dispute.[54]

Through seven years of acrimony, including several rounds of petitions and counterclaims, the status of the couple's estate remained unclear. As of December 1856, it was appraised at 1:304$220, of which 1:296$000 remained to be divided after costs. Of the total value, 1:100$000 was accounted for by two of Ignacia's father's slaves, Antonio Quilimane and Gertrudes Angola, with the rest in furniture and musical instruments. After all her efforts, if the partilha was ever completed, Ignacia emerged from this process with 607$000 to her name—a far cry from the level of wealth attained by her father.[55]

Perhaps for this reason, she appears to have ignored the legal decision in the partilha and sought to prove that her divorce with João Baptista had set aside her inheritance during the course of settling her father's estate. In response, João Baptista cried foul and Ignacia answered by sending him to discuss matters with Antonio Fernandes, the tutor. We do not know the final result of this dispute, but it seems quite possible that Ignacia managed to keep some of her inheritance hidden to the bitter chagrin of her former husband.[56]

Orphans and Tutors

The majority of the cases in the estate sample involved minor children and were therefore adjudicated in the orphans' court. It should be noted that the death of one parent, not both, was sufficient to place children under the authority of the orphans' judge, who, along with the executor of the estate, was charged with maintaining records of expenditures on minor children through their majority. Consequently, we have records not only of the size of the decedent's estate and its division among the heirs but also detailed records of what happened to the estate over time. Turning again to Dutra's case, this section follows the trail of his wealth over the ensuing years as his family struggled to maintain its social position. Fortune and social standing were tenuous for the middling wealthholders of Dutra's time. Legal strictures requiring equal division of property could vitiate the profitability of a family enterprise; when there were many children, as with Dutra, the amount of wealth inherited by each heir was a shadow of what their parents had accumulated. Bad luck, changing times, and illness could also take a toll on a family's fortunes. All this comes clear in the lives of Dutra's children in the years following his death.

At the top of the list of problems confronting the family was the status of their father's barbershop on Rua da Alfândega, number 163. Although it clearly did well while he was alive, it was in deep trouble soon after his death. Freeing the five most skilled slaves in the shop raised the cost of business by transferring the portion of their earnings that had previously been remitted to Dutra to the former slaves themselves. On top of this, bad luck struck the family (and the entire city) when yellow fever broke out with a vengeance in 1850. The effects of illness were pronounced on the shop's bottom line. In January 1850, the business grossed 76$000 with a healthy compliment of workers. By May, the shop's gross fell dramatically to 39$000. In the three months prior to the fever striking the shop, the average gross from barbering and other services was 73$000; once the fever hit in April, the remaining months of 1850 averaged just 45$000 gross income—resulting in a total for the ten-month period January to October of 530$000. Meanwhile, over the same period, expenditure ran to 1:064$000.[57]

Complete ruin was avoided, however, through the continued earnings of the band. From January to October 1850, Dutra's band brought in 1:036$000 gross, more than covering the losses sustained in the barbershop. Illness probably cut into the earnings of the band as well in the months of April and May, although the month in which gross receipts was lowest in the barbershop coincides with the month in which earnings were highest from the band—perhaps indicating that there was a trade-off in time spent playing music versus barbering.

Total income over expenditure in the family business came to 502$000—about twice the yearly wage of a skilled urban tradesman. Added to this sum was 484$000 in rent obtained from Dutra's two residential properties—these were rented for 16$000 and 30$000 respectively and the proceeds from their rental were to cover the living expenses of Dutra's five minor children: to wit, the two boys were to receive 8$000 per month each from one property and the three girls to receive 10$000 each from the other. The problem, for the family, was that it had grown accustomed to a standard of living more in keeping with an intact fortune of 15:000$000 and a prosperous small business. Daily expenses ran at a rate of 3$000 (956$000 for the whole period in question)—for food, domestic services such as ironing, and additional supplies for the nurses employed from February through May to tend the sick children and slaves alike.[58] On top of this, all the children save Alexandre received medical care from Doctor Antonio Dias da Costa, whose mother ended up renting one of Dutra's houses, as well as tutoring or schooling at substantial cost. These expenses, no doubt perceived as entirely necessary for a family of middling wealth, added up to 288$000.[59] It is noteworthy that this family of middling wealth opted for a "real" doctor to treat its members and slaves during the yellow fever outbreak, when they presumably could have relied on their barber-surgeons free of charge. This, I argue, along with the spending on schooling, highlights the way in which the family had adopted the social, medical, and educational patterns of the city's middling and upper groups.

All told, the family's income came to 2:051$000 between January and October 1850; its expenses came to 2:403$000, resulting in a deficit of 352$000. Given all the difficulties surrounding the barbershop—illness, the flight of the slave José—this deficit was not in itself profoundly troubling. Each of Dutra's heirs received 1:732$500 in the settlement of his estate.[60] At a rate of 59$000 each, they could afford to sustain such deficits until they were all grown and either employed or married. The catch was that their wealth, and income, was not in liquid assets at first, which could be drawn down as needed. Over time, without the robust stream of income from Dutra's shop and band, did the heirs inevitably draw down their inheritances?

When Antonio Fernandes gave his accounting of the surviving girls' estates in 1860, he reported that Leopoldina and Maria had 642$000 and 710$000 respectively in the bank. Keeping in mind that they each held a one-third share in the house on Rua do Saco do Alferes, worth approximately one conto, it appears that they were able to maintain their capital over the decade following their father's death.[61] Antonio Fernandes, tutor of the minor children, noted a liquidity problem, however, in his report on the status of the estate in November 1850. According to his report, the difficulty resided in the fact that yellow fever rendered it impossible to sell the slaves of the five minor children on the market—sick slaves sold at a steep discount—and, likewise, lowered their productivity in the barbershop and band.[62]

The year 1851 proved worse again for the family, as tragedy struck with the death of Fructuosa, daughter of Dutra and Anna Maria Matildes. The funerals of children of the middle groups tended to be truly modest affairs; given rates of infant and youth mortality in Rio, it could hardly have been otherwise. The most expensive item in poor Fructuosa's funeral was her death shroud, representing the order of Our Lady of the Good Death. Her coffin was hired, as was the carriage that carried her to her resting place in a crypt in the Campo do Caju. All told, her funeral cost just under 20$000.[63]

The grim process of divvying up her part of Dutra's estate followed on the heels of her death. Because she was a "natural" child, born out of wedlock, her mother Anna Maria had to petition the court for the rights to her child's estate. In the end, her rights as a mother were vindicated, and she was awarded Fructuosa's inheritance, including one-third of the house on Rua do Saco do Alferes. The irony here is obvious. Only with the death of her child did Anna Maria become, by extension, a legal heir of Dutra.[64]

Her relationship with Dutra's executor, Antonio Fenandes, appears to have been somewhat complicated by the fact that she now shared the equivalent of a one-third stake in the estate of her other two children Maria and Leopoldina. Whereas she now controlled Fructuosa's share, the inheritance of her living children remained in the power of their tutor! In one exchange in the mid-1850s, she is seen negotiating with Antonio Fernandes regarding the settlement of her portion of the inheritance vis-à-vis the shares of her daughters. Antonio clearly saw his role as tutor as paramount to Anna Maria's role as mother, calling the girls "my pupils." He also resisted selling the house according to Anna Maria's wishes, electing instead to pay the mother for the upkeep of her children from the rents derived from the property.[65] In the end, this turned out to be a poor choice of strategy on Antonio Fernandes's part, as Anna Maria mortgaged her share of the house at a high rate of interest. For Anna Maria's part, she did not live long to enjoy the bitter fruit of her youngest daughter's death, as she followed Fructuosa to the grave in 1856.

Marriage, Inheritance, and Conflicts of Interest

As Dutra's children attained adulthood, their position vis-à-vis their inheritance shifted according to their gender and civil status. Maria Mathildes, Dutra's second daughter, married Estevão Barroso Pereira, in 1862. The problem for the young couple, regarding Maria's inheritance, was that it was tied up in the house she had inherited along with her sisters, which, in turn was mortgaged to the tune of 700$000 at 2 percent per month.[66] This debt had been contracted by Maria's mother, Anna Maria Mathildes, after the death of Fructuosa had placed her in control of one-third of the house. Although this undoubtedly eased their mother's financial problems at the time, the mortgaging of part of the house caused problems for her daughters. As Antonio Fernandes da Silva, tutor of the younger Leopoldina put it: such an interest rate was "quite heavy" and would have the consequence, in time, of "absorbing the entire value of the house."[67] The solution, proposed by Antonio Fernandes, was to pay his charge's portion of the debt in cash and thus free her from the obligation to pay the debt and interest.

It is worth noting that Maria and Leopoldina did not share the same civil status at this point, but were both represented in these deliberations by men. Maria, married before her twenty-first birthday, was never emancipated, passing from the paternalistic power of her tutor to the patriarchal authority of her husband; Leopoldina, still a minor, was represented by Antonio Fernandes. For women, the pathway to independent control of wealth was narrow, and, as the case of their mother all too clearly demonstrates, entangled in a complex array of family relationships. It is no accident that Dutra's daughters faced a complicated future with respect to their inheritance.

For Dutra's sons, things went much more smoothly, as they did not have to worry about losing direct control of their inheritance through marriage and, moreover, found themselves insulated from the problems associated with Anna Maria Mathildes. Indeed, the brothers inherited equal shares in the other house on Rua do Saco do Alferes. In 1855, the eldest, Manoel, turned twenty-one and obtained his legal emancipation (*carta de emancipação*).[68] Two years later, Alexandre followed his brother's footsteps into adulthood.[69]

The future, for the young men, was, nevertheless, none too bright. They came into their small inheritances but could no longer depend on their father's business for income. Manoel followed his father's footsteps and trained as a barber-surgeon. The shop, however, had ceased to function as early as 1851. According to a complaint lodged by Sebastião Navarro de Andrade, on behalf of Manoel, the shop had been closed since May 1851 and many of the items therein "stolen" or misplaced. Even the leeches applied by the barbers came into the dispute, as the complaint alleged that Antonio Fernandes was understating the income generated from bleedings by reporting $400 rather than $800 réis as the charge per application of the *bichas*. To add insult to injury, the complaint continued with the information that the freed slaves that had made up the core of the old enterprise were now in business for themselves in another shop rented on Rua do Fogo.[70] Clearly, whatever Antonio Dutra's intentions had been with regard to the disposition of his estate and the care of his heirs, things had not gone well for the family in the aftermath of his death.

Other estate inventories from the period depict middling and poorer families in a range of complicated and sometimes conflicted situations upon the death of the head of the household. For the poorest of families, it was possible that their inheritance would prove negative: they would owe rather than receive an inheritance. Poor survivors would sometimes renounce their right to an inheritance if it was too small to justify the costs of an appraisal and court fees.[71] Alternatively, an inventory process could be set off by a testamentary recognition of a natural child—placing matters under the jurisdiction of the orphans' judge. In one case, a "natural" child was recognized, but the estate proved too small to yield an inheritance.[72] In another instance, the heirs were the former slave and her child, recognized as lover and son, in the final testament of Lourenço José do Amaral in 1821.[73]

Among middling and rich wealthholders, an additional wrinkle was introduced whenever the decedent was on his or her second (or third) marriage. In these instances, complicated inheritance scenarios played out with parts of the estate earmarked for the children of the first marriage and other parts set for the children of the second. For example, the estate of Angelo José de Morais was divided among his second wife and her three children along with another three children by his first marriage. His second wife, in keeping with inheritance laws, received one-half of the estate, whereas her children received only half as much as his children from his first marriage. In this, equity was attained because it was assumed that the three children with smaller inheritances would eventually receive their mother's estate.[74] In what must have been an extremely unusual case, a divorced decedent, João Bartholomeu Klier, owner of a successful shop selling musical instruments, left part of his discretionary estate to his former wife and another portion to his children by that union.[75]

These diverse examples highlight the diversity of outcomes possible under Brazilian inheritance law, as well as a sense of the range of situations that families of decedents found themselves in at the lower and middle ranges of wealthholding. Although the tale of Dutra's estate is unusual, it opens a window on the often-prolonged process of death and dying. Moreover, it highlights the way in which civil status and gender crosscut families in mid-nineteenth-century Rio de Janeiro.

7

FAMILY AND GENDER

A long with wealth, the three most important determinants of a person's social position in Rio de Janeiro were their parents, their civil status, and their gender. Although it was possible for someone like Dutra, a former slave who became a barber, to transcend these categories, for most Cariocas, these markers provide a reliable guide to a person's status. Most married women did not exercise the freedom and determination shown by Ignacia when she challenged her husband in court; most slaves did not gain their freedom and become barbers and bandleaders. Rather, the social universe of Rio de Janeiro mapped people in place according, foremost, to their civil status and gender.

The family was a central institution in Brazilian life during the nineteenth century. For the wealthy, this meant close supervision of unmarried young women, the careful arrangement of marriages (often endogamous), and the placement of sons in positions of political and economic power. Visitors to Rio de Janeiro commented on the timidity of women in the early years of the nineteenth century. They also noted, over time, a tendency for women to emerge from the walls of the patriarchal manor. Thus, physical sequestration and lack of education gave way to a less restricted, but nonetheless controlled existence determined by what was considered proper behavior and proper company.[1] Alliances were formed among elite families through marriage and business ties.[2] At the top, then, of Rio society, were a few score of truly wealthy and powerful families. In the 1810s and 1820s, these families were often linked closely to the Portuguese crown—holders of rents granted by the king and his ministers—and some were associated with the great families of Portugal. By the 1840s, however, the elite families of Dutra's world were more likely to be headed by native Brazilian merchants, planters, and politicians.[3]

Below the level of the great families, with their patents of nobility and connections to the emperor, were the many households of middling wealth.[4] Politically and economically insignificant when taken individually, this group of families nonetheless comprised, as a group, the core of Rio de Janeiro's small-business and service economy. Most families in this group—those headed by men—were eligible to vote for electors in Brazil's indirect elections of the period. This group therefore exercised some political power in a limited fashion.[5] The truly distinguishing characteristic of middling families is their diversity. From the Horatio Alger story of Antonio Dutra to the cosseted scion of a wealthy merchant, wealthholders in the middle 60 percent of the distribution covered every possible social and cultural category.

By definition, poor families hardly figured as wealthholders. They did, however, form the absolute majority of families in Rio de Janeiro. Again, poverty meant a range of social positions from the impoverished but respectable widow to the truly destitute dipsomaniac. Slaves, too, formed families, which provided them a refuge within the system as well as a potential means to exit it.[6] Many slaves who obtained their freedom went on to purchase the freedom of their children and loved ones.[7] A few slaves went so far as to marry, obtain their freedom, and then petition for ecclesiastical divorce—tracing out nearly the whole range of possible positions regarding civil status and family life.[8]

Family Structure and Inheritance

Looked at from the perspective of their heirs, a wealthholder was only as rich as their prospective share in his or her estate. Dutra, with a gross estate of over 15:000$000 in 1849, was well off by contemporary standards; his estate placed him in the top 40 percent of all wealthholders for the period 1845–54—which, by extension, put him in the top 10 to 20 percent of all households in Rio de Janeiro. Yet, for his children, this proved far too little to afford a 15:000$000 lifestyle. Their accounts were frequently in deficit and their tutor, Antonio Fernandes, was forever juggling their estate to make ends meet. Just the issue of buying shoes and clothes raised problems, much less continuing the piano lessons and private schooling to which they were accustomed.[9]

The key point is that the value of a middling estate was not always easily divisible. Slaves could be distributed more or less evenly; although, for orphans, this could be risky if a slave fell ill, died, or ran away. For example, Benedito, the slave left to Dutra's daughter Maria Mathildes in her father's will, fell ill in 1850 and the cost of his rehabilitation came to 110$000.[10] Other forms of wealth, such as houses and businesses were not so easily divided, although houses could be apportioned in shares among heirs. Often, a combination of holdings that worked well for the decedent in his or her lifetime did not function nearly as well for the heirs once the estate was dismembered.

In the case of decedents with few children, the problem of division was minimized. When José Thomas Rodrigues, a Portuguese-born naval officer, passed away in 1849, his only daughter received the balance of his 7:184$000 estate—minus a single slave freed for "good services rendered" for thirty-six years.[11] At the other extreme, the widower Francisco de Macedo Freire divided his estate among twelve heirs, each receiving just 914$000. In this way, a wealthier man while alive left a much smaller estate to his many children. Resident of the outlying rural district of Guaratiba, Francisco's estate comprised twelve slaves, a farmhouse, and various small plantings of manioc, plantains, and oranges.[12] In this instance, it is likely that most of the children remained on the farm and that the productive core of land and slaves remained intact—the returns from which accrued to each heir proportionally. At some point, however, the children would want to marry and move to houses of their own. As the Brazilian saying goes, "quem casa quer casa," those who marry want a home of their own. Slaves would have to be sold and other arrangements made to allow them to carry their inheritance with them to their new home.

Not all estates were divided among spouses and children. Sometimes the decedent had neither, and the estate passed back up the generational tree. In other cases, traditional family structure was lacking and testators tried to tailor their unorthodox lives to the spirit of inheritance law and cultural convention. An expressive instance of the posthumous creation of "family" though wealth transfer is found in the inheritance record of João Baptista, resident on Rua do Pedregulho and deceased in 1855.

Single, but with three children by two women, João Baptista settled an equal 498$000 on each of his "natural" children and 200$000 to one mother and 300$000 to the other, Maria Peixoto, who, as it happened, was a freed slave of the executor of his estate. To tie things up, Baptista requested that his lover's former master serve as tutor for his two minor children by this union. We can only wonder how this arrangement went over with Maria, given that her former master was now given newfound power over her and her children. At the very least, João Baptista settled a small sum on her as well—perhaps to help preserve her independence.[13]

In a similar case, but drawn from an upper-middle-class estate, Ignacio Caetano de Araujo bequeathed 9:556$000 on each of his children upon his death in 1849. Ignacio had never married. What is more, his offspring were born to one of his slaves. Upon his death, in accordance with his testament, his lover and mother of his two children was freed. She did not receive an inheritance. Ignacio's remaining six slaves were auctioned off and the proceeds credited to his children's accounts.[14]

Family size, and the number of legatees depended, in some small part, on wealth: the richer the decedent, the more heirs in their estate. Middling wealthholders, nevertheless, had about as many heirs and legatees as did the wealthy, creating great difficulties for families with a tenuous purchase on middle-group status.

Children

The status of children in Rio de Janeiro depended, fundamentally, on the wealth and civil status of their parents. Best off were the children of wealthy married couples. In these instances, children stood to inherit an equal portion of their parent's estate, with one-half usually reserved for the surviving spouse. With a surviving parent to act as their "tutor," they were less vulnerable to manipulation by a tutor from outside the nuclear family. From their perspective, the only problem was that they were kept from inheriting their full share of the estate until the death of both of their parents. But, as they were wealthy enough from their share of half of the estate, they were not likely to be impeded in charting an independent life once they attained adulthood.

For children of middling wealthholders, the initial distribution from the estate on the death of one parent often did not suffice to launch them on an independent course. In the middle of the wealth distribution, children were lucky to inherit 2:000$000—not nearly enough to maintain their status in Rio's social structure.[15] Meanwhile, if there was a surviving parent, he or she also struggled to make do with half of the original estate. Because the law demanded that the tutors of "orphans" maintain strict accounts with their inheritances, widows had fewer options when it came to putting their wealth to work. They could risk their own capital in business ventures, but the estates of their minor children tended to be limited to safer investments in real estate, slaves, and bank accounts—indeed, it was the job of the tutor and the orphans' court to monitor the accounts of minor children and safeguard them from malfeasance or risky investments.

Insofar as the data permit, we can conclude from the estate samples undergirding this book that children born out of wedlock did not suffer inordinately in relation to their legitimate counterparts. To be sure, many "natural" children failed to be recognized in the testaments of decedents, so our knowledge of what happened to illegitimate children is limited to those who were recognized. In these cases, natural children had all the rights of the legitimate ones. They received equal shares of their father's estate; they had tutors appointed to look after their interests and education. Paradoxically, because their mothers were not usually named as legatees in the testaments, they stood to inherit their full share of their fathers' estates outright, rather than have to wait for the death of both parents—as was the case with Dutra's heirs.

An exception to this rule occurred in the cases where their father was married but had children with other women or otherwise chose to distribute his estate in an alternative fashion. For instance, when Placido Adão da Silva died in 1820, he left 180$000 for his wife and 168$000 to his illegitimate son.[16] Another poor decedent, Ildefonso Teixeira da Cunha, divided his estate among two illegitimate children and a freed slave. The children each received 304$000 and the slave 200$000. Although it is not certain, Ildefonso was probably a liberto. His two children were classified as black, and one, aged six, was listed as a *liberta*—that is, she was born a slave. It is entirely possible that she was born to a slave mother and that Ildefonso himself was already a free man, yet it is suggestive to look closely at this case. Whether or not Ildefonso was a freedman, he owned two slaves, one of which he freed with a small sum of money to boot; the other, listed as an old woman, was auctioned off. Charity apparently had its limits. The favored slave got freedom and money at the expense of Ildefonso's heirs, the unlucky old woman was sold in order to distribute the proceeds to the children.[17]

Finally, there were cases in which children of more than one marriage stood to inherit. For the middling landowner Angelo José de Moraes, this meant that his children did not all inherit equal shares of his estate. Owner of land in the rural districts of Inhauma and Engenho Novo, he left a total estate worth 39:832$000 to his second wife, Ignes Carlota de Moraes, and ten children. Three of his offspring were from his first marriage, and each received approximately 3:300$000. Another three children with his second wife received approximately 1:590$000. Last, his four stepchildren got 762$000 each. His second wife, meanwhile, retained 15:485$000 of the couple's estate.[18] Presumably, upon her death, the order of inheritance would have reversed, with her own children inheriting the lion's share of her wealth—helping to balance out the unequal division in the first instance. In any event, with ten children from three different marriages, the family fortune stood to be dispersed on the death of both parents. The children would eventually want to marry and have homes of their own, and the family's assets would be broken up, with the slaves and land auctioned off and the productive core of the estate dismembered.

The Socioeconomic Consequences of Inheritance Laws

Brazilian inheritance law required the equal division of estates among children, but this practice did not lead to greater equality over time.[19] On the surface, one might assume that the division of large estates would undermine the status of wealthy families. After all, a 50:000$000 estate divided among five children created five middling fortunes in the place of a substantial one. Yet, in reality, the division of estates led to greater, not lower, levels of inequality. On one level, this is a statistical illusion, because the division of an estate makes inequality among all families appear to rise. For instance, the father dies, leaving 100$000 to his wife and 50$000 to each of two children. What had been one observation at 200$000 has now become three observations; yet, in life the father controlled all the wealth, so inequality has really fallen within the family. However, if we place our three hypothetical heirs in a larger universe of hundreds or thousands of heirs with similar properties, the effect will be to raise inequality, as there are relatively more "poor" observations owing to the lopsided division of estates.

The reasons behind this somewhat counterintuitive result are simple. First, the number of heirs among the rich was no greater than among middling and poorer wealthholders. Thus, the division of great estates was replicated throughout the social hierarchy. The fact that widows and widowers generally retained one-half of the family's estate meant that relative inequality increased *among all heirs*— although in many ways this is a statistical illusion, given that the "lower" inequality observed prior to the division of the estates was predicated on the monopolization of wealth and resources in the hands, most often, of the *pater familias*. Analysis of the division of estates in the inventory samples for Rio de Janeiro helps clarify these matters.

For the period 1815–25, the data indicate that 119 estates were divided among 506 legatees—including extended family members and others outside of the nuclear family. The top 20 percent of the estates prior to division accounted for 76.3 percent of total wealth, whereas after division, the top 20 percent of legatees controlled 80.6 percent. In the 1850s, we have data on the division of 207 estates among 1,025 legatees. Prior to division, the top 20 percent held 67.5

percent of total wealth, whereas afterward this same fraction held 75.6 percent of all wealth. In both periods, the division of estates actually appears to have increased the concentration of wealth measured in terms of inequality among the entire universe of heirs.

To reiterate, the key to understanding this pattern of greater inequality among heirs is the institutional framework for inheritance. The stipulation that spouses retain half or more of the couple's estate, depending on whether they had children, meant that fortunes were not broken up immediately upon the death of one partner to the marriage. Inheritance law, which superficially appeared to have been fairly egalitarian with regard to the equal division among children, also served to increase inequality within families and, therefore, among all heirs. In the 1820s sample, married decedents in the top 20 percent of the distribution controlled 77.6 percent of the wealth in their category, whereas among their heirs, the top 20 percent held 82.2 percent. The top 20 percent of heirs of widows and singles, by contrast, held 69.6 percent of the wealth in their category. These findings are somewhat limited by the size of the sample: just 78 heirs were indicated for nonmarried decedents (widows, widowers, and singles). Our data for the 1850s are more robust, with 306 heirs to widows, widowers, and singles and 664 heirs to married decedents. The wealthiest 20 percent of married decedents held 78.9 percent of the wealth in their category, whereas the heirs of nonmarried decedents in the top 20 percent held just 72.8 percent of the wealth in their category.[20] Wealthy widows and widowers concentrated wealth at the expense of a more equal division among all heirs—this allowed richer families, in particular, to maintain their status in spite of the dilution of their wealth owing to inheritance laws.

A worthwhile question to ask at this point is whether there was a tipping point below which the size of inheritances set the heirs on a downward trajectory in the social hierarchy. Clearly, this was the case with Dutra's children as their tutor struggled to keep them clothed, fed, and educated. There is a technical literature on the subject of the intergenerational transfer of wealth and its inequality effects. In this literature, the basic distinction turns on whether an inheritance of a given amount is sufficient to set the heir on an upward path of wealth accumulation or whether, on the contrary, the inheritance is bound to be spent over the course of one or more generations.[21] Although we must recognize that luck, timing, and hard work all played a role in the formation of wealth, it is fairly evident that very large estates could be passed along in much diluted form and still supply heirs with the foundation for future wealth. Alternatively, when middling estates were dismembered, heirs faced an uphill battle to maintain their social position, much less improve it.

A simple model of income and consumption helps to define the parameters of social advance or decline on the basis of inheritance. Inheritances above 20:000$000, in constant 1850 values, probably sufficed to maintain a person's social status and allow for improvement during the lifecycle—particularly if a goodly portion of the estate was invested in income-generating assets. A minor child with an inheritance of 20:000$000 could look forward to beginning their adult life with an income of 1:000 to 1:500$000 per year on the basis of rents, income, and interest on their estate.[22] At worst, this would afford them a decent standard of living even if they chose not to work. An income of 1:000$000 was the equivalent, circa 1849, of the labor of seven unskilled laborers. At best, they would conceivably have up to 1:000$000 per year to invest. In the course of twenty or thirty years, this could easily translate into a fortune of 50:000$000 or more.

Heirs to fortunes of 50:000$000 or more would have a hard time, no matter how poorly they managed their wealth, falling down the social ladder—although some particularly inept businessmen and investors no doubt managed this feat. Added to the advantages of being born with a fair amount of wealth, was the likelihood that intermarriage among wealthy families would serve to reconstitute large estates. Two heirs with 20:000$000 each could marry and hasten the return to high-wealth status—and, if their union was endogamous, the family patrimony could be preserved intact from one generation to the next. In the real world of Rio de Janeiro in the 1850s, heirs to fortunes in the top 20 percent of the distribution stood to inherit an average of 22:427$000—more than enough, by these calculations, to maintain one's status and, with a good marriage and a modicum of thrift, return to the top ranks of wealthholding. These heirs were not, on the whole, a downwardly mobile lot.

Things were much different for middling wealthholders and their heirs. Whereas a fortune of 10:000$000 to 20:000$000 formed the basis for a respectable life, once divided among the average of five heirs, the next generation found the going tough if they wanted to improve their situation or attain the level of affluence enjoyed by their parents. This was especially the case for families without recourse to education and the skills prized in public employment and commerce. Certainly, it was better to start adult life with two contos; but the time, work, and luck required to turn this back into an estate of ten contos or more was much greater than the equivalent time required to reconstitute a larger estate.

Fundamentally, the discretionary income that could be turned to investment was much smaller for this group. Moreover, as time went on, the most accessible form of investment, slaves, rose dramatically in price. A 2:000$000 inheritance, prior to the 1850s, was usually made up of a small house, or a portion of a larger home, a slave or two, some cheap furnishings, and perhaps a little cash. By the mid-1850s, 2:000$000 would barely account for a pair of slaves. If the heir chose to live in their inherited domicile, they would have to forego the potential stream of rents from the property (although many, no doubt sublet rooms).[23] At the very best, they could count on 200$000 to 300$000 per year in income from their assets. Their home could appreciate in value, but because they owned just one and needed a place to live, this was an illiquid asset. A slave could be inherited at a value of 500$000 in the 1840s and sold for 1:000$000 in the 1850s, but where would the 500$000 profit be invested? Houses were too expensive and stocks and bonds were rarely held by Rio's poorer residents. Holding cash was a bad idea with the threat of inflation ever looming on the horizon.

For poorer heirs, then, their adult lives were spent clawing their way back up the social ladder with hard work and luck—the same way their parents generally rose in life. As the economy shifted in the late 1840s and beyond, the avenues to social ascent narrowed. The strategy of accumulating slaves was impeded by high prices; commerce became more competitive and required greater sophistication and stocks of capital—often brought across the Atlantic by European immigrants. In the 1850s, the mean inheritance for members of the upper-middle group (the second 20 percent of the distribution) amounted to 6:212$000: enough, perhaps, to contract a marriage of equals and maintain one's status, difficult, however, to return to the status of one's parents. For the middle 60 percent of the distribution as a whole, the mean inheritance was 3:804$000, roughly equivalent to the value of the median house owned by members of this group.

Changing economic conditions profoundly affected the prospective fortunes of heirs in Rio de Janeiro. If a middling inheritance in the 1820s amounted to 1:500$000, this amount went much further than the equivalent 3:000$000 in the 1850s: the former sufficed to purchase ten slaves, the latter bought just three or four. Meanwhile, the cost of living had risen dramatically in the city—leaving middling heirs little room for error in the 1850s. If rent had to be paid, it would come to twice as much in real terms as in the 1820s. Food prices had increased commensurately, putting additional strain on the finances of small wealthholders. All the while, real wages were barely higher than a generation before. Middling and poorer heirs in the 1850s faced significant obstacles in their struggle to maintain their social status and wealth.

Women and Wealth

Rio de Janeiro's society, for all its complexity, also broke down along some very simple lines. Distinctions based on civil status served to place people in general categories: slave or free, married or single. For wealthholders, civil status was a critical determinant of the size of estates. Married decedents, in Dutra's time (late 1840s), possessed more than twice the wealth of their widowed counterparts. Brazilian inheritance law explains the difference. In the case of married decedents, the value reported represented the entire estate accumulated by the couple; widow's estates were often smaller—if children were involved—because some of the community property had already been distributed on the death of their spouse.

The place of women in Dutra's world depended a great deal on their civil status—as the sagas of his lover Maria Mathildes and his daughter Ignacia make clear. For the ten-year period around Dutra's death, 1845–54, independent women decedents (single and widowed) accounted for 13 percent of all estates. If we include married women's estates, the percentage of women in the wealthholding sample rises to 30 percent. In the 1820s, women decedents of all types accounted for 42 percent of wealthholders in the sample, with 12 percent representing widows and singles. Women played a significant role in wealthholding and affected social structures accordingly. About one in eight decedents was a woman with independent control of her estate.

The relationship between women and overall patterns of wealthholding was surprisingly unstable over the period 1815–60. Whereas our sample size appears robust for the analysis of many aspects of wealthholding, gender differences do not appear to follow easily identifiable trends. On the one hand, more "independent" women, widows and singles, appear over time, perhaps indicating changing social patterns. On the other hand, the wealth of women oscillates widely from period to period. Dutra's own period, from 1845–49, marks the lowest point for women wealthholders in terms of their mean wealth relative to men. Yet, in the expanded period, 1845–54, women, on average, held more mean wealth than did their male counterparts. Even discounting the wealthiest woman as an outlier,

Table 11

Wealth and Civil Status in Rio de Janeiro, 1845–1849

	N obs.	N Slaves	Urban Real Estate	Slaves	Rural Property	Cash and Bank Deposits	Stocks and Bonds	Business Assets	Debts	Credits	Furn. and Precious Metals	Other	Total
						TOTAL WEALTH BY CIVIL STATUS							
married	62	737	672,824	245,987	139,583	123,373	90,472	57,195	(239,064)	343,026	64,767	29,383	1,527,547
widowed	23	162	128,306	51,469	42,934	41,438	23,364	1,201	(53,685)	16,536	12,099	10,566	274,228
single	30	239	138,929	80,075	43,644	27,428	65,389	3,957	(32,556)	86,282	16,648	3,902	433,698
						MEAN WEALTH BY CIVIL STATUS							
married	62	12	10,852	3,968	2,251	1,990	1,459	923	(3,856)	5,533	1,045	474	24,638
widowed	23	7	5,579	2,238	1,867	1,802	1,016	52	(2,334)	719	526	459	11,923
single	30	8	4,631	2,669	1,455	914	2,180	132	(1,085)	2,876	555	130	14,457

Source: Inventarios, Rio de Janeiro, AN.
Note: Values reported in constant 1850 mil-réis.

women for this ten-year period held almost exactly as much wealth on average as did men. Unmarried women, widows and singles, did hold less wealth than did their married counterparts, but this was the same with men. Looked at a third way, during the period 1850 to 1860, and restricting our analysis to the middle 90 percent of the wealth distribution in the sample (to avoid the potential for wild oscillations due to outliers, which becomes more of a problem when we break down the sample into smaller components based on gender and civil status), we derive the results reported in Table 12.

According to this analysis, male decedents tended to hold slightly more wealth than their female counterparts during the 1850s. The presence of outliers can change this portrait dramatically. Nevertheless, leaving aside this problem for the moment, it emerges that single women fared the worst by far in this analysis. It is also clear that women did not participate in nearly the same degree as men in the informal credit networks that lubricated the wheels of exchange and investment in the city. A generation before, when Dutra arrived in Rio de Janeiro and the city was half as large and somewhat poorer, the picture that emerges of women and wealth is just as mixed. The number of independent women wealthholders, whether by choice or necessity, was about the same in the 1820s as it had been in the 1850s, accounting for 12 percent of all decedents in the sample (21 of 172). Yet, unlike the women of the 1850s, female decedents in early nineteenth-century Brazil held far less wealth than their male counterparts—17:970$000 per man and 11:452$000 per woman.

On the whole, the economic growth and social mobility described for Rio de Janeiro in the first chapters of this book appear to have influenced the fortunes of women as well as men. Women were the minority of wealthholders, and independent women accounted for fewer than one in seven estates. By the 1840s and 1850s, however, the chief differences between women's and men's wealth came down to the allocation of wealth among categories of wealth rather than in the mean values. Men, on average, owned more financial wealth and women owned more real estate wealth. In particular, wealthy women tended to own large amounts of rural land—but the high mean shown in this category is really a statistical illusion, as independent women owned practically no rural property at all. Counting married female decedents as landowners is not entirely meaningless, but it is misleading.

For example, Claudianna Maria da Luz's inheritance record includes 12:790$000 in land and another 1:014$000 in coffee plantings

Table 12

Mean Wealth and Gender in Rio de Janeiro:
Middle 90 Percent of Wealthholders, 1850–1860

	N obs.	Urban Real Estate	Slaves	Stocks and Bonds	Debts	Credits	Total
women	88	7,136	3,758	1,359	862	773	18,158
men	174	9,446	3,915	1,809	3,322	2,775	23,385
women/men	0.51	0.76	0.96	0.75	0.26	0.28	
married women	46						20,159
single women	8						10,943
widows	22						16,821

Source: Inventarios, Rio de Janeiro, AN.
Notes: Values reported in constant 1850 mil-réis; the number of women with information on civil status does not equal the total number of women in the sample.

out of a total estate valued at 24:502$000.[24] On the one hand, Claudianna was legally the "owner" of one-half of the community property in her marriage. So we cannot entirely discount her as a woman wealthholder. On the other hand, she was married at the time of her death, and the laws were clear that her husband had control of their community property. A more useful category of analysis, then, is that of independent women—widows or singles.

Independent Women Wealthholders

If we focus on widows and single women who died between 1845 and 1854, the overriding source of their wealth appears to be urban real estate. Slavery, oddly enough, appears to have been of minimal importance for this group. Most women, it seems, shied away from large amounts of credits or debits, holding, on average, less than one-third as much as men. This is in keeping with our major finding that women held fewer financial assets than did men. In this, they were in the same boat as middling wealthholders of Dutra's ilk: dependent on traditional forms of wealth, they lacked the financial acumen or cultural disposition to participate fully in Rio de Janeiro's burgeoning commercial economy.

To be sure, there were exceptions, especially among widows whose estates presumably reflected some of the financial strategies adopted by their late husbands. Ana Theodora Mascarenhas Barros, a wealthy widow, held bonds worth 10:008$000 in an estate valued at 115:370$000.[25] Widows were also more likely than single women to owe or to be owed significant debts.

Few single women held wealth. In the period 1815–25, just 6 out of 176 estate inventories pertained to single women. Later, in the 1850s, just 16 out of 363 fit this category. In short, single women made up 3 to 4 percent of all decedents in the samples gathered through the middle part of the nineteenth century. It was only in the 1880s that immigration and social change raised the percentage of single women among the inventoried population (16 out of 144 cases). Because the estate inventories prior to the 1880s do not generally give the age of the decedent, it is impossible to know how many of these single women were children at the time of their inventories. Limited data from the 1880s indicates that perhaps one-quarter were under the age of twenty.

During the middle years of the nineteenth century, single women wealthholders exhibited several noteworthy characteristics relative to other men and women in Rio de Janeiro. Not only were they poorer, on average, than any other group, but also they tended to own female slaves at a much higher rate than other groups. Although we lack specific information regarding the profession of most of the single women in the samples, it is likely that ownership of female slaves was tied to these women's own labor. Just as Dutra's male-dominated slaveholding was associated with the gendered categorization of his barbering business, it is easy to imagine single women slaveholders employing female slaves in their own gender-determined enterprises. On the whole, although the number of observations for single women is small, it appears that single women's slaveholdings were 78 percent female whereas single men's slaveholdings were just 28 percent female—in contrast, among married decedents, the figure was about 37 percent.[26]

Notwithstanding our uncertainty regarding the age of single women decedents in the 1820s and 1850s, it is well worth looking more closely at a few cases in order to describe the range of positions such women found themselves in. We begin with the instructive case of Carlota Augusta de Barros, deceased in 1853. Carlota's estate cuts against the grain inasmuch as it consisted almost entirely of bonds worth 18:782$000 in an estate valued at 19:447$000 to be distributed among a huge list of kin and nonkin legatees. Her cousin, Luiz

Mariano de Oliveira, served as executor, and it was to his children that the lion's share of the estate fell. A total of twelve other people, ranging from sisters to friends, received smaller sums. Finally, and perhaps most generously, she freed her only slave—although she did not, as many testators took care to do, settle a small amount on this newly freed slave.[27] Embedded in this record we see clearly the importance of piety and generosity in the testaments of single women. Carlota took care to leave a small amount to many of her friends, to free her slave, and to leave a sum for masses to be conducted for her eternal salvation. Other, poorer women, followed similar strategies. Catharina Luiza de Menezes, before her death in 1845, took care in her testament to allocate her meager estate to her sole heir as well as to four godchildren and to leave a bit for the saying of masses.[28]

Finally, there were single women with children. Such was the case of Candida Perpetua da Gloria, deceased in 1853. Candida's estate was small but not insignificant, amounting to 3:132$000, most of which was accounted for by her home. Her only son, classified in her testament as "insane," received the balance of her estate, to be administered by his tutor, José Alves da Silva. Before her death, it appears from the inventory that Candida lived by renting part of her house to a boarder and by the wages earned by her one slave. Like Carlota, in the example above, she freed her slave in her testament, adding, importantly, the condition that her bondswoman continue to serve her son for ten years.[29]

Looking at the 1880s sample, with information on age, we can extend our description of single women wealthholders, highlighting the way general trends in wealthholding toward modern financial instruments were manifest in this subgroup of the population. At the bottom of the social spectrum were poor women like Martiniana Maria Jacinta de Souza, native of the state of Rio and last resident on Rua Senhor dos Passos. At the time of her death in 1889, Martiniana's meager possessions totaled 125$000 in the Caixa Econômica. Aged fifty, she left behind no children and her estate went to her two brothers.[30] Higher on the scale, Amelia Avelina de Jesus died in 1889, leaving an estate of 3:419$000 (in bonds, no less) to her eleven children. Her *companheiro* (lover), João da Silva Alves, was nominated as executor, but he received nothing himself. With eleven children, Amelia was probably in her forties or fifties at the time of her death. At the higher end of the social spectrum, a few single women do appear in the record. Mary Isabella Ford, a twenty-six-year-old Brazilian woman resident on Rua da Passagem, died in 1888 with an estate valued at 17:983$000 in stock.[31] It is notable that, by the 1880s, the widespread ownership of stocks and bonds had filtered down to single women. In the 1840s and 1850s, very few women of any civil status held such instruments, although there were exceptions as in the case of Carlota Augusta de Barros. It is tempting to speculate that these single women wealthholders inherited their wealth in stocks and bonds rather than purchased them themselves.

Dowries

During the colonial era, dowries provided families with daughters with a powerful means to influence their position in society. The "marriage bargain," as Muriel Nazzari defines it, was transformed over the first half of the nineteenth century. From an institution based on family alliances and the transfer of wealth via daughters, it gradually took on a "modern" form in which personal relationships were paramount and brides brought little, if anything, of monetary value to the marriage.[32]

Nazzari's excellent analysis of the disappearing dowry in São Paulo can be extended to Rio de Janeiro, albeit in a slightly different period. Whereas São Paulo's transformation into a commercial metropolis occurred over the second half of the nineteenth century, Rio was well on its way at the time of independence. In the sample for 1815–25, there were just ten dowries (present in 6 percent of all estates) worth an average of 5:584$000. By the 1850s, there were only nine dowries (present in 2 percent of all estates) worth a mean value of 4,955$000. Dowries were of limited importance in the marriage bargain in Rio de Janeiro at the beginning of the nineteenth century and declined in importance over the course of time.

The same forces that Nazzari identifies in the disappearance of the dowry in São Paulo were probably at work in Rio. Foremost, the rise of commerce and entrepreneurship made individual men less dependent on capital brought to the marriage by their wives in the form of dowries.[33] In an associated development, urbanization meant that the family was undermined as a primary economic unit for production. Consumption, not production, became its distinguishing characteristic—as can be seen quite clearly in the family structure of Dutra's household, where the work was done by Dutra himself and his slaves rather than by family members. Ideologically, too, Brazilian thinking about marriage changed in the nineteenth century—placing more emphasis on personal ties. Finally, as Nazzari suggests, the dowry placed fetters on the free disposition of property that was the basis of the emerging market economy in southeastern Brazil.[34]

Did losing their dowries substantially affect the fortunes of women in Rio de Janeiro? Clearly, in terms of their status relative to their husbands, the loss of this independent source of wealth was a blow to women. Yet, the main avenue for women to obtain wealth was through the institution of community property, which reigned supreme with few exceptions in cases of prenuptial contracts, and inheritance. In philosophical terms, the difference between a woman entering a marriage with a substantial inheritance and one with a dowry was not too great. Although her inheritance became part of the couples' community property, and thereby passed into the direct control of her husband, a substantial inheritance no doubt helped in finding a good marriage match.

It is true for Rio, as Nazzari found in São Paulo, that marriage contracts in the nineteenth century tended to favor the interests of men rather than women. In the exceptional cases of separation of property, women invariably came out on the short end. In 1890, for instance, the lawyer and capitalist Carlos Frederico Taylor died leaving a wife and a son. Under traditional community property, his wife should have received one-half of their estate valued at a total of 1,372:410$000. Instead, with a prenuptial contract and separation of property, she got her dowry, worth 50:000$000, the house and furnishings worth 48:998$000, and 30:000$000 in cash for a total of 128:998$000—less than 10 percent of the couple's estate. Meanwhile, the son received 980:197$000.[35] Less spectacular, was the case of Julia Amelie D'Oliveira, whose small-merchant husband died in 1886 under the regime of separate property with a total of 6:646$000. In her case, the couple's entire estate was in the hands of her husband.[36]

Our analysis of the consequences of inheritance law, civil status, and gender for the distribution of wealth yields three major findings. First, the likelihood of a given family's continued status as middling or upper-level wealthholders was quite sensitive to the size of the estate and the number of heirs. Middling estates faced the continual threat of extinction by dilution on the death of the primary wealthholder. A second finding concerns the importance of civil status to determining levels of wealthholding. Married decedents typically reported considerably more wealth than did widows and widowers or singles. The third finding concerns gender. Emília Viotti da Costa identified the "myth of the helpless woman" as one of the enduring misconceptions regarding Brazil in the nineteenth century.[37] My research confirms da Costa's argument, while, at the same time, adding further complexity. Women were not helpless when it came to wealth; yet, neither did they enjoy the same relative position and status as men. They held a great deal of wealth, most of it in the form of community property with their spouse or inherited wealth from their husbands and parents. Moreover, they tended to hold less wealth in the form of stocks, bonds, business assets, and credit. With some notable exceptions, women wealthholders must therefore be characterized as somewhat "passive" and "traditional" relative to men—doubtlessly owing in large part to the patriarchal context in which they lived. The consequences of this tendency, over the long run, placed women at an ever-greater disadvantage relative to their male counterparts as the economy of the city became increasingly complex and tied into broader national and international markets.

Many questions remain. Two of the most important issues revolve around the role of inheritance institutions in patterning wealthholding and social structure and the consequent effect of wealth inequality on the economic development of Brazil. It is possible that the practice of equally partitioned estates undermined the formation of capital in Brazil prior to the era of joint-stock companies and sophisticated financial institutions. There were ways around the problem, and some great fortunes were amassed and passed on relatively intact to the next generation. Yet, inheritance may have beaten on the foundations of even the greatest fortunes over time, eroding their coherence and efficiency.

In addition to this, the role of women in the structuring of Brazilian society in the nineteenth century remains an enticing but poorly illuminated terrain of analysis. Much good work has been done along these lines: Nazzari's research on the dowry and Dain Borges's work on the family in Bahia jump to mind.[38] Yet, there is so much more work to be done. Again, the position of women in elite families may hold the key to understanding a whole series of questions about the intergenerational transfer of wealth and business enterprises, but such women are unlikely to elicit much interest in today's researchers. Furthermore, the impact of massive European immigration, skewed toward adult males, deserves careful analysis in connection with patterns of wealthholding on the other end of the gender equation.

8

CONCLUƧION

In writing this book I often wondered what Antonio Dutra would think were he to know that, someday in the distant future, an historian comfortably ensconced in a university in California would attempt to tell the story of his life. I have often doubted that he would approve of my rendering of his experience. He would probably find my constant denunciations of the slave system grating, although he was, himself, a slave at one time. One can only imagine how he would have viewed his daughter Ignacia's antics in the months and years after his death. In my telling, with the benefit of hindsight and a thousand probate records, his life and death illuminated a dimly perceived world of middling wealth and slaveholding in Rio de Janeiro. From his perspective at the time, he could hardly have known how "representative" his wealthholding was. Fundamentally, Dutra and the thousands of other decedents, family members, and slaves in my samples wove a social and economic structure with their lives that emerges, in partial terms, in this book. I have chosen wealth as the warp of this study; the weft of life is much more complicated.

Notwithstanding these limitations, and with all due reverence to the complex reality of the lived experience of the people of Rio de Janeiro during the nineteenth century, I attempted in this book to overcome some of the distance between that "other country" of the past. By focusing on Dutra and others of middling wealth, I aimed to cast light on a broader, more representative, and yet very diverse part of the population. The broad conclusions of the book can be summarized in three areas. First, analysis of estate inventories indicates that middling wealthholders, of which Dutra was one at the time of his death in 1849, experienced a period of expanding social mobility through about 1850 followed by a prolonged contraction of their opportunities. The factors behind this transformation were, in simple terms, the economic transformation of southeastern Brazil and the institutional changes that ended the slave trade and opened the way to modern forms of finance.

Second, and more speculatively, it appears that wealth inequality rose among wealthholders during the nineteenth century. This finding is sensitive, however, to the way we define the distribution of wealth. Counting slaves as wealth and not potential wealthholders, as Dutra and his ilk assuredly did, the wide distribution of slaves among owners lowered wealth inequality among those with wealth and provided a springboard for social mobility. A former slave turned barber-surgeon like Dutra could, through the acquisition of slaves and the expropriation of their labor, become a relatively wealthy man.

Third, in our analysis of death, dying, gender, and the distribution of estates among heirs we have uncovered further tendencies that undercut the status of middling wealthholders and constrained certain categories of people. The division of estates according to Brazilian inheritance law tended to fragment middling estates, which, owing to their tenuous status, tended to be quite fragile and susceptible to small calamities. Dutra's children appear to have had a hard go at life after his death. The business suffered, slaves and children fell sick, and generations and factions in the family feuded over the proper use of the estate's fragmented assets. What is more, in the general scheme of things, our research indicates that women decedents were systematically poorer than their male counterparts, with less access to credit and other sophisticated financial resources.

Beyond these basic considerations, the results of the research resonate with current debates about the timing and extent of economic growth and the origins and development of the abolitionist movement in Brazil. In Dutra's time, Rio de Janeiro underwent a profound transformation from a small, merchant-bureaucratic city to a booming metropolis. Trade-led growth reconfigured the economy, lifted incomes, and raised the level of financial sophistication in the city. The growth in volume of trade flowing through Rio de Janeiro outstripped the rate of increase in the population throughout much of the nineteenth century. Thus, although "export-led" growth did not occur in Brazil as a whole, it probably did take place in the southeastern part of the country, especially in Rio de Janeiro and São Paulo.[1] Indeed, it was precisely in this region that the social return to railroads was consistently the highest, indicating the high level of domestic and foreign trade carried on there.[2] The flow of goods into the city, whether for export or consumption, occasioned the vast expansion of Rio de Janeiro's warehousing, wholesaling, and retail sectors; it also underwrote the expansion of informal and, later on, formal credit markets centered in the city. To the extent that other towns and cities in the southeastern region were able to mimic Rio de Janeiro on a smaller scale, they too could grow in wealth on the basis of special-ization and trade.

At the same time, rapid urbanization led to an explosion in prop-erty values and an expansion of the service sector. Small business, construction, and administration provided jobs and opportunity for those aspiring to middling status. These internal dynamics, in turn, were powerfully affected by institutional changes in slavery and property rights. When Great Britain and Brazil combined to suppress the Atlantic slave trade in 1850, the price of slaves rocketed upward and their accessibility, as the first rung on the ladder to fortune, was restricted. Dutra's world, built on a combination of relatively cheap slave labor and urban opportunity, began to unravel.

The very wealthy, with a large stake in the urban property market and the financial acumen required to weather this change, solidified their position at the top of Carioca society. Middling wealthholders, although still an important group, gazed across a widening divide of wealth, status, and skills. In the short run, their heavy investment in slaves cushioned their fall relative to their wealthy counterparts—as slave values rose nearly as fast as urban properties. Yet, the high degree of social mobility evident in the period before 1850 began to constrict. Equally importantly, the demographic profile of the city began to shift with the arrival of great numbers of mainly Portuguese immigrants. The predominance of slaves and freed per-sons in nearly all occupations eroded and the likelihood of a former slave like Antonio Dutra rising to social respectability and relative fortune declined.

With regard to the question of abolition, our analysis helps to explain why the movement to end slavery was delayed for so long in Brazil. In simple terms, the data presented in this book reveals the great extent to which middling wealthholders depended on slavery for their wealth and income. We tend to think of a middle group com-prising urban professionals, state employees, and owners of small businesses. Indeed, this is the image of the urban middle groups that informs most of the historiography: these are the firebrands who will challenge slavery; these are the young law graduates who will imbue turn-of-the-century Rio de Janeiro with reform; these are the soldiers and engineers who will remake the political and urban reality of the city. Yet, at least through the 1870s, the middle sectors were more likely than not heavily dependent on slavery. This is not, by any means, to argue for a reductionist accounting in which the "objective" material conditions of an individual suffice to explain his or her class position. It is, however, to suggest that knowing whether the vast majority of "middle-class" residents of Rio owned slaves is of material importance in evaluating claims about this class's purported abolitionist tendencies. Even if the majority of abolitionists can be shown to have come from the middle sectors of society, this does not in any way indicate that the middle sectors as a whole shared these views or were even organically disposed to them.

Along these lines, the great diversity of backgrounds and occupations found in the middle groups implies that the main thing that they really had in common for much of the nineteenth century was a commitment to the institution of slavery and to a model of social relations and mobility predicated on it. If forward-thinking statesmen like Jozé Bonifácio de Andrada e Silva wanted the gradual abolition of slavery, they faced potential opposition not just from the landed elites but also the vast and diverse swath of urban and rural Brazil that depended on small and middling slaveholding for its wealth and social mobility.[3] After all, as Richard Graham convincingly shows, the electorate in nineteenth-century Brazil was quite a bit larger and more diverse than is commonly assumed—with as much as 50 percent of eligible adult males listed on electoral rolls circa 1870.[4] The income qualification, set at 100$000 prior to 1846 and 200$000 thereafter served to bar only "vagabonds" and servants, in the pool of free adult males.[5] Most of the male wealthholders in our samples earned at least enough income to qualify as voters, and between 80 and 90 percent of them owned at least one slave.

The question for students of political culture is how these two very different stakeholders in the slave system related to one another. Were the landed elites emboldened in their opposition to proponents of abolition (or restrictions of any kind on slavery, including the Atlantic trade) by the inchoate but numerous mass of middling wealthholders in their shadow? Conversely, did small and middling slaveholders free ride on the political efforts of their rich and recalcitrant cousins? Paying attention to the middle sectors in a substantive and systematic way leads us to seek their voice in political matters and shifts the focus (partially) away from the political history that has focused almost entirely on elites. Such work has already begun, but more needs to be done.[6]

Ironies of History

Our detailed examination of Antonio Dutra and his family revealed several striking ironies about life in Rio de Janeiro in the first half of the nineteenth century. Foremost is the fact that slavery was both a

horrible institution built on exploitation and coercion and a powerful avenue for social advancement. The rise to fortune of a former
slave like Dutra would have been inconceivable without slavery
itself. In a better world, without slavery, the middling groups in Rio
society would have looked very different indeed.

A second irony in Dutra's family history turns on the ambiguous
position of women and children in the universe of wealthholding. On
the one hand, his daughter Ignacia showed an amazing degree of freedom in her decision to exclude her wayward husband from his con-
ventional role as executor of her father's estate and to cap this off by
successfully suing for divorce. On the other hand, Dutra's lover, Anna
Maria Matildes, had to wait for the death of one of her children before
she saw a cent of Antonio's substantial estate. Legal considerations
and cultural norms crosscut Dutra's family, and, in all likelihood,
many others like it.

The final irony is that fortune, like freedom, could be fleeting for
the middling wealthholders of Rio. After a life of struggle, the middling status of a family could deteriorate over the course of a few
months or years. Here, cultural practices were of paramount importance. In a preindustrial society like Rio's, middling wealthholders
mimicked their wealthier counterparts not only in sending their children to music lessons and joining charitable societies but also in
having large numbers of offspring. The rich could afford to have an
average of five heirs; the middling groups could not. A middling fortune was quickly dispersed and depleted in a way that a great fortune was not. Perhaps in Dutra's time of greater social mobility,
middling families counted on finding a good place for their children
without depending on passing on a large inheritance. In the 1830s and
1840s, when Dutra was building his family along with his fortune, it
was easy enough to imagine his sons and daughters following the
same arc. As his estate inventory makes clear, his sons had a hard time
of it in the 1850s. How much of this was due to their dispositions, we
cannot say for certain. Were they the lazy and unmotivated adoles-
cents described in the documents? Or were they confronted by a
vastly restricted world of relative poverty and lack of opportunity?

Alexandre managed to become a municipal guard, but rose no
higher. Even the slaves he freed faced daunting challenges in their
new lives. No doubt their condition was vastly improved by freedom.
They kept what they earned; they went as they pleased; some banded
together to open a rival barbershop. Yet, others still worked in the barbershop and all faced the problem of finding housing in an expensive
city. They had little prospect of following in Dutra's footsteps and

attaining fortune and a modicum of status through the acquisition of slaves of their own in the transformed city of the 1850s and beyond. Slaves were too expensive, the cost of living was high, barber-surgeons were losing out to the "formal" medical establishment, and the era of barber bands was drawing to a close.[7]

APPENDIX
SAMPLING PROCEDURES AND SENSITIVITY ANALYSIS

Estate inventories provide a uniquely valuable source of data on wealthholding in nineteenth-century Latin America. Their systematic use, however, is complicated by three basic problems. These are, in increasing order of difficulty: (1) the problem of consistency over time, as the types of decedents inventoried can alter according to changes in the law, demographic patterns, or unaccountable factors such as the loss of records; (2) the problem of age and censoring, as it is possible that the inventoried population is older and wealthier than the living; and (3) the problem of coverage, as we often do not know how many people among the living held wealth to begin with. Together, these three problems can undermine the reliability of estimates based on estate inventory samples and lead to biased and misleading conclusions about the pace and scale of changes in wealthholding over time.[1]

Historical studies that utilize estate inventories from Brazil almost never perform the most rudimentary of sensitivity tests regarding their data. Indeed, in spite of all the hard work that has gone into collecting estate inventory data over the years, much of what has been published along these lines must be taken with a grain of salt. Without naming names, common problems in the literature can be boiled down to:

I. Big conclusions based on small samples.
II. Selection bias in the sampling procedure itself.
III. Failure to adjust (for age, censoring, etc.) and deflate values or failure to conduct sensitivity tests on use of different deflators.
IV. Failure to conduct sensitivity tests in general and to check results against independent measures.

This appendix explains the method by which I obtained my estate inventory samples and the reasons why I argue that the data contained in them is, with adjustment, reasonably consistent, unbiased, and representative.

Collecting and Coding the Sample

The underlying estate inventory data utilized in this book derive from the records kept in Brazil's National Archive in Rio de Janeiro. There are thousands of inventories in this archive, cataloged in alphabetical order by last name. In order to draw our sample, we first estimated how many records would appear for a given year during the periods in which we were interested. We then decided on how many records we needed per year and per period in order to be assured of a large and representative sample. In the end, we selected every other estate inventory for the period 1815–25 and every third inventory for the periods 1845–60 and 1885–95; we also drew a smaller sample for the period 1868–73. Our aim was to obtain a minimum of 20 and an average of 30 usable cases per year, and a minimum of 100 and an average of 200 cases per period or sub period (for example, 1845–49). In the end, our samples yielded 176 observations for the first period and 483 for the second. We drew a smaller sample of 87 observations for the third period simply in order to create a benchmark for change between the second and last major periods. The final period, which straddles the end of slavery and the declaration of the Republic, yielded a sample of 362 observations. In the course of analyzing the data, we also divided these samples into sub periods when deemed necessary. Thus, for instance, the period 1845–49 is bracketed off and analyzed on its own in order to render a portrait of wealthholding around the time of Dutra's death.

We adopted this procedure purposefully in order to ensure large samples (note, when considering whether our samples are "large," that 100 inventories require between 200 and 400 hours of labor to transcribe, code, and process) and to avoid problems associated with basing the analysis on shorter periods. A sample drawn from a shorter period would be more susceptible to variation owing to random events (deaths due to an epidemic) or short and rapid changes in exchange rates or deflators. It merits mention that, combined (N=1,109), the inventory sample used in this book is larger than any other sample hitherto gathered for the study of wealth in nineteenth-century Brazil, let alone in Rio de Janeiro. In addition, as will emerge in the remainder of this appendix, the samples drawn for Rio de Janeiro and their interpretation have been buttressed by an additional 492 estate inventories from important commercial centers in the neighboring province of Minas Gerais.

In order to get an idea of how many inventories were made during the period under review, our analysis indicated that approximately

45 estate inventories exist for each year in the 1820s and that about 120 exist for each year in the 1840s and 1850s. Unfortunately, we have no way of knowing whether these represent all the inventories that were created during those periods of the nineteenth century. Indeed, it is likely that some unknown number were destroyed, another unknown quantity lost, and still more hidden away in notarial archives. In spite of this uncertainty, we can see that the number of cases per year appears to track the growth in the population of the city, which is inconclusive but somewhat reassuring. Additionally, we can venture a rough guess as to the percentage of decedents in a given year who were likely to be subject to an inventory process. These figures are, necessarily, very rough owing to limitations in the data. It appears, however, that about 2,500 adults (age twenty and up) died in Rio de Janeiro in 1847.[2] Of these, a large number were slaves. Among the free population, then, there were probably about 1,500 free adult decedents.[3] On this basis, the inventories would appear to cover about 120 out of 1,500 possible decedents—or 8 percent.[4] Looked at another way, the mortality rate among the free in the 1840s was approximately 30 per 1,000.[5] With about 20,000 households in 1847, the number of decedents who were heads of households or married to heads of households would be on the order of 1,050 (630 heads, 420 spouses, in keeping with the ratio of married decedents in the samples). In this scenario, the inventories would account for 11 percent of all decedents likely to be eligible for the process.

Measures of Consistency

The first question researchers should ask when dealing with inventory samples that cover an extended period of time is whether they are consistent in type, origin, and nominal characteristics. In Brazil, the law required inventories in some instances and not in others; there was also a gray area where inventories might or might not be required. In addition to this, the population of Rio de Janeiro was growing and perhaps changing in terms of its characteristics. A change in the law or a change in demography could, conceivably, alter the distribution of inventoried decedents. We do not have perfect, direct measures, for consistency; however, we can asses this problem indirectly by looking at the jurisdictional origins of inventories over time, the civil status of the decedents, and their gender.

Most inventories involved decedents with minor children and thus fell under the authority of the orphans' judge. The proportion of inventories under this legal rubric remained almost constant over core periods under review: 82 percent of all inventories in the period 1815–25 came from the orphans' judge; 81 percent of all cases in the period 1850–60 were filed in the same court; in the 1870s, this proportion fell somewhat to 66 percent. Another measure of consistency involves the civil status of decedents in the sample. A dramatic rise in the number of single or widowed decedents could affect our estimates. Yet, the number of married decedents in the sample periods is virtually identical: 62 percent in the 1820s; 64 percent in the 1850s; and 62 percent in the 1870s. Finally, the gender of decedents in the samples does not vary too radically over time, with male decedents predominating—accounting for 57 percent of cases in the 1820s, 65 percent in the 1850s, and 59 percent in the 1870s. On the whole, the samples are strikingly consistent over time, and the potential bias injected by changing composition along nominal axes seems limited. At worst, there are 12 percent too many males in the 1850–60 sample—assuming a long-run trend of 58 percent male decedents. Men held more wealth, on average, than women, so a fraction of the increase in wealth registered between the 1820s and 1850s could be attributable to this factor. However, according to the values in the sample, the effect was minimal: men in the 1850s sample held, on average, just 3 percent more wealth than their female counterparts, most of whom, of course, were married.

Measures of Age Bias and Censoring

The inventoried population is likely to be older and wealthier than the living population. Is age bias a significant problem in our samples? From the outset this is an extremely difficult problem to address. Prior to the 1870s, few inventories contain information about the decedent's age. Knowing that roughly two-thirds of cases involve married decedents and that more than 80 percent involve minor children, we can come to some very general conclusions about the likely age range of the majority of decedents in the samples prior to the 1870s. Yet, perhaps it is best to begin with the periods for which we do have some data regarding the age of the decedents in our samples. For the period 1868–73, we have age information on just 22 of 87 decedents for which detailed property reckonings exist. The mean age of this small group is 49.5 years. In the period 1885–89, the mean age of decedents is 47.5 (N=51). Slightly out of the period covered by this book, in the early 1890s, the mean age of decedents was 50.5 (N=111).

These averages are consistent with our expectations based on inferences from other parts of Brazil where we have census data regarding the age of heads of households. In the *município* (county) of São João de Rei, in Minas Gerais—admittedly not a perfect match with a metropolis such as Rio—the mean age of *living* heads of households was 42.4 years. Among the known wealthholding population (slaveholding heads of households, 42 percent of all households) the mean age was 45.2 years; among heads of households without slaves, the mean age was 40.9.[6] The wealthholding population (slaveholders as a proxy), as expected, was slightly older than the population without evident wealth. However, the most important finding from this analysis of age and wealth (slaveholding) in São José is that wealth, measured by slaves, does not appear to be significantly affected by age bias. Plotting the number of slaves held by each household by age, Figure A1, does not exhibit a pattern of significant age bias.

This finding is doubly consistent with the argument made in this book: the optimal size of slaveholding in a nonplantation environment, such as São João (or Rio city) is limited by slave agency and the high cost and scarcity of housing in the case of urban settings; thus, according to this hypothesis, slaveholders will accumulate bondspersons only up to a certain point, after which, as they age, they maintain roughly the same number of slaves. As a corollary to this, we predict that slave wealth will be a poor predictor of overall wealth, especially in urban environments. Returning to Rio de Janeiro, we see the limited predictive value of slave wealth relative to total wealth depicted in Figure A2.

❖❖❖❖

Figure A1
Slaveholding by Age: São João (Minas) 1831/32

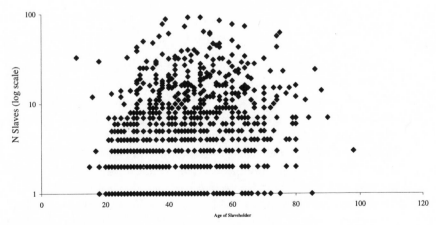

Source: Paiva dataset.

Figure A2
Nonhuman Wealth as a Function of Slave Wealth

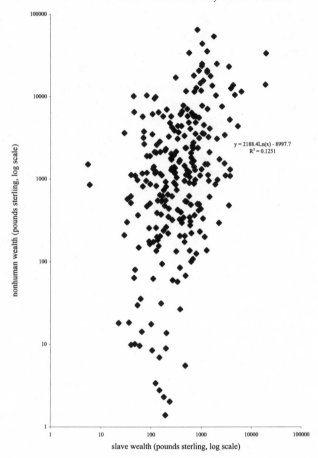

$y = 2188.4\text{Ln}(x) - 8997.7$
$R^2 = 0.1251$

nonhuman wealth (pounds sterling, log scale)

slave wealth (pounds sterling, log scale)

Source: Inventories, Rio de Janeiro, AN.

The consequences of this finding are both helpful and problematic with regard to the problems of bias and coverage in our samples. The dispersed patterns indicated in Figures A1 and A2 help assure us that age bias is less of a problem than we originally suspected. Even if a certain age group is overrepresented in the estate samples, it is likely to contain a broad range of wealthholding types and yield estimates that are not terribly biased. This is not to say that age bias is not an issue, it is only to argue that it is less of an issue than is often supposed. The only other study I am aware of that attempts to account for age bias in estate inventories in Rio de Janeiro during the nineteenth century is Silveira's analysis of wealth and inequality from

1870 to 1980. According to Silveira's estimates, inequality attributable to age varied, as a factor in overall inequality, from 35 percent in the 1870s to 8 percent in the 1900s.[7] Although Silveira's analysis is careful, and his samples are large, his estimate regarding the age-wealth relationship in the 1870s is based on a series of inferences regarding the age of the decedents (age information is largely lacking for this period).[8] Thus, it seems much more likely that the contribution of age to inequality was similar in the 1870s to that in the 1900s and beyond, where Silveira never reports a contribution above 12 percent. To be sure, his discussion of the age-inequality problem is focused on the contribution of age to the observed inequality in his samples, and not, precisely, the relative frequency of decedents in different age bands and their wealth or the effect of age bias relative to the living population. Nevertheless, in the last analysis these are basically two ways of talking about the same thing, and the age-wealth effect derived by Silveira for the living population is 21 percent on average, 17 percent circa 1900.[9]

The lack of fit between slave wealth and total wealth is potentially troubling if we wish to argue that the estate inventory samples are representative of the wealth of living slaveholders. If our theory about the accumulation of slaves in the urban environment is correct, our older sample of decedents will have had ample time to expand their wealthholding in other areas, whereas the younger, living population, will contain many wealthholders still in the process of accumulating slaves—and this group will generally be poorer than the estate sample.

The degree to which this may be a problem can be approached indirectly by returning, again, to São João. With the caveat that we are referring to an interior county in the province of Minas Gerais, and not a metropolis on the order of Rio de Janeiro, it is instructive to compare the size distribution of slaveholding among the living and among decedents in this region.[10] Although we can only draw rough inferences from these figures to the probable distribution of slaveholding among heads of households in Rio de Janeiro, it is nonetheless plausible to assume that roughly the same tendency was manifest in Brazil's capital during the first half of the nineteenth century. The living population of wealthholders was slightly younger, on average, and slightly poorer.

Returning to Rio de Janeiro, I also collected data on 111 decedents for which age could be determined for the period 1890–95. Although we must take care in projecting these findings backward into the period of the empire (1889 marked the first year of the Republic in Brazil), it is nonetheless reassuring to see the lack of a clear pattern regarding

Table A1

Distribution of Slaves Among the Living: Município of São João del Rei, 1831/32

Age Range	% of Slave Holders	% all Households	% Slaves	Mean Slave Holding
<30	14.5	17.2	6.4	3.44
30-39	22.3	24.4	20.6	7.23
40-49	25.3	23.3	25.9	7.99
50-59	18.8	17.5	24.2	10.07
60-69	13.0	11.7	15.3	9.2
>70	6.1	5.9	7.6	9.76
Total	100	100	100	7.82

Source: Clotilde de Paiva dataset, listas nominativas, São João del Rei (Minas Gerais), 1831/32.

Note: The data do not include the town of São João del Rei, which was not included in the imanuscript census of 1831/32.

Table A2

Distribution of Slaves: Census and Inventory Samples, São João and São José

Percent of all owners by interval of slaves owned

N slaves owned	c.1820, inventories	c.1855, inventories	census c. 1831/32
fewer than 6	43.8	51.6	61.2
6 to 10	22.3	19.0	18.6
11 to 20	17.4	12.1	12.8
21 to 40	9.1	11.3	5.2
more than 40	7.4	6.0	2.3
% slaves in >40	53.1	60.6	37.7

Source: Paiva dataset and inventories, São João del Rei and São José (Minas Gerais).

wealth and age in this decedent sample—indeed, this is in keeping with Silveira's findings for the 1900s, where his decomposition of inequality shows age contributing 8 percent to overall inequality. By saying this, I am not by any means claiming that age bias did not exist: I merely wish to underscore that the preponderance of the evidence points to this as a relatively minor source of distortion in the estate samples.

Censoring, the technical term for the omission of estates (or values in particular categories) below a certain level of wealth, appears to be less of a problem. First, many small estates are recorded in the samples. Second, the minimum values recorded in each sample period do not deviate greatly. Third, the proportion of small estates does not change too dramatically—although it does increase over time, perhaps indicating a greater propensity for decedents to be inventoried owing to stronger and more efficient legal mechanisms. One measure of this tendency is the percentage of estates worth less than 100 pounds sterling—which rises from 14 percent in the 1850s to 25 percent in the 1880s. The most fundamental problem, then, is wrapped up in the same problem as age bias—too few observations in the sample at the bottom of the distribution relative to the living population of wealthholders. Unfortunately, we are not in a position to estimate the precise degree of censoring going on at the bottom of our samples. We can, however, remove an arbitrary percentage of estates

◈◈◈◈

Figure A3
Age and Wealth: Rio de Janeiro, 1890–1895

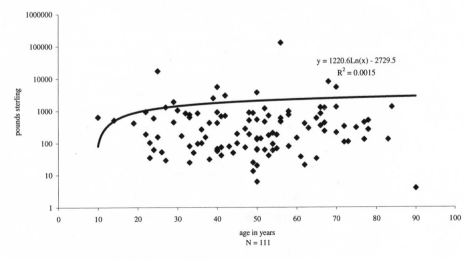

Source: Inventories, Rio de Janeiro, AN.

at the top and bottom to see whether outliers or censoring are driving changes in our wealth estimates over time.

Cutting out the richest and poorest quintiles, leaving our middle 60 percent of the distribution that I argue represents the middle groups, results in the same general tendency in terms of growth in wealth over time as with the entire sample. The annual rate of growth in real (Lobo-pound sterling deflator) mean *net* wealth was 1.7 percent in the full samples over the periods 1815–25 and 1850–60 (calculated as the growth in the mean from c. 1820 to c. 1855, or thirty-five years); for the middle 60 percent, the rate of growth was 1.5 percent per annum. This provides rather imprecise but compelling evidence that the observed changes in levels of wealth over time are not driven by outliers or radical changes in censoring at the bottom of the distribution.

The Problem of Coverage

In light of the foregoing, we are in a position to claim that our estate inventory samples are reasonably consistent and only slightly biased with regard to age and wealth. We still need to ask, however, what portion of the overall population these samples represent.[11] What percentage of households held at least some wealth? How do our samples relate to this population? What effect does counting slaves as potential wealthholders have on our estimates? Is it possible to craft measures of inequality given the degree of uncertainty belied by these questions? In the concluding pages of this appendix, answers to these questions are ventured. From the outset, however, it is necessary to underscore that much of what follows is speculative—guesswork informed by faint empirical signposts.

In the body of this book, it has been assumed as a stylized fact that half of the households in Rio de Janeiro held wealth and the other half did not (I do not wish to suggest that the zero case households went about naked, just that the value of their possessions was close to zero).[12] On top of this, it is also assumed that the estate inventory samples are roughly representative of the 50 percent of households with wealth.[13] The extended discussion of consistency and bias issues already developed in this appendix is intended to bolster the credibility of this claim. Nevertheless, it is immediately evident that margins of error in these assumptions are probably too large to sustain any but the simplest claims about levels of wealth and change over time. What if 60 percent of households own nothing? What if the estate samples censor many small estates? On a basic level, these questions are unanswerable: we do not possess the requisite data to answer them convincingly.

We can, however, create rough confidence intervals for some of our larger claims about wealthholding and its transformation over time. Table A3 presents a matrix of possible outcomes based on different assumptions about the proportion of the population holding wealth, the degree of age bias, and the level of censoring at the bottom end of the distribution at two key points in our analysis: circa 1820 and circa 1855.

The value of this exercise is that it helps identify the most reasonable parameters for our overall assessment of wealthholding in Rio de Janeiro. The most conservative estimates, which assume that 40 percent of households held wealth and that age bias and censoring, if accounted for, would lower the mean by 20 percent, result in figures that are quite consistent with the expected ratio of wealth to income—somewhere between 3- and 4-to-1.[14] Our per-head income estimate, however, is also quite conservative, as it is based on the annualized rental income of an unskilled slave. Bairoch's well-known rule of thumb for deriving GDP per head is 200 times the daily unskilled wage (200w), but this is meant to capture per head income in poor, largely agrarian societies.[15] Our estimate is similar, inasmuch as we assume that per-head income can be estimated from unskilled wages; however, our calculation is based on the annual slave rental "wage" rather than 200w. Surely the presence of thousands of skilled workers and entrepreneurs in Rio de Janeiro would tend to revise our estimate of per-head income in the city higher than the hire rate of unskilled slaves. In this case, if we maintain a 3.5-to-1 ratio of wealth to income, it is quite likely that the values for censoring and proportion of households with wealth would cluster in the middle of the matrices presented above. A definitive answer to these questions will have to await further archival work in the reconstruction of price and wage history in Brazil.

The Problem of Inflation

To the extent that the reader has been convinced to this point of the reliability of the estate samples utilized in this book, and still has patience for more detail, we can also venture a small digression regarding prices and the possible biasing effects of choosing one or the other deflators. Unfortunately, many books that utilize estate inventory data do not attempt to account for inflation. Others consider using a conversion to pounds sterling or dollars to be sufficient. Now, to be sure, it is better to convert to pounds than to compare nominal values when speaking of wealthholding in Brazil over the course

Table A3

The Sensitivity of Wealth Estimates for Rio de Janeiro

NOMINAL WEALTH PER HOUSEHOLD

	c. 1820			c. 1855		
	percent households with wealth					
censoring and age effect	40	50	60	40	50	60
0	2,959	3,699	4,438	14,407	18,009	21,610
0.95	2,811	3,514	4,216	13,686	17,108	20,530
0.9	2,663	3,329	3,994	12,966	16,208	19,449
0.85	2,515	3,144	3,772	12,246	15,307	18,369
0.8	2,367	2,959	3,551	11,525	14,407	17,288

NOMINAL WEALTH PER HEAD

	c. 1820			c. 1855		
	percent households with wealth					
censoring and age effect	40	50	60	40	50	60
0	375	469	563	1,518	1,898	2,277
0.95	356	445	534	1,442	1,803	2,163
0.9	338	422	506	1,366	1,708	2,049
0.85	319	398	478	1,290	1,613	1,936
0.8	300	375	450	1,214	1,518	1,822
N per household	7.9	7.9	7.9	9.5	9.5	9.5

NOMINAL WEALTH/INCOME RATIO
(Unskilled slave rental rate)

	c. 1820			c. 1855		
	percent households with wealth					
censoring and age effect	40	50	60	40	50	60
0	4.2	5.2	6.3	5.3	6.6	7.9
0.95	4.0	5.0	6.0	5.0	6.3	7.5
0.9	3.8	4.7	5.7	4.7	5.9	7.1
0.85	3.6	4.4	5.3	4.5	5.6	6.7
0.8	3.3	4.2	5.0	4.2	5.3	6.3
Wage, in mil-réis	89.6	89.6	89.6	288.0	288.0	288.0

Source: Estate Inventories, 1815–25 and 1850–60, Rio de Janeiro, AN; and *Jornal do Commercio*, rental advertisements.
Note: all values expressed in current mil-réis.

of the nineteenth century—and I have done this myself in this appendix. However, as other scholars have noted, the exchange rate does not accord precisely to the rate of change in internal prices, particularly for nontraded goods—so over the long term, the exchange rate is not a very good deflator. An alternative would be to adopt one or another price index that has been developed for Brazil in the nineteenth century. Here the problem is that these indices vary greatly in quality and their effect on the resulting estimates can be dramatic. Figure A4 presents the problem in graphical form.

Eyeballing Figure A4 above, one must conclude that either most deflators are wildly off the mark, or Lobo's index, which, to be fair, is a version of a consumer price index, is an unreliable outlier. Any estimates based wholly or in part on Lobo's data will be systematically biased against finding evidence of real growth in wages or wealth.[16] Nonetheless, in an effort to bias the results against my own hypothesis that wealth grew, I have used Lobo's index (accounting for 55 percent of my index), in conjunction with the exchange rate (45 percent), to deflate the values reported in the tables in the body of this book.[17]

The Problem of Measuring Inequality

Finally, we arrive at the question of whether age bias, censoring, and degree of coverage undermine our ability to make claims about levels of inequality and changes in distribution over time. With respect to the former, we are indeed limited in what we can say about overall levels of inequality because we do not know how many zero cases there actually were (among households, potential wealthholders, and so on), we do not know precisely how much age bias affects the distribution in the estate sample, and we do not know how much censoring has distorted the bottom of the distribution. We can make educated guesses about all of these matters, but we will not come to any hard and fast conclusions. With regard to the question of change over time, we are on stronger ground. There are good reasons to believe that the conditions of *ceteris paribus* hold well enough to allow comparisons between one sample distribution and another. Adding more zero cases in similar proportion to the 1820s and 1880s datasets will not change the result in terms of the tendency observed to greater inequality. There is a problem only when the parameters change over time: more or less censoring; more or less age bias. Here, again, we can do no better than construct estimates based on a range of reasonable assumptions.

For instance, it is possible that the censoring problem changed over time. In the 1850s sample, 86 percent of all estates were worth at least

Figure A4
Measures of Inflation in Brazil, 1800s

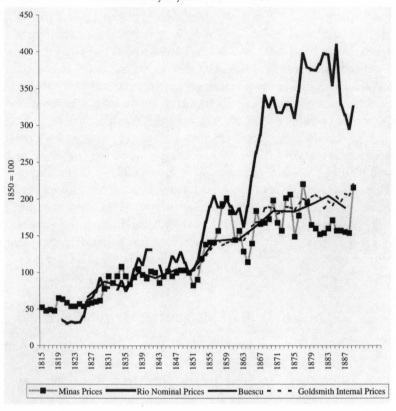

Sources: Alencastro 2001 (Minas); Lobo 1978 (Rio nominal); Buescu 1973
(Rio wholesale); Goldsmith 1986 (Brazil).

100 pounds sterling; by the 1880s this percentage had fallen to 75 percent. Could it be that the higher degree of inequality measured in the 1880s sample is driven by the fact that more small estates are present at the bottom of the distribution? If we remove all estates below 100 pounds and recalculate our distribution, our result is much the same: the top 10 percent raised its share, by this measure, from 57.6 percent of net wealth in the 1850s to 63.8 percent in the late 1880s. Clearly the observed increase in inequality is not being driven primarily by more observations at the bottom of the distribution in the 1880s. It would require a major change in coverage levels, censoring, or age bias to swamp our findings of substantial rising inequality in the 1870s and 1880s. Therefore, we can be fairly confident in our claim that wealth inequality rose over the last half of the nineteenth century.

Concluding Thoughts

The use of estate inventories in the analysis of wealthholding and social structure has long been a staple of economic history. The proper use of these materials depends on their systematic collection and careful sensitivity testing. Estate samples must be large enough to generate sufficient observations in each category of analysis. Moreover, they must be analyzed for age, censoring, and coverage bias. It is not possible to banish bias and uncertainty from this analysis; scholars working with estate inventory samples must, by the nature of their materials, acknowledge these problems and attempt to minimize their effects. In order to accomplish this goal, it is the firm position of this author that researchers working with quantitative data should render their analysis as transparently as possible. This requires a frank discussion of the source of the raw data, the steps taken to transform raw data into processed estimates, and the range of other possible outcomes in light of alternative specifications.

NOTES

Chapter 1

1. Inventory of Antonio José Dutra, 1849, caixa 68, n. 171, Rio de Janeiro, Arquivo Nacional (AN).
2. Traslado de apensos dos autos de inventário do finado Antonio José Dutra, 1849, caixa 2680, n. 341, Rio de Janeiro, AN.
3. An exception to this is Mattoso's *Bahia*. For examinations of the complexity of slaveholding in colonial Brazil, see Paiva, *Escravidão*; Nizza da Silva, *História da família*; Metcalf, *Family and Frontier*; for a study that treats the colonial period and empire in equal proportion, see Nazzari, *Disappearance of the Dowry*. The experience of slaves, freedmen, and free colored during colonial times is taken up in A. J. R. Russell-Wood's *The Black Man in Slavery and Freedom*.
4. Slenes, "Demography and Economics of Brazilian Slavery"; Conrad, *Destruction of Brazilian Slavery*; and Toplin, *Abolition* are excellent studies, but all focus on the period after 1850. The most influential modern interpretation of the transition from slave to free labor remains Viotti da Costa's *Da senzala*. There is a distinction in the literature between the abolition of the Atlantic slave trade in 1850 and the emancipation of the slaves in Brazil in 1888. Drescher's essay, "Brazilian Abolition"; and Bethell's *Abolition* cover the earlier decades in detail.
5. Stein, *Vassouras*; Dean, *Rio Claro*. An important exception to the focus on the coffee economy as the engine of growth in Brazil prior to 1860 is Fragoso's *Homens de grossa aventura*. The importance of sugar, rather than coffee alone, for the province of Rio de Janeiro and its elite is also explored in Needell, "Party Formation and State-Making."
6. Important works in this genre include: Karasch, *Slave Life in Rio de Janeiro*; S. L. Graham, *House and Street*; Reis and Silva, *Negociação e conflito*; Nogueira da Silva, *Negro na rua*; Algranti, *O feitor ausente*; Chaloub, *Visões*; and Soares, *A capoeira escrava*.
7. An exception is Barman's *Brazil*. Important studies of elite politics prior to 1850, with less emphasis on the role of the urban middle groups, include Carvalho, *Construção da ordem*; and Mattos, *Tempo saquarema*.
8. See, for example, Klein and Luna, "Free Colored in a Slave Society." For Bahia, see Barickman, "Cores do escravismo." For a good

overview of the legal and social dimensions of the lives of freed persons in particular, see Mattoso, *To Be a Slave*, esp. ch. 7; as well as Russell-Wood, *The Black Man*, ch. 4. Eduardo Silva's *Prince of the People* provides a window on the culture and consciousness of the free colored in Rio de Janeiro during the later years of the nineteenth century. Beyond the borders of Brazil, there is a growing literature on the experiences of the free colored in other slave societies. For an overview of some recent findings, see *Against the Odds: Free Blacks in the Slave Societies of the Americas*, special issue in *Slavery and Abolition*, ed. Jane G. Landers, 17, no. 1 (1996).

9. Although correct in general terms, Mary Karasch's claim that slaves were the "source of their owners' wealth and capital" needs to be qualified inasmuch as the salience of slave wealth among elites was actually smaller than among poorer slaveholders. Moreover, although the rich did accumulate "as many 'man-machines' as possible," there were limits to the size of urban slaveholdings and richer owners tended to invest more heavily in real estate and financial instruments than in slaves. Karasch, *Slave Life*, 185.

10. Mattoso, *Bahia, Século XIX*, 629.

11. Costa, *Brazilian Empire*, 91, 161.

12. Ibid., 164.

13. Ibid., 162. For the propensity of freed persons to purchase slaves and the general failure of the literature to deal with the subject, see, for example, Barickman, "Cores do escravismo," esp. 7–8.

14. R. Graham, *Patronage and Politics*, 32–33.

15. Karasch notes, for instance, that prior to 1850, freed persons could easily obtain slaves in the low-cost environment of the first half of the nineteenth century, "but after 1850 when slave prices rose sharply, slaveownership was more difficult" (Karasch, *Slave Life*, 211).

16. Figures cited in Atack and Passell, *New Economic View*, 305. As the authors note, vast differences in mortality and fertility meant that the ratio of all slaves living in Brazil and in the United States circa 1825 was virtually one to one. Six times as many slaves went to Brazil from Africa, but, in the end, more slaves lived in the United States in 1825 (36 percent of the total for the Americas) than in Brazil (31 percent).

17. Klein, *Middle Passage*, 55, covering the years 1795 to 1811.

18. Ibid., 76.

19. Karasch, *Slave Life*, 62, 66.

20. Recent contributions highlighting the importance of the free-colored population include de Paiva and Klein's articles on Minas Gerais: "Freedmen in a Slave Economy"; and Klein and de Paiva, "Slave and Free in Nineteenth-Century Minas." For São Paulo and Minas, see

Klein and Luna, "Free Colored in a Slave Society." For Bahia, see Barickman, "Cores do escravismo."

21. The free-colored population made up about 19 percent of the population in New Orleans circa 1840 and slaves made up another 23 percent; Domínguez, *White by Definition*, 116. Recent work along these lines includes, Barickman's *Bahian Counterpoint*; Luna, *Minas Gerais*; Marcondes, "Small and Medium Slaveholding in the Coffee Plantations"; and Versiani and Vergolino, "Slave Holdings in Nineteenth-Century Brazilian Northeast."

22. Schwartz, "Patterns of Slaveholding."

23. Martins and Martins, "Slavery in a Nonexport Economy"; Libby, *Transformação e trabalho*. In neither case do these authors suggest that slavery was good for development; rather, they argue that it was not incompatible with economic activity (evinced by continued slave imports and small-scale craft production in Minas Gerais).

24. The most important contribution along these lines is Fragoso's *Homens de grossa aventura*.

25. For example, Karasch, *Slave Life*, 345; S. L. Graham, *House and Street*; Nogueira da Silva, *Negro na rua*; Algranti, *Feitor ausente*, 85–95; and Chaloub, *Visões de liberdade*.

26. Owensby, *Intimate Ironies*, 8.

27. The diversity of the middle sectors and their lack of "class consciousness" are suggested in Hahner, *Poverty and Politics*, 16–17 and 290–91.

28. An example of the fruitful use of extraordinary case studies to reveal hidden aspects of nineteenth-century Brazil's social world is S. L. Graham's *Caetana Says No*.

29. For an interpretation of these underlying factors with an emphasis on the interaction of factor endowments and institutions, see Engerman and Sokoloff, "Paths of Growth Among New World Economies," 27. North, *Institutions, Institutional Change, and Economic Performance*.

30. In making this assertion, I follow Stein and Stein, *Colonial Heritage of Latin America*; and Haber and Klein, "Economic Consequences of Brazilian Independence." Starting from very different positions, both sets of authors end up emphasizing the continuity in social and economic structures following independence.

31. The degree of European immigration to Rio de Janeiro is difficult to estimate for the period under consideration. Many contemporary documents lump freed slaves in with free immigrants in their calculations of the foreign-born free population. Gladys Ribeiro provides data on Portuguese immigrants who registered with the police in Rio de Janeiro between 1820 and 1834. According to her calculations, 3,808 Portuguese registered during this period, with the bulk

arriving after 1825. More to the point, examining the registry of arriving immigrants for January 1828 through May 1829, Ribeiro counted 2,564 Portuguese destined for the interior (*campo*) and 1,778 destined for the city (Ribeiro, *Liberdade em construção*, 187). Although we lack consistent time series for European immigration, it is fair to say that thousands entered and stayed in Rio de Janeiro during the period covered by this book and that their numbers increased dramatically as the century wore on.

32. The best treatment of D. Pedro II is found in Barman's *Citizen Emperor*. R. Graham analyzes political consolidation in the time of D. Pedro II in *Patronage and Politics*, esp. ch. 2, writing: "Those who owned property in early-nineteenth-century Brazil held ambivalent views about central government . . . Despite hesitations and reversals, by the 1840s they had unambiguously decided to throw in their lot with central power" (43). Needell's recent work on the origins and development of the Conservative Party points to the same conclusion, with the added insight that D. Pedro II's rise to power was, in many ways, eventuated by the ideology and practice of the Conservatives. I am grateful to Professor Needell for furnishing me with draft copies of chapters of his forthcoming book, from which these insights flow.

33. A good example of this is Moya's book *Cousins and Strangers*, wherein Moya combines a quantitative study of immigration to Buenos Aires with a nuanced analysis of the sociopolitical and cultural coordinates of immigrant life. In the study of Brazil, Mattoso's *Bahia, Século XIX* adheres to a "total history" paradigm that reaches across the divide between social and cultural history in the tradition of the *Annales* school. The classic in the Brazilian field remains, however, Stanley Stein's *Vassouras*, wherein economy, society, politics, and culture are woven together with unmatched verve.

34. Bloch, *Historian's Craft*, 26. "The good historian is like the giant of the fairy tale. He knows that whenever he catches the scent of human flesh, there his quarry lies."

Chapter 2

1. Calculating the precise population of the city of Rio de Janeiro is made difficult by the fact that largely rural districts that later became part of the urban core are either included or excluded in published estimates. Karasch, citing 1821 population estimates, reports a total of 86,323 residents (40,376 slaves) (Karasch, *Slave Life*, 62); citing the same source, Nogueira da Silva reports 79,321 residents, excluding the semirural districts of Lagoa and Engenho Velho (Nogueira da Silva, *Negro na rua*, 53).

2. Walsh, *Notices of Brazil*, 1:79–80.

3. Ibid., 1:83–85.

4. Ibid., 1:86–87.

5. Freyre, *Mansions and Shanties*, 45, 109–10.

6. For a discussion of slave mobility in Rio's urban milieu, see Karasch, *Slave Life*, 185–213. There may have been a downside to their status for urban slaves inasmuch as marriage and stable family life may have been more difficult given their dispersal in small groups and the frequencies of sales in the urban milieu. Slenes argues, along these lines, that slaves on large plantations actually had the best prospects of forging their own family units (*Na senzala, uma flor*, 109–15).

7. Karasch, *Slave Life*, 345.

8. S. L. Graham, *House and Street*, 74.

9. Ibid., 81–82. For a discussion of the legal aspects of manumission and its revocability, see Mattoso, *To Be a Slave*, 158–64.

10. Traslado de apensos dos autos de inventário do finado Antonio José Dutra, 17 July 1849, caixa 2680, n. 341, AN, Rio de Janeiro; apelação cível de João Baptista Moreira da Silva contra Antonio Fernandes da Silva, caixa 1143, n. 4622, AN, Rio de Janeiro.

11. Dutra's eldest daughter, Ignacia, was born a slave. We cannot be sure from this fact, however, that Dutra himself was still a slave at this time.

12. Because almost any slave from the Zaire River region was classified as a "Congo" in Brazil, it is impossible to place Dutra's origins more precisely than West Central Africa. The fact that he evidently departed from Luanda gives some indication that he was from a BaKongo group in northern Angola. In any case, about half of all slaves listed in the custom-house registries for 1821–22 were from Angola (and about 10 percent specifically from Luanda) (Karasch, *Slave Life*, 14).

13. The pervasive stench of death at both ends of the Atlantic slave trade is highlighted in Miller, *Way of Death*, 391.

14. The "voyage of no return" is due to Miller, *Way of Death*, ch. 11. Although his metaphor is apt for most slaves, it is slightly misleading, inasmuch as Dutra's voyage of no return also included an exit from slavery and the donning of a new mask as a slaveholder.

15. Miller, *Way of Death*, 513.

16. Ibid., 402–5.

17. Travelers' accounts tell a grim tale of sickly and malnourished slaves arriving in the market. The mental strain was also great and suicides were common (Karasch, *Slave Life*, 40). For a clear discussion of the Atlantic slave trade during the first decades of the nineteenth century, see Klein, *Middle Passage*.

18. Reproduced in Conrad, *Children of God's Fire*, 23–28. Published slave narratives, unfortunately, are virtually nonexistent in Brazil. In fact, Baquaqua's narrative was published in Detroit.
19. Karasch, *Slave Life*, 36–39.
20. Ibid., 40–41.
21. Walsh, *Notices of Brazil*, 2:179.
22. This estimate assumes that Dutra arrived between 1815 and 1820 and was sold for the average price of a fifteen- to twenty-nine-year-old male slave. Source for prices: Estate Inventories, Rio de Janeiro, AN.
23. Karasch, *Slave Life*, 44–50. For a good discussion of the politics surrounding the legal ending of the slave trade in 1831, see Bethell, *Abolition of the Brazilian Slave Trade*, esp. 62–70.
24. This discussion of the transformations wrought in Rio de Janeiro by the arrival of the Portuguese court is drawn from Schultz, *Tropical Versailles*, esp. ch. 4.
25. A clear discussion of the political demise of D. Pedro I's regime is found in Needell, "Party Formation and State-Making," 267–70. D. Pedro I's personal life was also the source of discontent, as he carried on a very public affair with a mistress, Domitila, with whom he had several children. The repercussions of his "polygamy" are tellingly described in Lewin, *Surprise Heirs*, esp. 144–60.
26. Fragoso, *Homens de grossa aventura*, 137, calculated from Table 12–2.
27. Ibid., 143.
28. Ibid., 145.
29. Ibid., 146.
30. *Anuário Estatístico*, 1939/40 (Rio de Janeiro: IBGE, 1940), 1358 (exports), and 1293 (population).
31. Ibid., 135; exchange rate calculated from *Anuário Estatístico*, 1374.
32. The estimate assumes imports of twenty thousand slaves valued at 150$000 each. Price estimate based on slave values reported in postmortem estate inventories, Rio de Janeiro, Arquivo Nacional. See Appendix for a detailed discussion of estate inventories in the sample.
33. Luccock, *Notes on Rio de Janeiro*, 41–42.
34. Ibid., 41–42.
35. Ibid., 106.
36. An exception is S. L. Graham's *House and Street*.
37. See, for example, col. 126, maço 129, Relação dos credores . . . com as obras de reparos da igreja matriz de Angra dos Reis, 1870, Arquivo do Estado, Rio de Janeiro. In this case, twenty-one workers were employed, including ten slaves. Wages for slave and free workers were, on average, indistinguishable in this case. For similarity in slave and free wages in other regions, see Mattoso, *Bahia, Século XIX*, 539.

38. For a classic and insightful interpretation of the continuum from resistance to accommodation in slave societies, see Mintz, *Caribbean Transformations*, 75–81.
39. Slaveholders understandably shared the assumption that freedom was, in a sense, defined by slave ownership in slavery-saturated Brazil. S. L. Graham's analysis of the testament of Ignacia Delfina Wernek underscores the prevalence of this notion. Ignacia, in settling her estate on the family of her house slave Bernardina, went to great lengths to ensure that she would be supplied with slaves of her own (S. L. Graham, *Caetana Says No*, 120).
40. Conrad, *Children of God's Fire*, 302; Luccock, *Notes on Rio de Janeiro*, 103; Karasch, *Slave Life*, 202–3.
41. Luccock, *Notes on Rio de Janeiro*, 103.42. Ibid., 104–5.
43. Fragoso, *Homens de grossa aventura*, 37, 131–49.
44. Pimenta, "Entre sangradores e doutores," 94.
45. Eschwege, *Pluto Brasiliensis*, 437.
46. Inventory of José Sebastião de Castro, 1818, caixa 1403, n. 369, Rio de Janeiro, AN; Eschwege, *Pluto Brasiliensis*, 437.
47. Inventory of Antonio José Dutra, 1849, caixa. 68, n. 171, Rio de Janeiro, AN. For an overview of street vendors in general, see Karasch, *Slave Life*, 206–7.
48. For the lowly status of porters of water and refuse, see Karasch, *Slave Life*, 191.
49. Luccock, *Notes on Rio de Janeiro*, 108–9.
50. Karasch, *Slave Life*, 189.
51. Luccock claims, with some exaggeration, that even artisans disdained carrying their tools in public, as the conveyance of objects of any size was considered the labor of slaves. Luccock, *Notes on Rio de Janeiro*, 108. R. Graham picks up the theme of this distinction in *Patronage and Politics*, 33–34.
52. Mattoso, *Bahia, Século XIX*, 132.
53. Costa, *Brazilian Empire*, 247–48; Mattoso, *Bahia, Século XIX*, 140.
54. *Constituições do Brasil*, 20–21. According to Article 91 of the Constitution of 1824, voters in the first level of elections (*eleições primárias*) had to be native or naturalized Brazilians over the age of twenty-five (twenty-one if married or military officers). In addition, voters had to be "independent" from parental control (that is, not living with their parents or otherwise living as the servants of others) and able to prove an income of 100$000 per annum. Note that free slaves were explicitly prohibited from voting in the second level of elections for deputies and senators and that this level of voting required an income of 200$000 (Art. 94). For voting by freed slaves, see Karasch, *Slave Life*, 75–76.

55. The best treatment of this theme remains Degler's *Neither Black nor White*.

56. S. L. Graham, *House and Street*, 26.

57. This finding confirms Graham's claim that residential segregation increased over the course of the nineteenth century (S. L. Graham, *House and Street*, 26–27). Likewise, according to Needell, Rio de Janeiro's elite began to shift out of the old city center, where they had mixed with middling and poor residents, to the more exclusive southern neighborhoods by the 1840s and 1850s. Indeed, the first successful tramline was built in 1868 to serve these neighborhoods (Needell, *Tropical Belle Époque*, 152).

58. Census figures from Karasch, *Slave Life*, 62. Note that the mean number of slaves per owner is lower when restricted to urban-type owners alone.

59. Data for this discussion derive from Karasch, *Slave Life*, 26.

60. This calculation simply divides the mean number of slaves per household reported by Karasch by the mean number estimated from estate inventories.

61. Inventory of João Gomes Barbosa, 1822, caixa 909, n. 870, Rio de Janeiro, AN.

62. Inventory of Joanna Apolinaria, 1822, maço 429, n. 8456, Rio de Janeiro, AN.

63. Inventory of Claudio Gabriel, 1818, maço 2294, n. 386, Engenho Novo, Rio de Janeiro, AN.

64. Inventory of Rita Joaquina do Espirito Santo, 1823/25, maço 458, n. 8749, Rio de Janeiro, AN.

65. Luccock, *Notes on Rio de Janeiro*, 118–19.

66. Ibid., 119.

67. Luccock, *Notes on Rio de Janeiro*, 120–21.

68. Inventory of Rita Mathildes do Sacramento, 1825, caixa 1130, n. 9636, Rio de Janeiro, AN.

69. For the old argument about imitative consumption, see Prado Júnior, *História Econômica do Brasil*, 136–37.

70. Needell, *Tropical Belle Epoque*, 163–64.

71. It is unclear which of these values, the sum of the nominal reckoning or the *formal de partilha*, forms the basis of other works based on Brazilian estate inventories. There is a slight difference between the values obtained from these two different sources of information.

72. The exact numbers of observation for each sample period are the following: 176 for 1815–25; 120 for 1845–49; 363 for 1850–60; 96 for 1868–73; and 143 for 1885–88.

73. Note, however, that the opposite may just as well have been the case.

Douglas Libby and Afonso de Alencastro Graça Filho have uncovered some evidence for censoring at the top end of the wealth distribution in Minas Gerais, cited in Libby, "Minas na mira dos brasilianistas," 296.

74. For example, the minimum total value of personal items in the estate inventories of Rio de Janeiro was 4$000 in the 1820s and 1$000 in the 1850s. In most cases, the inventories include items of extremely low value. Moreover, there is evidence that censoring was not a dramatically changing problem. If the percentage of estates below a certain value changed dramatically, this would indicate a major change in the rate of censoring. In the 1820s, 14 percent of estates were worth 100 pounds or less; in the 1850s, this number had fallen to 7 percent. Yet, because average wealth nearly doubled, this change is predicted. Additionally, these are both small percentages of the total sample, and marginal changes of this sort will not have a major effect on the estimates.

75. There are approximately 45 inventories per year in the National Archive in Rio de Janeiro for the period 1815–25; for the 1850–60 period, there are about 120 inventories per year. The estimate of 8 percent is based on inventoried decedents divided by free adult decedents, numbering roughly 1,500 in the late 1840s (based on data on mortality in Karasch, *Slave Life*, 101). The estimate of 11 percent is derived by dividing 120 inventories into the likely number of deceased heads of households or their spouses: 21,000 households x 1.67 (heads and spouses) x mortality rate of 30 per 1000 (from Karasch, Slave Life, 94) = 11 percent.

76. On this score, the inventory samples appear remarkably consistent: 82 percent of all cases in the 1815–25 period pertained to the orphans' court; 81 percent of all cases in the 1850–60 period were from the same forum. Further evidence of consistency is found in the proportion of married decedents in the samples: 62 percent were married circa 1820 and 64 percent were married circa 1855; again, this consistency over time suggests that the samples can be compared reliably.

77. Inventory of Manoel de Oliveira Machado, 1819, maço 439, n. 8470, Rio de Janeiro, AN.

78. Inventory of Claudio Gabriel, 1818, maço 2294, n. 386, Rio de Janeiro, AN.

79. Inventory of Maria de Oliveira Gonçalves, 1825, maço 427, n. 8273, Rio de Janeiro, AN; and Inventory of Eugenia Thereza Filgueiras de Barbosa Ribeiro e Cirne, 1824, caixa 613, n. 6995, Rio de Janeiro, AN.

80. Inventory of Josefa Maria da Conceição, 1816, caixa 3264, n. 57, Rio de Janeiro, AN. For other examples, see inventory of Peregrina de Castro, Guaratiba, 1819, maço 476, n. 9174–5, Rio de Janeiro, AN, with seven slaves worth 614$000, a house worth 20$000, and plantings of

coffee and oranges worth 100$000; and Inventory of Francisco José Leal, São Gonçalo, 1817, maço 285, n. 5194, Rio de Janeiro, AN, with four slaves worth 473$000, houses worth 420$000, and plantings valued at 91$000.

81. Karasch, *Slave Life*, 185.
82. See Table 7.
83. Cited in Karasch, "Slave Life in Rio de Janeiro," 135–36.
84. Bergad, *Slavery*, 69, 207–8.

Chapter 3

1. Figures cited in Karasch, *Slave Life*, 166.
2. IBGE, *Anuário Estatístico do Brasil* 1939/40, 1358, 1374.
3. IBGE, *Anuário Estatístico do Brasil* 1939/40.
4. Karasch, *Slave Life*, 29, n. 1. Slave imports were nearly as high in the later 1820s. See, for example, Fragoso, *Homens de grossa aventura*, 145–46; and Klein, *Middle Passage*, 76.
5. Karasch, *Slave Life*, 26, 30.
6. Census totals reported in Karasch, *Slave Life*, 69.
7. *Jornal do Commercio*, Rio de Janeiro: 1/4/49, 4; 1/8/49, 4; 1/14/49, 4; 1/17/49, 4; 3/13/49, 4.
8. Carvalho de Mello, "Rates of Return," 2:68.
9. Zimmerman, "Advertising Gender," 7. The number of observations in the sample for 1850 was 211.
10. Ibid., 5.
11. Source: inventory sample (116 observations), Rio de Janeiro, AN.
12. I am grateful to Kari Zimmerman for sharing her dataset of rental and sale advertisements, on which this claim is based. Slave commission agents operated sophisticated sale and rental enterprises in Rio de Janeiro throughout the period under review. Their businesses were clustered in the old city center, *Almanak [Laemmert] . . .* 1845 and 1870.
13. Computer file generously provided by Zimmerman.
14. Freyre, *Escravo nos anúncios de jornais brasileiros*.
15. *Jornal do Commercio*, Rio de Janeiro, 3 January 1870.
16. Karasch, *Slave Life*, 66.
17. The tendency of freedmen to own barbering businesses is noted in Karasch, *Slave Life*, 238; and Pimenta, "Entre sangradores e doutores," 94.
18. For a similar case, this time in Bahia circa 1817, of a freeman with a barbering business and band, see Reis, *Death Is a Festival*, 76, 79. Mattoso provides a transcript of a liberto barber-surgeon's last will and testament in *To Be a Slave*, 213–20. Fryer's overview of Afro-Brazilian

music also underscores the popularity of barber-musicians during the nineteenth century (Fryer, *Rhythms of Resistance*, 139–41). See also, Tinhorão, *História social da música popular brasileira*, esp. 155–75, on the popular music of Rio's barber-surgeons in the nineteenth century.

19. Karasch, *Slave Life*, 69. For a detailed history of the Portuguese in Rio de Janeiro in the first half of the nineteenth century, see Ribeiro, *Liberdade em construção*.

20. Karasch, *Slave Life*, 69. For partial but illuminating lists of foreign and national enterprises on a yearly basis, see the *Almanak [Laemmert]*.

21. Needell, *Tropical Belle Epoque*, 166–71.

22. These changes are examined in detail in Needell, Tropical Belle Epoque, 141–43.

23. Ibid., 152–53.

24. These values are culled from my housing sample, N=175, for 1845–49.

25. Rents ranged from 5 to 15 percent of the value of the property per year—with most clustering around 7 to 8 percent. A house worth 1:000$000 could be had for less than 100$000 per annum. For perspective, note that, in the 1840s, day laborers earned about 150$000 per year in Rio de Janeiro. Holloway's research in the police archives of Rio suggests that the area around the Saco do Alferes was known for "criminals and vagrants," *Policing Rio*, 123.

26. Values derived from 175 house values and addresses listed in the estate sample for the years 1845–49.

27. Data from *Almanak [Laemmert]*. For a fine description of Rua do Ouvidor and its role in the construction of middle- and upper-class identity, see Needell, *Tropical Belle Epoque*, 164–66.

28. *Almanak [Laemmert]*, author's machine-readable database.

29. IBGE, *Anuário Estatístico do Brasil* 1939/40, 1353.

30. Price and wage indices are found in Lobo, *História do Rio de Janeiro*, 752–828.

31. Two of Lobo's price indexes show a decline in the price level from 1839 to 1849. Lobo, *História do Rio de Janeiro*, 728.

32. Ibid., 752–53, 774. Caution must be used when interpreting the wage figures provided in Lobo's study. First, her three price indexes vary wildly and she makes no allowance for substitution of cheaper goods in each of her price baskets. Second, many of the wage figures reported are clearly estimates or interpolations. Nevertheless, it appears that real wage growth occurred for urban workers such as carpenters and stonemasons.

33. For a clear statement of the problems associated with the use of probate (inventory) samples, see Lindert, "An Algorithm for Probate Sampling," esp. 657–68.

34. Inventory of Antonio José Dutra, 1849, caixa 68, n. 171, Rio de Janeiro, AN.
35. Fragoso, *Homens de grossa aventura*, 275.
36. I am not the first to suggest that rising slave prices served as an impediment to social mobility among the population of the free, including freed persons. See, for example, Karasch, *Slave Life*, 367; and Drescher, "Brazilian Abolition," 444.
37. Bergad, *Slavery*, 203.
38. Carvalho de Mello, "Economics of Labor." For a published version of these results, see Carvalho de Mello, "Rates of Return," 63–79, esp. 66–68.
39. Bergad, *Slavery*, 204.
40. Carvalho de Mello reports the following days worked and costs for an "urban" *negro de ganho* working in agriculture circa 1873: 276 workdays, 55$800 food, 41$000 lodging, 11$190 clothes, 12$500 medical, 10$000 tax, 25$110 commission and advertising fees, in "Rates of Return," 68. The total cost of maintenance in this example, including the full cost of food, was 211$400 out of gross earnings of 334$800, or 63 percent, leaving a "profit" of 37 percent to be shared between slave and master.
41. Inventory of José Sebastião de Castro, 1818, caixa 1403, n. 369, Rio de Janeiro, AN; the traveler Eschwege reported similar hire rates for skilled ($900 to 1$200 per day) and unskilled ($300) slaves circa 1811 (Eschwege, *Pluto Brasiliensis*, 437).
42. *Jornal do Commercio*, Jan. 1849.
43. As Carvalho de Mello notes, the internal rate of return on slaves was consistently 13 percent or better, which surpassed the alternative rate of 10 percent (Carvalho de Mello, "Rates of Return," 74).
44. Inventory of Anna Theodora Mascarenhas Barros, 1855, caixa 3604, n. 24, Rio de Janeiro, AN.
45. For a classic and insightful interpretation of the continuum from resistance to accommodation in slave societies, see Mintz, *Caribbean Transformations*, 75–81.
46. For the challenge of monitoring urban slaves and the relative autonomy of servants, both slave and free, see S. L. Graham, *House and Street*, 61–62; Mary Karasch also examines this issue in detail in *Slave Life*, ch. 5, and, regarding the mobility of slaves and the difficulty in monitoring them, 307.
47. For an analysis of the role of coercion in maintaining social control in nineteenth-century Rio de Janeiro, see Holloway, *Policing Rio de Janeiro*.
48. For a detailed discussion of slave runaways in Rio de Janeiro, see Karasch, *Slave Life*, 304–11.

49. In addition, as Reis and Silva point out, many runaways did not plan to flee for good; rather, their flight was a short, strategic action to call attention to a grievance they had with their owner (Reis and Silva, *Negociação e conflito*, 64–65).

50. *Jornal do Commercio*, Rio de Janeiro, complete months of January and July 1840. Inasmuch as slave prices are a guide, the peak earning years for male slaves in Rio de Janeiro were from about fifteen to forty years of age.

51. Ibid. The average price of a prime male slave in 1848–49 was 449$ (N=51).

52. Carvalho de Mello reports that 5.5 percent of workdays were lost to illness on coffee plantations during the 1870s (Carvalho de Mello, "Rates of Return," 68).

53. Inventory of Antonio José Dutra, 1849, caixa 3999, n. 171, Rio de Janeiro, AN.

54. S. L. Graham, *House and Street*, 12.

55. Inventory of Gregorio José de Abreu, 1846, caixa 4140, n. 1416, Rio de Janeiro, AN.

56. Inventory of Ignacio Caetano de Araujo, 1849, caixa 4145, n. 1504, Rio de Janeiro, AN.

57. Inventory of Antonio José Dutra, 1849, caixa 3999, n. 171, Rio de Janeiro, AN.

58. Inventory of Cantilda Carlota Pereira do Lago, 1847, caixa 725, n. 4060, Rio de Janeiro, AN.

59. For example, Luccock, *Notes on Rio de Janeiro*, 106.

60. *Recenseamento geral do Brasil, 1872*; and Karasch, *Slave Life*, 69.

61. *Recenseamento de 1872*, 15.

62. For a discussion of this phenomenon in the Atlantic economy as a whole, see O'Rourke and Williamson, *Globalization and History*, 59–64.

Chapter 4

1. The literature on the suppression of the trade is extensive. A good account with an emphasis on the role of the British is found in Bethell, *Abolition of the Brazilian Slave Trade*, esp. ch. 12.

2. For a good discussion of the genesis of this law, see Costa, *Brazilian Empire*, 78–83.

3. The commercial code of 1850 is described in R. Graham, *Britain*, 25. Note that the commercial code still required royal authorization for the formation of joint-stock companies. For this reason, the stock exchange remained a limited vehicle for capital formation until the 1880s.

4. Summerhill, *Order Against Progress*.

5. Indeed, as Lewin points out, the gradual shift that took place in the wealthholding patterns of the urban elite set the foundation for changing perceptions regarding inheritance law (Lewin, *Surprise Heirs*, 303). Although economic change did not *cause* social change in a mechanical way, it made new laws regarding everything from commerce and land tenure to inheritance more palatable to the political elite in the late 1840s and through the 1850s.

6. IBGE, *Anuário Estatístico do Brasil*, 1939/40, 1358.

7. Ibid., 1374.

8. The value of goods shipped outside of Brazil was 56,259:000$000 circa 1849, of which Rio de Janeiro accounted for 27,329:000$000. The next two most important ports, Salvador and Recife, in the Northeast, accounted for 18,185:000$000 combined. R. Graham, *Britain*, 15.

9. IBGE, *Anuário Estatístico do Brasil*, 1939/40, 1336.

10. IBGE, *Anuário Estatístico do Brasil*, 1939/40, 1353.

11. Values reported in constant 1850 mil-réis—the range depends on the choice of deflator used in the calculation.

12. Such growth may have been common throughout much of the New World during the first half of the nineteenth century. Lyman Johnson, for instance, records a five-fold increase in mean wealthholding in Buenos Aires Province over the period 1829–30 to 1855–56. Preliminary results reported in Johnson, "Pampa Transformed," 12.

13. For c. 1820, calculation based on Eschwege, *Pluto brasilensis*; for 1860, calculation based on rental advertisements in the *Jornal do Commercio*, Rio de Janeiro.

14. Taking 1850 = 100 as the basis of analysis, in Mircea Buescu, *300 anos de inflação*, 223.

15. Elizabeth Kuznesof finds much the same pattern for São Paulo in the 1820s and 1830s, where she notes that rural producers shifted dramatically from subsistence to market production (Kuznesof, *Household Economy*, 150).

16. The nexus between Rio de Janeiro and an expanded hinterland, extending as far south as Rio Grande do Sul's cattle ranches and inland to Minas Gerais, is persuasively described in Fragoso, *Homens de grossa aventura*, esp. 163–71.

17. As Summerhill points out, the idea of "export-led" growth is often misspecified with regard to Brazil in the second half of the nineteenth century (Summerhill, *Order Against Progress*, 154–55). In fact, for Brazil as a whole, Summerhill calculates that exports per head actually *declined* during the period 1861 to 1913 *relative* to GDP per head. Export-led growth presupposes a rising, not falling, share of exports in GDP. However, exports per head relative to GDP probably rose in

the Southeast, contributing "export-led" growth to the overall performance of the economy in Rio de Janeiro and São Paulo.

18. Mattoso, *Bahia, Século XIX*, 613–16.

19. Goldsmith reports real tangible wealth growth of 2.2 percent (Goldsmith, *Income and Wealth*, 269). Lee Soltow reports real per-head growth in wealthholding at 1.9 percent in the United States during a similar span (Soltow, *Distribution of Wealth and Income*, 38).

20. Growth in real wealth is not the same as growth in per-head incomes. It is possible that the rate of growth in the latter was lower and that the spread in the ratio of wealth to income widened over the period under review.

21. Both of these calculations assume that 60 percent of gross wages are spent on maintenance and/or retained by the slaves.

22. With credits and debits the percentage rises to 64.

23. Clearly these are heroic assumptions, meant to set the basic orders of magnitude and parameters of discussion. We have reason to believe that at least half of households owned some assets; indeed, a third or more owned slaves. Yet the wealth distribution of the inventoried population may not have been equal to the distribution among the living and there are good reasons to think that it differed somewhat because the sampled decedents were likely older and perhaps wealthier than the living population. For a detailed discussion of the use of estate inventories and their relationship to wealth among the living, please see the discussion in Chapter 3.

24. See, for example, Schwartz, "Colonial Past," 188, citing Alice P. Canabrava.

25. Libby, *Transformação*, 131, n. 30.

26. Bergad, *Slavery*, 69.

27. Measured by the Gini coefficient, inequality with slaves was 0.711 and without was 0.747.

28. According to the estate inventory samples, 88 percent of inventoried decedents owned at least one slave circa 1820. This figure had fallen to 80 percent by the 1850s, only to plummet further to 48 percent in the early 1870s when the combination of high prices and scarcity severely limited access to slaves.

29. Data from estate inventories, Rio de Janeiro, AN. These calculations assume that two-story residences have the same area on each floor. This may understate value to area slightly inasmuch as some upper floors were smaller than the footprint of the building. Calculations do not include outbuildings or yards.

30. Note that the annual rate of increase (1820–55) in value per square meter according to this calculation is just 3.4 percent whereas the

mean nominal value of housing in the estate samples rose by about 5 percent during the same span. This gap could be explained by flaws in either set of data, although the much smaller sample size for the per-meter calculations (14 and 35) seems most suspect (for the inventory samples there are 107 and 226 observations respectively for 1815–25 and 1850–60); it could also be attributable to a slight shift in the composition of the inventory samples. Perhaps these figures are best taken, then, as upper and lower bounds for the rise in the value of urban real estate.

31. For example, Candido Maria da Silva's estate inventory indicates ownership of four properties on Rua da Imperatriz, with a high value of 4$000 and a low value of 1$209 (caixa 4027–666, Rio de Janeiro, AN).

32. Karasch, *Slave Life*, 62, 66.

33. Ibid., 128.

34. S. L. Graham, *House and Street*, 26. Additional information, including several revealing quotations from public figures can be found in Hahner, *Poverty and Politics*, 25–26. According to the data cited in Hahner, there were approximately two people per room in Rio's tenements, with the greater part of this population composed of foreign immigrants.

35. S. L. Graham, *House and Street*, 24, 26.

36. *Relatorio . . . provincial de São Paulo pela commissão central de estatística*, 25.

37. Inventory of Anna Theodora Mascarenhas de Barros, 1855, caixa 3604, n. 24, Rio de Janeiro, AN. Carpenters earned approximately 275$000 per year circa 1855.

38. Karasch reports that slaves often constructed their own rudimentary housing on Rio's steep hillsides (Karasch, *Slave Life*, 128).

39. Walsh, *Notices of Brazil*, 256–57.

40. Carvalho de Mello, "Rates of Return," 68.

41. R. Graham, *Britain*, 25–26.

42. Costa, *Da Senzala*; R. Graham, *Britain*, 25

43. Calógeras, *Política Monetária*, Quadro Sinótico das Operações dos Bancos de Emissão, inserted between 98–99.

44. Calógeras, *Política Monetária*, 145.

45. A possible objection to the theory proposed here is that these shifts were driven by something other than slave prices. Perhaps the age of slaves was associated with total wealth, not slave wealth or slave prices, per se. This objection is amply rebutted by the fact that total wealth has no predictive power whatsoever with regard to the age structure of slaveholding. From 1855–60, when the wealth of the city had been transformed by export growth and the beginning of railroad construction, the mean age of slaves was thirty-one, regardless

of whether the total wealth of the owner was less than 5:000$000, less than 10:000$000, more than 20:000$000, or limited only to cases of widows (presumably older owners). Every case results in the same mean of thirty-one years. The number of slaves owned is the only category that has a measurable effect on the mean age of slaveholdings.

46. IBGE, *Anuário Estatístico do Brasil*, 1939/40, 1358 and 1375.

47. These figures refer to all wealthholders in the category (middle 60 percent). The greater number of wealthholders with zero wealth in slaves in the 1870s depresses the average percentage relative to the 1850s figure. Omitting zero cases does little to change the overall trend: in the 1850s, among slaveholders in the middle 60 percent of the distribution, slave wealth accounted for 38 percent of net wealth; circa 1870, slave wealth accounted for 23 percent of net wealth for the same group.

48. These are rough percentages derived by counting all slaves owned by rural landowners as "rural" slaves and all other slaves as "urban." To be sure, the urban residences of rural landowners in the sample were home to some of their slaves. Unfortunately, the documents rarely distinguish the location of slaves on their owner's various properties.

49. Inventory of Maria do Carmo Louzada Macedo, 1885, caixa 4283, n. 450, Rio de Janeiro, AN.

50. Inventory of Francisco Belizário Soares de Souza, 1889, caixa 4257, n. 2778, Rio de Janeiro, AN.

51. Inventory of Francisco José da Cruz, 1887, caixa 4137, n. 1340, Rio de Janeiro, AN.

52. Stein, *Vassouras*, esp. ch. 9.

53. Brazil, *Recenseamento de 1890*.

54. Inventory of Carlota Dorissou, 1888, caixa 4061, n. 741, Rio de Janeiro, AN; Inventory of Domingos Aristide Guilherme, 1889, caixa 4082, n. 938, Rio de Janeiro, AN.

55. For a thorough analysis of the Portuguese in Rio de Janeiro during the first half of the nineteenth century, see Ribeiro, *Liberdade,* 56. Brazil, *Recenseamento* 1890, 161.

56. Brazil, *Recenseamento* 1890, 161.

57. Examples include Inventory of Felipe Manoel Mendes, maço 419, n. 7943; Inventory of Izabel Carolina de Figueiredo Mascarenhas, maço 419, n. 7923; and Inventory of Guilhermina Alves Teixeira, maço 418, n. 5031.

58. Pimenta, "Entre sangradores e doutores," 97–99.

59. Tinhorão, *História social*, 170.

60. This is precisely the segment of the population Owensby suggests was growing rapidly and forming as a class during the last part of

the nineteenth century and first part of the twentieth, *Intimate Ironies*, 26–35.

Chapter 5

1. For the late development of banking in Brazil, see Triner, *Banking and Economic Development*.
2. For data concerning internal aspects of Rio de Janeiro's economy, see Fragoso, *Homens de grossa aventura*, esp. ch. 2.
3. This point has been stressed throughout the first section of this book. Contemporary accounts also stressed the way slavery opened the door to wealthholding and social advancement. See, for example, Luccock, *Notes on Rio de Janeiro*, 106; Schlichthorst, *Rio de Janeiro wie es ist*, 162–200.
4. An insightful and theoretically informed discussion of the role of notaries and credit is found in Hoffman, Postel-Vinay, and Rosenthal's recent work. As the authors point out, the "dichotomy between impersonal relationships under capitalism and the personal links and traditional financial structures in preindustrial societies" has tended to be overdrawn (*Priceless Markets*, 2). In other words, just because Brazil lacked modern financial institutions should not lead us to conclude that other forms of credit were lacking or unimportant.
5. Threats to property rights could come from two basic directions: the state (or a dominant faction) could predate on property rights, as it did to a degree in 1808 when the Portuguese court arrived in Rio; conversely, a weak state could fail to enforce property rights and parties could turn to violence and other forms of private enforcement. Crimes against property such as theft tended to involve small sums, often the theft of clothing, food, or small amounts of cash *from* slaves as they went about their business (Alegranti, *Feitor ausente*, 177).
6. This is not to deny the often-chaotic political situation in Brazil prior to about 1850. For recent treatments of this theme, see Costa, *Brazilian Empire*, 61–68; Barman, *Citizen Emperor*, ch. 3; and Kraay, *Race, State, and Armed Forces*.
7. For a discussion of the process of wealth accumulation over the lifecycle in another region of Brazil, see Marcondes, *Arte de accumular*.
8. The profitability of slavery has long been a source of some controversy, although most estimates end up near 15 percent. Carvalho de Mello calculated a return of 13 percent per annum for 1873 (Carvalho de Mello, "Economics of Labor," 50 66). Nathaniel Leff's interpretation of Carvalho de Mello's figures results in an estimate of a 16 percent return (Leff, *Underdevelopment and Development*, 50).

9. Prior to 1850, our data on urban wages are extremely sketchy. Lobo's *História do Rio de Janeiro*, 752–828, provides estimates dating back to 1802 for several urban professions. Unfortunately, the manner in which the data are presented leads us to doubt their accuracy and utility—as the yearly mean varies wildly in many cases and the mean wage remains the same for decades at a time in some cases. Clearly, Lobo did the best she could with limited data; however, it makes more sense to adopt Goldsmith's more reasonable per-head GDP estimates beginning in 1850 and project these values back to the 1810s and 1820s checking our estimates against archival records and travelers accounts that specify wages in Rio de Janeiro.

10. Estate Inventories, Rio de Janeiro, AN.

11. Goldsmith, *Brasil 1850–1984*, 22–23, 30–31.

12. Lobo, *História do Rio de Janeiro*, 2:803–4. This rate of increase comports with our estimate in Table 9.

13. For the classic study of expropriation of slave labor, see Fogel and Engerman, *Time on the Cross*, 154. In their study, Fogel and Engerman estimate that a slaves' earnings, discounted back to birth and accounting for rearing costs, came to just 30 dollars. See also, Vedder, "Slave Exploitation (Expropriation) Rate," 455. Most studies of the rate of expropriation for U.S. slaves exceed 50 percent of the slaves marginal product (Atack and Passell, *New Economic View*, 335).

14. Carvalho de Mello, "Rates of Return," 74–75.

15. Bergad, *Slavery*, 188–89.

16. This estimate is very rough. It is informed, however, by two salient facts. First, circa 1849, about two-thirds of the slave population in Rio de Janeiro was African-born, so the overall costs of child rearing were lower than they would have been without the slave trade and flows of older slaves from Africa. Nevertheless, the ratio between the price of slaves aged 0–7 and 8–30 was about 1:3, indicating that the costs of rearing children factored heavily in the calculation of prices. Second, we know that slaves resisted in myriad ways, and that their efforts must have cut into average returns when they ran away, shirked, or stole. Settling on a figure of 7.5 percent has the advantage of depicting slavery as about as remunerative, all things considered, as real estate.

17. Census figures reported in Karasch, *Slave Life*, 66.

18. Estate inventory sample, Rio de Janeiro, AN. See, also, Table 8.

19. The total welfare effects of abolition in 1850, spread over Brazilian society, would have been different. Because slaves outnumbered owners by a factor of 5 or more, we must conclude that, leaving aside the moral improvement associated with abolition, material redistribution alone would have benefited far more people than it hurt.

20. For example, in the late 1840s, the middle 60 percent of wealthholders in the sample owed 67 percent of the value of all debts but lent out just 17 percent of the value of all loans. Interest charged on these loans generally varied from 1 to 2 percent per month. Scattered examples of interest rates charged on informal credit are found in the lists of debtors in estate inventories. The inventory of Domingos da Costa Guimarães, 1855, caixa 1484, n. 3442, Rio de Janeiro, AN, for instance, records an interest rate of 1.25 percent per month.

21. Inventory of Domingos José da Costa Guimarães, 1855, caixa 1484, n. 3442, Rio de Janeiro, AN.

22. Kotlikoff, "Quantitative Description," 40.

23. Fogel and Engerman, *Time on the Cross*, 70.

24. Inventory of José Ferreira Maia Sobrinho, 1856, caixa 4156–1794, Rio de Janeiro, AN. From the inventory, it is clear that part of the business functioned as a bakery; however, José Ferreira is also listed in the *Almanak [Laemmert] . . . 1845* as owner of an import-export business (*trapiches*), which is in keeping with the type of creditors listed in the estate.

25. Inventory of José Ferreira Maia Sobrinho, 1856, caixa 4156, n. 1794, Rio de Janeiro, AN.

26. Inventory of Domingos José da Costa Guimarães, 1855, caixa 1484, n. 3442, Rio de Janeiro, AN.

27. Karasch, *Slave Life*, 69.

28. See Table 4.

29. Nearby businesses on Rua da Alfândega, numbers 142, 193, 194, 174, and 143 respectively, cited in *Almanak [Laemmert] . . . 1845*.

30. Inventory of Antonio José Dutra, 1849, caixa 68, n. 171, Rio de Janeiro, AN.

31. Ibid., 3, for characterization of João Baptista's moral qualities. We suspect that João Baptista was semiliterate on the basis of his very tentative signature, his profession as a stonemason is given in the course of his and Ignacia's *partilha de divórcio* (separation of property), Inventory [divorce] of João Baptista Moreira da Silva and Ignacia Maria Antonia de Jesus Dutra, 1855 [1852–57], caixa 4122, n. 17, Rio de Janeiro, AN, 7–13.

32. Apelação cível de João Baptista Moreira da Silva contra Antonio Fernandes da Silva, 1850, Inventories, caixa 1143, n. 4622, Rio de Janeiro, AN. Ignacia's baptism is registered in Livro 6 de batismos de escravos (Sacramento), f. 30.

33. The ages of Dutra's other children were sixteen, fourteen, seven, and four years, and fifteen months. Inventory of Antonio José Dutra, 1849, caixa 68, n. 171, Rio de Janeiro, AN, 3.

34. Apelação civil de João Baptista Moreira da Silva contra Antonio

Fernandes, 1850. Joaquim José de Castro, tabelião público do Judicial e notas, em 1/10/1850, certificado: Livro de Registro 44, p. 92 verso. The text reads: "I am the owner of a slave named Ignacia, aged four or five . . . freed today for all and always as if she were born of a free womb, and seeing that this is done, I received 128 mil-réis." I am grateful to Silvana Jeha for providing me with a transcription of this document.

35. Ibid., 35–36, for the ages and genders of Dutra's slaves.

36. Inventory of Antonio José Dutra, 1849, caixa 68, n. 171, AN, Rio de Janeiro, 78–80.

37. Tinhorão, *História social*, 157–58.

38. Ibid., 173.

39. Lindley, *Narrativa de uma viagem*, 73; Debret, *Viagem pitoresca*, 151.

40. Melo Moraes Filho, *Festas e tradições*, 169.

41. Tinhorão, *História social*, 170.

42. The instruments played by the various members of Dutra's band reported in Inventory of Antonio José Dutra, 1849, caixa 68, n. 171, AN, Rio de Janeiro, 45–69.

43. Inventory of Antonio José Dutra, 1849, caixa 68, n. 171, AN, Rio de Janeiro. The time required to obtain the title of barber-surgeon was two years of training according to Pimenta, "Barbeiro's," 368, n. 8.

44. In his testament itself, Dutra freed five slaves, Joaquim Rebello, Joaquim Congo, Domingos and Felipe Moçambique, and Antonio Quilimane—the second names referring to their African origins with the exception of the first (Traslado de apensos dos autos de inventário do finado Antonio José Dutra, 1849, AN, Rio de Janeiro, caixa 2680, n. 341). In the *auto de partilha*, dated 8 February 1850, Carlota Cabinda, a sixth slave, and her nineteen-month-old child Alexandre were also freed (Inventory of Antonio José Dutra, 1849, caixa 68, n. 171, Rio de Janeiro, AN, 45–50).

45. Inventory of José Joaquim Gaspar dos Reis, 1848, Rio de Janeiro, AN. According to contemporary estimates, there were thirty-seven funileiros in Rio circa 1852, cited in Lobo, *História do Rio de Janeiro*, table 3.24, 282.

46. Karasch cites the Cidade Nova as one of the poorest and most dangerous districts circa 1850 (Karasch, *Slave Life*, 166).

47. Kidder, *Sketches of Residence*.

48. Inventory of Joaquim José de Almeida Freitas, 1845, maço 287, n. 5236, Rio de Janeiro, AN.

49. Lobo, *História do Rio de Janeiro*, table 3.40, 315.

50. Inventory of José Francisco Silva, Rio de Janeiro, AN.

51. Inventory of Joaquina Roza da Silva Guimarães, 1849, caixa 3618, n. 1, Rio de Janeiro, AN.

52. Lobo, *História do Rio de Janeiro*, 342.
53. Ibid.
54. Ibid.
55. According to Lobo's statistics, the vast majority of businesses in these lists were small in terms of capital and presumably in employees. Most businesses in the 1850s declared less than 1 conto in capital. See, especially, Lobo's discussion of small businesses (Lobo, *História do Rio de Janeiro*, 170–209).
56. Ibid., 265.
57. Inventory of Francisco José Gonçalves, 1848, caixa 4135, n. 1292, Rio de Janeiro, AN.
58. Inventory of Antonio José Dutra, 1849, caixa 68, n. 171, Rio de Janeiro, AN, 133–34.
59. Ibid., 78–80.
60. See Table 4 and discussion in the text.
61. Inventory of José Jordão da Costa, 1847, caixa 4165, n. 1943, Rio de Janeiro, AN.
62. Inventory of José Thomas Rodrigues, 1849, maço 381, n. 6756, Rio de Janeiro, AN.
63. Brazil, Ministerio da Guerra, *Relatório . . . 1845*, Mappa dos Empregados do Hospital da Guarnição da Corte, seus vencimentos annuaes, e rações diarias, s/n indexed page N 7.
64. Ibid., Mappa dos Ordenados . . . do Arsenal de Guerra da Corte, N 7.
65. Brazil, Ministerio da Fazenda, *Relatorio . . . 1825*, 232.
66. Brazil, Ministerio da Guerra, *Relatorio . . . 1845*, N 7.

Chapter 6

1. Assis, *Posthumous Memoirs*.
2. An excellent discussion of the cultural practices surrounding death and funerals in Brazil as a whole can be found in Reis's "Cotidiano da morte no Brasil oitocentista." For a detailed analysis of death, funeral practices, and urban social structure and unrest, see Reis, *Death Is a Festival*.
3. As S. L. Graham notes, nineteenth-century Brazilian society was extremely legalistic, generating massive quantities of formal notarized documents regarding practically every aspect of life (S. L. Graham, *Caetana Says No*, xxi).
4. According to Reis, the ideal testament in the nineteenth century was undertaken well before death in order to plan for any eventuality and to avoid dying intestate. However, as one expects, most testaments appear to have been drawn up in response to sickness and the fear of death (Reis, *Death Is a Festival*, 71–73).

5. For an analysis of the intricacies of the law of succession over time, see Lewin, *Surprise Heirs*.

6. S. L. Graham, *Caetana Says No*, 104–5.

7. Inventory of Manoel Rodrigues dos Santos, 1854, caixa 3603, n. 115, Rio de Janeiro, AN.

8. Traslado de apensos dos autos de inventário do finado Antonio José Dutra, 17 July 1849, caixa 2680, n. 341, Rio de Janeiro, AN. The rhetoric displayed in Dutra's testament is similar to that reported in Reis's research on testaments in Bahia during the first half of the nineteenth century (Reis, *Death Is a Festival*, 72–73). As Reis points out, the testator often referred to fear of an imminent and inevitable death when composing these opening lines.

9. Inventory of Antonio José Dutra, 1849, caixa 68, n. 171, Rio de Janeiro, AN.

10. For the pledge to help free slaves in the brotherhoods, see Russell-Wood, *Black Man*, 38. A copy of the statutes of Dutra's brotherhood is available online, and Dutra's name appears as a signatory to the statutes of 1831. Among the articles listed therein, article 24 details the workings of the brotherhood's savings chest devoted to helping slaves obtain their freedom: "Do modo de proceder a liberdade dos cativos." I am grateful to Silvana Jeha for drawing my attention to the website of this brotherhood (Jeha, "Ganhar a Vida: Uma história do africano Antonio José Dutra e sua família, Rio de Janeiro, século XIX," unpublished manuscript, 3). For the arrival of Candomblé with Bahian slaves in the 1850s, see Karasch, *Slave Life*, 266.

11. The procedure by which captives were given the catechism and baptized prior to embarkation is described in Miller, *Way of Death*, 402–4.

12. For a through account of the Antonian movement, see Thornton, *The Kongolese Saint Anthony*, esp. ch. 5.

13. The location of the black Saint Anthony is noted in Karasch, *Slave Life*, 270.

14. Christianity became the religion of the Kongolese elite in the sixteenth century under King Afonso (1506–43), Hilton, *Kingdom of Kongo*, 60–66.

15. Miller, *Way of Death*, 404–5.

16. Reis describes the same tendencies in greater detail in *Death Is a Festival*, esp. ch. 7.

17. Notice published in the *Jornal do Commercio*, Rio de Janeiro, 4 January 1849, 3.

18. *Jornal do Commercio*, 20 July 1849, 4.

19. In 1849 alone, 2,239 bodies were buried in the cemetery of the Santa Casa, many felled by the yellow fever epidemic that swept the city in

1849 and 1850. José da Costa Carvalho, Ministerio do Imperio, *Relatorio do anno de 1849*, mapa 12.

20. For the burial of slaves, see Karasch, *Slave Life*, 221. For the wealthy, Luccock reports that burial always took place within family tombs inside churchyards (Luccock, *Notes on Rio de Janeiro*, 55).

21. Reis's analysis of burials by church and by race clearly indicates distribution by color and class in Bahia circa 1835–36, (Reis, *Death Is a Festival*, 174–82).

22. Karasch, *Slave Life*, 335.

23. Luccock, *Notes on Rio de Janeiro*, 55.

24. Reis, *Death Is a Festival*, 82–84.

25. Ibid., 109.

26. Luccock, *Notes on Rio de Janeiro*, 56–57.

27. Reis, *Death Is a Festival*, 322–23.

28. Ibid., 186.

29. Another kind of complication involved estates in which there were no direct heirs on the side of the decedent, such as children or grandchildren, and the entire estate fell to the surviving spouse. In such cases, members of the decedents extended family sometimes sought to lay claim to a portion of the estate (Inventory of Francisco Martins de Siqueira, 1855, caixa 1391, n. 220, Rio de Janeiro, AN).

30. For a detailed analysis of the problem of "illegitimacy" and inheritance, see Lewin, *Surprise Heirs*. According to Lewin's careful research, a good deal of change took place in the course of the nineteenth century with regard to the rules regarding succession and "natural" children. Lewin cautions against using the term "illegitimate" because it tends to be misleading for nineteenth-century Brazil (xxv–xxvi).

31. Although it is possible that some cases of separation of property slipped through the coding procedure, research in Rio de Janeiro's estate inventories identified just 2 such cases out of a sample of 199 cases for which such detailed information was sought.

32. These auctions were commonly advertised in the local papers. In the year Dutra died, examples can be seen in the *Jornal do Commercio*, 14 January 1849, 4; 13 March 1849, 3.

33. Inventory of Antonio José Dutra, 1849, caixa 68, n. 171, Rio de Janeiro, AN, 24.

34. *Almanak [Laemmert] . . . 1845*.

35. Inventory of Antonio José Dutra, 1849, caixa 68, n. 171, Rio de Janeiro, AN, 2. João Baptista's testimony to the contrary is found in Inventory of Ignacia Maria Antonia de Jesus Dutra and João Baptista Moreira da Silva, 1857, caixa 4122, n. 17, Rio de Janeiro, AN, 7–13.

36. Ignacia's miscarriage was attended by Doctor Antonio Dias da Costa.

37. The story of Ignacia's childhood is recounted in Jeha, "Ganhar a Vida," 7. The source of this information is not unproblematic, inasmuch as it is João Baptista himself. Nevertheless, there seems no reason to think he would lie about this aspect of her past. Apelação cível de João Baptista Moreira da Silva contra Antonio Fernandes da Silva, caixa 1143, n. 4622, Rio de Janeiro, AN. Divorce in the modern sense was not possible. The purpose of ecclesiastical divorce in nineteenth-century Brazil was to allow for separation of estates and the emancipation of female petitioners from their husband's legal authority. Signatures of Ignacia Antonia Maria de Jesus and João Baptista Moreira da Silva found on pages 6 and 15 respectively, Inventory of Antonio José Dutra, 1849, caixa 68, n. 171, Rio de Janeiro, AN.

38. Inventory of Antonio José Dutra, 1849, caixa 68, n. 171, Rio de Janeiro, AN, 13–15.

39. Ibid., marginal notations throughout the manuscript, esp. page 6.

40. Ibid., 15–16. Antonio Fernandes was not mentioned in Dutra's testament. Therefore, for his labors, he requested a legally stipulated payment known as a *vintena*, 43.

41. For other expressive instances of women's agency, see S. L. Graham, *Caetana Says No*.

42. Inventory of Antonio José Dutra, 1849, caixa 68, n. 171, Rio de Janeiro, AN, 32–41.

43. Ibid., 93–100.

44. Ibid., 78–80.

45. See, for example, Karasch, *Slave Life*, 345.

46. Inventory of Antonio José Dutra, 1849, caixa 68, n. 171, Rio de Janeiro, AN, 45–68.

47. Inventory of Antonio José Dutra, 1849, caixa 68, n. 171, Rio de Janeiro, AN, 121.

48. Inventory of Antonio José Dutra, 1849, caixa 68, n. 171, Rio de Janeiro, AN, 44–69; and Traslado de apensos dos autos de inventário do finado Antonio José Dutra, 1849, caixa 2680, n. 341, Rio de Janeiro, AN.

49. Even priests recognized their "natural" children after some palaver about the "weakness of the flesh." They did not name their lovers. See, for example, Inventory of Padre Manoel Gomes Souto, 1845, maço 6209, n. 448, Rio de Janeiro, AN.

50. Inventory of Antonio José Dutra, 1849, caixa 68, n. 171, Rio de Janeiro, AN.

51. Inventory of Antonio José Dutra, 1849, caixa 68, n. 171, Rio de Janeiro, AN, 29. Antonio da Silva reports that the divorce case (*libelo de divórcio*) of Ignacia and João Baptista was wending its way through the ecclesiastical court. Another divorce case, from about the same

period, involved Emilia Teixiera de Seixas, who obtained a divorce on the grounds of adultery—her husband was caught in an affair with an actress (1859, caixa 285, n. 183, Rio de Janeiro, AN).

52. Inventory of João Baptista Moreira da Silva and Ignacia Maria Antonia de Jesus Dutra, 1855 [actual dates cover 1852–1857], caixa 4122, n. 17, Rio de Janeiro, AN, 18–23.

53. Ibid., 29–32.

54. Ibid., transcrição de auto de apelação, sentença de acordo, July 19, 1852, 68.

55. Ibid., auto da partilha, 90.

56. Ibid., processo anexo, 1.

57. Inventory of Antonio José Dutra, 1849, caixa 68, n. 171, Rio de Janeiro, AN, 78.

58. Ibid., 78–80.

59. Ibid.

60. Ibid., 45–68

61. Ibid.,189.

62. Ibid., 80.

63. Ibid., 126–29.

64. Ibid., 157–72.

65. Ibid., 178.

66. Ibid., 202.

67. Ibid., 203.

68. Ibid., 175.

69. Ibid., 187.

70. Ibid., 140.

71. This was the case with the wife of Antonio Rodrigues da Mota Cunha, caixa 612, n. 6988, Rio de Janeiro, AN.

72. Inventory of Floriano dos Santos, 1825, maço 381, n. 6752, Rio de Janeiro, AN.

73. Inventory of Lourenço José do Amaral, 1821, caixa 1130, n. 9633, Rio de Janeiro, AN.

74. Inventory of Angelo José de Morais, 1858, caixa 4012, n. 385, Rio de Janeiro, AN.

75. Inventory of João Bartholomeu Klier, 1855, caixa 4104, n. 1600, Rio de Janeiro, AN.

Chapter 7

1. See, for example, Debret, *Viagem pitoresca e histórica ao Brasil*, 4:128–29.

2. For the practice of endogamy and elite family networks, see Mattoso, *Bahia, Século XIX*, 178–92; for the family as a business concern, see

Nazzari, *Disappearance of the Dowry*, 6–7; for the general importance of the family in Brazilian social structure, see Costa, *Brazilian Empire*, 265; for an outstanding social and cultural history of the family in Brazil, see Borges, *Family in Bahia*.

3. The rise of a class of planters and merchants in Rio de Janeiro is analyzed in detail in Fragoso, *Homens de grossa aventura*.

4. Note that titles of nobility were not inheritable in Imperial Brazil.

5. Prior to 1881 (the Lei Saraiva), elections in the empire were indirect. A property qualification limited the indirect vote substantially, but many barbers, clerks, and public functionaries, to name a few subaltern categories, voted in the primary elections. The second stage of elections was very restricted. In the city of Rio de Janeiro, for the 1869–72 voting period, there were just 359 registered electors, *Almanak [Laemmert] . . . 1870*, part 2, 317.

6. Karasch, *Slave Life*, 287–94; Slenes, *Na senzala, uma flor*, esp. ch. 3, presents a masterful discussion of the uses of marriage from the point of view of the slaves themselves.

7. Karasch, *Slave Life*, 347–48.

8. This case is drawn from S. L. Graham's "Honor Among Slaves," 207–23.

9. Inventory of Antonio José Dutra, 1849, caixa 68, n. 171, Rio de Janeiro, AN, 87–88.

10. Ibid., 103–12.

11. Inventory of José Thomas Rodrigues, 1849, maço 381, n. 6756, Rio de Janeiro, AN.

12. Inventory of Francisco de Macedo Freire, 1854, caixa 4136, n. 1297, Rio de Janeiro, AN.

13. Inventory of João Baptista, 1855, caixa 4105, n. 1605, Rio de Janeiro, AN.

14. Inventory of Ignacio Caetano de Araujo, 1849, caixa 4145, n. 1504, Rio de Janeiro, AN.

15. According to the estate inventory sample for Rio de Janeiro in the 1850s, the average heir received 1:977$000 from the division of estates worth between 5:000$000 and 20:000$000.

16. Inventory of Placido Adão da Silva, 1820, maço 2289, n. 2095, Rio de Janeiro, AN.

17. Inventory of Ildefonso Teixeira da Cunha, 1858, caixa 4012, n. 385, Rio de Janeiro, AN.

18. Inventory of Angelo José de Moraes, 1857, caixa 4143, n. 1472, Rio de Janeiro, AN.

19. For a definitive account of the evolution of Brazilian inheritance law in the nineteenth century, as well as its basic definitions, see Lewin, *Surprise Heirs*, esp. xxvi–xxvii for basic definitions and distinctions.

For a discussion of the strategies employed by wealthy families to mitigate the effects of inheritance law in another part of Brazil, see Borges, *Family in Bahia*, ch. 7.

20. All figures are derived from the estate inventory sample. Source: Inventories, Rio de Janeiro, AN.

21. For a good introduction to this literature, see Champernowne and Cowell, *Economic Inequality*, esp. 198–249. The authors model the behavior of inheritance inequality over time on the mythical isle of Mutt, where heirs follow paths to ruin or glory according to stochastic models.

22. This range of income is suggested by the average rates of return, in terms of income streams and leaving aside capital gains and depreciation, found in the ownership of real property (between 7 and 10 percent), slaves (10 to 15 percent), credit (as high as 18 percent), and bonds (6 to 9 percent).

23. S. L. Graham provides evidence of subletting among the poor in "Honor Among Slaves," 208.

24. Inventory of Claudianna Maria da Luz, 1852, caixa 1384, n. 134, Rio de Janeiro, AN.

25. Inventory of Ana Theodora Mascarenhas Barros, 1855, caixa 3602, n. 24, Rio de Janeiro, AN.

26. Data from estate inventory sample, 1850–60, Rio de Janeiro, AN.

27. Inventory of Carlota Augusta de Barros, 1853, caixa 4027, n. 655, Rio de Janeiro, AN. Lindert warns us against using inventories that seem incomplete, for example, containing only bonds, "Probate Sampling," 658. In this instance, however, it seems possible that Carlota's estate was complete (it includes her personal property) and that she lived on interest payments from her bonds. It is odd, however, that a person of her wealth would not own her own residence.

28. Inventory of Catharina Luiza de Menezes, 1845, caixa 333, n. 2945, Rio de Janeiro, AN.

29. Inventory of Candida Perpetua da Gloria, 1853, caixa 4061, n. 746, Rio de Janeiro, AN.

30. Inventory of Martiniana Maria Jacinta de Souza, 1889, maço 391, n. 7003, Rio de Janeiro, AN.

31. Inventory of Mary Isabella Ford, 1888, maço 419, n. 7928, Rio de Janeiro, AN.

32. Nazzari, *Disappearance of the Dowry*, 130–31.

33. Ibid., 164.

34. Ibid., 165–66.

35. Inventory of Carlos Frederico Taylor, 1890, caixa 4066, n. 840, Rio de Janeiro, AN.

36. Inventory of Antonio Ferreira da Silva, 1886, caixa 2748, n. 10, Rio de Janeiro, AN.
37. Costa, *Brazilian Empire*, ch. 10.
38. Borges, *Family in Bahia*.

Chapter 8

1. The argument against "export-led" growth as a general phenomenon in nineteenth-century Brazil is made persuasively by Summerhill, *Order Against Progress*, 136–38; in suggesting that a higher rate of growth obtained in the Southeast I follow Leff's classic analysis, *Underdevelopment and Development*.
2. Summerhill, *Order Against Progress*, 102. The highest social rates for return were found on railroads in the Southeast. Because these railroads linked already relatively dynamic regions and because there was great demand for transport services (for domestic and export markets) these railroads generated higher returns than railroads in many other parts of Brazil. It is important to bear in mind that there were exceptions to this pattern.
3. For a good overview of Bonifácio and his political context, see Costa, *Brazilian Empire*, ch. 2. According to Viotti da Costa, Bonifácio, one of the fathers of Brazilian independence, was a complicated man, whose political views placed in him conflict with both radicals and conservatives. A strong opponent of the continuation of the slave trade during the 1820s and 1830s, Bonifácio ended up disappointed, because the trade not only continued but increased as the power of the planter oligarchy expanded.
4. R. Graham, *Patronage*, 109.
5. Ibid., 104, quoting José Antonio Pimenta Bueno.
6. For an excellent examination of the political culture of the first years of the Old Republic, viewed from below, see Carvalho's *Bestializados*. An important variation on this theme in Argentina is found in Sabato's *Many and Few*.
7. The high prices of slaves and elevated living costs of the later years of the empire are well established. As for the decline of the barber-surgeons, see Pimenta, "Entre sangradores e doutores," 97–99. Note that Pimenta does not suggest that they disappeared, only that they gradually lost their "respectability." For the decline of the barber bands, see Tinhorão, *História social*, 170.

Appendix

1. For a clear overview of the problems associated with using probate (inventory) samples, along with a useful list of recommended practices, see Lindert, "Probate Sampling."
2. Estimate based on Karasch, *Slave Life*, 101.
3. Calculation assumes that slave and free populations had similar mortality rates. This measure biases against finding that the inventory samples represent a large portion of the inventory-eligible population because slave mortality was about 33 percent higher than among the free, circa 1847.
4. The number of sampled inventories per year in the 1840s and 1850s varied from year to year, however, the average number was 40 observations, including cases for which parts or all of the data were lost or illegible. Because we selected every third inventory, it follows that there are approximately 120 cases per year in the National Archive for these periods.
5. Karasch, *Slave Life*, 109. According to Karash's estimates, the mortality rate among the free was 31 per 1,000. This figure, however, is biased upward by the high mortality rate among children.
6. Data from Clotilde de Paiva, machine readable version of the 1831/32 provincial census.
7. Silveira, "Distribution," 80.
8. Silveira himself admits the tenuousness of these estimates ("Distribution," 40–41). It is noteworthy that the share of decedents estimated in the under-thirty age band falls from 40 percent in the 1870s sample to 13 percent in the 1900s sample—clearly this introduces a significant distortion.
9. Silveira, "Distribution," 114.
10. The choice of São João is not entirely arbitrary. This county was one of the most dynamic in all of Minas Gerais during the nineteenth century (Filho, *Princesa do oeste*). Moreover, the mean number of slaves per slaveholding household in this region (7.82) is similar to the likely mean in Rio de Janeiro if, following Karasch, we assume 3.6 slaves per household overall, and 40 percent of households with slaves, resulting in an estimated mean of 9 slaves per household. The estate samples consistently return a mean of between 8 and 11 slaves per household for Rio de Janeiro, or 6 or 7 slaves per household when rural landowners are excluded from the calculation—further suggesting that the estate sample is roughly representative of the distribution of wealth among the living.

11. For the best discussion of this problem in the context of Rio de Janeiro, see Silveira, "Distribution," esp. ch. 4.
12. Silveira comes to a similar conclusion: the distribution among the inventoried population roughly mirrors the distribution among the living. Moreover, he considers 30 and 50 percent zero-wealth scenarios as *extreme* assumptions (Silveira, "Distribution," 106, 110).
13. Adjusting for estimated age and censoring effects. This process remains extremely rough in the case of Rio de Janeiro (city) where we lack nominal census returns and cannot therefore connect our estate inventory samples with independent measures of wealth.
14. See Jones, *Wealth of a Nation to Be*, for a discussion of likely income-to-wealth ratios. The wealth-income ratio may also change over time. See Soltow, *Distribution*, 197.
15. For a clear description of Bairoch's rule and an example of its application in a Latin American setting, see Salvucci, "Mexican National Income." 15. For a good discussion of this problem and an excellent example of how it can be addressed, see Summerhill, *Order Against Progress*, 86–90.
16. Summerhill comes to a similar conclusion in *Order Against Progress*, 86.
17. In this, I follow a similar method to Leff, *Underdevelopment*, 33, 42, 97–101, and 123; however, I use the exchange rate rather than British wholesale prices as the "external" component of my index.

BIBLIOGRAPHY

Adelman, Jeremy. *Colonial Legacies: The Problem of Persistence in Latin America*. New York: Routledge, 1999.

Alencastro, Luiz Felipe de. *História da vida privada no Brasil*, Vol. 2, *Império: A corte e a modernidade nacional*. São Paulo: Companhia das Letras, 1997.

Algranti, Leila Mezan. *O feitor ausente: Estudos sobre a escravidão urbana no Rio de Janeiro, 1808–1822*. Petrópolis, Brazil: Editora Vozes, 1988.

Almanak [Laemmert] administrativo, mercantil e industrial da Corte e Provincia do Rio de Janeiro para o anno de 1870. Rio de Janeiro: Laemmert, 1870.

Almanak [Laemmert] administrativo, mercantil e industrial do Rio de Janeiro para o anno de 1845. Rio de Janeiro: Laemmert, 1845.

Assis, Machado de. *Posthumous Memoirs*. 1880. New York: Oxford University Press, 1998.

Atack, Jeremy, and Peter Passell. *A New Economic View of American History*. New York: W. W. Norton, 1994.

Barickman, Bert. *A Bahian Counterpoint: Sugar, Tobacco, Cassava, and Slavery in the Recôncavo, 1780–1860*. Stanford, CA: Stanford University Press, 1999.

———. "As cores do escravismo: Escravistas "pretos," "pardos," e "cabras" no Recôncavo baiano, 1835." *População e Família* 2 (1999): 7–59.

Barman, Rodrick. *Brazil: The Forging of a Nation, 1798–1852*. Stanford, CA: Stanford University Press, 1988.

———. *Citizen Emperor: Pedro II and the Making of Brazil, 1825–81*. Stanford, CA: Standford University Press, 1999.

Bergad, Laird W. *Slavery and the Demographic and Economic History of Minas Gerais, Brazil, 1720–1888*. Cambridge: Cambridge University Press, 1999.

Bethell, Leslie. *The Abolition of the Brazilian Slave Trade: Britain, Brazil and the Slave Trade Question*. Cambridge: Cambridge University Press, 1970.

Borges, Dain. *The Family in Bahia, Brazil, 1870–1945*. Stanford, CA: Stanford University Press, 1992.

Botelho, Tarcísio Rodrigues. *História quantitativa e serial no Brasil*. Belo Horizonte: ANPUH-MG, 2001.

Brazil. Ministerio da Fazenda. *Relatorio . . . em fim do anno de 1825, com o orçamento da renda, e despeza que poderá ter lugar no corrente anno de*

1826. No publication information available, document available online at http://brazil.crl.edu/bsd.

———. Ministerio da Guerra. *Relatorio . . . do anno de 1845 apresentado á Assembléa Geral Legislativa na 3a sessão da 6a legislatura*. Rio de Janeiro: Typ. Nacional, 1846.

Brazil. Ministerio do Imperio. *Relatorio do anno de 1849 apresentado a assemblea geral legislative no 2a sessão da 8a legislature*. Rio de Janeiro: Typ. Nacional, 1850. Mapa 12.

Buescu, Mircea. *300 anos de inflação*. Rio de Janeiro: APEC, 1973.

Calógeras, João Pandiá. *A Política Monetária do Brasil*. São Paulo: Companhia Editora Nacional, 1960.

Carr, Lois Green. "Emigration and the Standard of Living: the Eighteenth-Century Chesapeake." In *The Early Modern Atlantic Economy*, ed. John McCusker and Phillip Morgan, 319–43. Cambridge: Cambridge University Press, 2001.

Carvalho, José Murillo de. *Os bestializados: O Rio de Janeiro e a República que não foi*. São Paulo: Companhia das Letras, 1999.

———. *A construção da ordem: A elite política imperial*. Rio de Janeiro: Campus, 1980.

Chaloub, Sidney. *Visões da liberdade: Uma história das últimas décadas da escravidão na corte*. São Paulo: Companhia das Letras, 1990.

Champernowne, D. G., and F. A. Cowell. *Economic Inequality and Income Distribution*. Cambridge: Cambridge University, 1998.

Conrad, Robert. *Children of God's Fire: A Documentary History of Black Slavery in Brazil*. Princeton, NJ: Princeton University Press, 1983.

———. *The Destruction of Brazilian Slavery, 1850–1888*. Berkeley: University of California Press, 1972.

Constituições do Brasil. São Paulo: Edição Saraiva, 1967.

Costa, Emília Viotti da. *The Brazilian Empire: Myths and Histories*. Chapel Hill: University of North Carolina Press, 2000.

———. *Da senzala à colônia*. São Paulo: DIFEL, 1966.

Dean, Warren. *Rio Claro: A Brazilian Plantation System, 1820–1920*. Stanford, CA: Stanford University Press, 1976.

Debret, Jean Baptiste. *Viagem pitoresca e histórica ao Brasil*. Trans. Sergio Milliet. 4 vols. São Paulo: Livraria Martins, 1940 [originally published as *Voyage Pittoresque et Historique au Brésil*, 3 vols.: Paris, 1834–39].

Degler, Carl. *Neither Black nor White: Slavery and Race Relations in Brazil and the United States*. New York: Macmillan, 1971.

Domínguez, Virginia R. *White by Definition: Social Classification in Creole Louisiana*. New Brunswick, NJ: Rutgers University Press, 1986.

Drescher, Seymour. "Brazilian Abolition in Comparative Perspective." *Hispanic American Historical Review* 68, no. 3 (1988): 429–60.

Engerman, Stanley, and Kenneth Sokoloff. "Paths of Growth Among New World Economies." In *How Latin America Fell Behind: Essays on the Economic Histories of Brazil and Mexico, 1800–1914*, ed. Stephen Haber, 260–304. Stanford, CA: Stanford University Press, 1997.

Eschwege, Ludwig Wilhelm Von. *Pluto brasilensis*. São Paulo: Companhia Editora Nacional, 1944.

Fogel, Robert, and Stanley Engerman. *Time on the Cross: The Economics of American Negro Slavery*. 2 vols. Boston: Little Brown, 1974.

Fragoso, João Luís Ribeiro. *Homens de grossa aventura: Acumulação e hierarquia na praça mercantil do Rio de Janeiro, 1790–1830*. Rio de Janeiro: Arquivo Nacional, 1992.

Freyre, Gilberto. *O escravo nos anúncios de jornais brasileiros do século XIX*, 2 ed. São Paulo: Companhia Editora Nacional, 1979.

———. *The Mansions and the Shanties: The Making of Modern Brazil (Sobrados e mucambos)*. New York: Alfred A. Knopf, 1963.

———. *The Masters and the Slaves: A Study in the Development of Brazilian Civilization (Casa-grande & Senzala)*. New York: Alfred A. Knopf, 1978.

Fryer, Peter. *Rhythms of Resistance: African Musical Heritage in Brazil*. Hanover, NH: University Press of New England for Wesleyan Press, 2000.

Goldsmith, Raymond. *Brasil 1850–1984: Desenvolvimento sobre um século de inflação*. São Paulo: Harper and Row and Bamerindus, 1986.

———. *Income and Wealth of the United States, Trends and Structure. Papers by Simon Kuznets and Robert Goldsmith*. Ed. Simon Kuznets. Cambridge: Bowes and Bowes, 1952.

Graça Filho, Afonso de Alencastro. *Princesa do oeste e o mito da decadência de Minas Gerais: São João del Rei (1831–1888)*. São Paulo: Annablume, 2002.

Graham, Richard. *Britain and the Onset of Modernization in Brazil, 1850–1914*. London: Cambridge University Press, 1968.

———. *Patronage and Politics in Nineteenth-Century Brazil*. Stanford, CA: Stanford University Press, 1990.

Graham, Sandra Lauderdale. *Caetana Says No: Women's Stories from a Brazilian Slave Society*. Cambridge: Cambridge University Press, 2002.

———. "Honor Among Slaves." In *The Faces of Honor: Sex, Shame, and Violence in Colonial Latin America*, ed. Lyman Johnson and Sonya Lipsett-Rivera, 201–28. Albuquerque: University of New Mexico Press, 1998.

———. *House and Street: The Domestic World of Servants and Masters in Nineteenth-Century Rio de Janeiro*. Cambridge: Cambridge University Press, 1987.

Haber, Stephen, and Herbert Klein. "Economic Consequences of Brazilian Independence." In *How Latin America Fell Behind: Essays on the Economic Histories of Brazil and Mexico, 1800–1914*, ed. Stephen Haber, 243–59. Stanford, CA: Stanford University Press, 1997.

Hahner, June. *Poverty and Politics: The Urban Poor in Brazil, 1870–1920*. Albuquerque: University of New Mexico Press, 1986.

Higgins, Kathleen. "Gender and the Manumission of Slaves in Colonial Brazil: The Prospects for Freedom in Sabará, Minas Gerais, 1710–1809." *Slavery and Abolition* 18, no. 2 (1997): 1–29.

Hilton, Anne. *The Kingdom of Kongo*. Oxford: Oxford University Press, 1985.

Hoffman, Philip, Gilles Postel-Vinay, and Jean-Laurent Rosenthal. *Priceless Markets: The Political Economy of Credit in Paris, 1660–1870*. Chicago: University of Chicago Press, 2000.

Holloway, Thomas. *Policing Rio de Janeiro: Repression and Resistance in a 19th-Century City*. Stanford, CA: Stanford University Press, 1993.

Huggins, Martha Knisely. *From Slavery to Vagrancy in Brazil: Crime and Social Control in the Third World*. New Brunswick, NJ: Rutgers University Press, 1985.

Jeha, Silvana. "Ganhar a Vida: Uma história do africano Antonio José Dutra e sua família, Rio de Janeiro, século XIX." Unpublished manuscript, Rio de Janeiro, 2004.

Jones, Alice Hanson. *Wealth of a Nation to Be: The American Colonies on the Eve of Revolution*. New York: Columbia University Press, 1980.

Karasch, Mary. "Slave Life in Rio de Janeiro, 1808–1850." PhD dissertation, University of Wisconsin, 1972.

———. *Slave Life in Rio de Janeiro, 1808–1850*. Princeton, NJ: Princeton University Press, 1987.

Kidder, Daniel P. *Sketches of Residence and Travels in Brazil, Embracing Historical and Geographical Notices of the Empire and its Several Provinces*. Philadelphia, PA: Sorin and Ball, 1845.

Klein, Herbert. *The Middle Passage: Comparative Studies in the Atlantic Slave Trade*. Princeton, NJ: Princeton University Press, 1978.

———. "Slave and Free in Nineteenth-Century Minas: Campanha in 1831." *Slavery and Abolition* 15, no. 1 (1994): 1–21.

Klein, Herbert, and Francisco Vidal Luna. "Free Colored in a Slave Society: São Paulo and Minas Gerais in the Early Nineteenth Century." *HAHR* 80, no. 4 (2000): 913–41.

Kotlikoff, Laurence J. "Quantitative Description of the New Orleans Slave Market, 1804–1862." In *Without Consent or Contract: The Rise and Fall of American Slavery, Markets and Production Technical Papers*, vol. 1, ed. Robert Fogel and Stanley Engerman. New York: W. W. Norton, 1992.

Kraay, Hendrick. *Race, State, and Armed Forces in Independence-Era Brazil: Bahia, 1790s–1840s*. Stanford, CA: Stanford University Press, 2001.

Kuznesof, Elizabeth. *Household Economy and Urban Development: São Paulo, 1765–1836*. Boulder, CO: Westview Press, 1986.

Leff, Nathaniel. *Underdevelopment and Development in Brazil*, Vol. 1: *Economic Structure and Change, 1822–1947*. London: Allen and Unwin, 1982.

Lewin, Linda. *Surprise Heirs II: Illegitimacy, Inheritance Rights, and Public Power in the Formation of Imperial Brazil, 1822–1889*. Stanford, CA: Stanford University Press, 2003.

Libby, Douglass. "Minas na mira dos brasilianistas." In *História quantitativa e serial no Brasil*, ed. Tarcísio Rodrigues Botelho et al., 279–304. Belo Horizonte: ANPUH-MG, 2001.

———. *Transformação e trabalho em uma economia escravista: Minas Gerais no século XIX*. São Paulo: Editora Brasiliense, 1988.

Lindert, Peter. "An Algorithm for Probate Sampling." *Journal of Interdisciplinary History* 11, no. 4 (1981): 649–68.

Lindley, Thomas. *Narrativa de uma viagem ao Brasil*. São Paulo : Editora Nacional, 1969.

Lobo, Eulália Maria Lahmeyer. *História do Rio de Janeiro: Do capital comercial ao capital industrial e financeiro*. Rio de Janeiro: IBMEC, 1978.

Luccock, John. *Notes on Rio de Janeiro and the Southern Parts of Brazil: Taken During a Residence of Ten Years in that Country, from 1808 to 1818*. London: n.p., 1820.

Luna, Francisco Vidal. *Minas Gerais: escravos e senhores*. São Paulo: IPE-USP, 1981.

Marcondes, Renato Leite. *A arte de acumular*. São Paulo: EDUSP, 2001.

———. "Small and Medium Slaveholding in the Coffee Plantations of the Vale do Paraíba (São Paulo, Brazil)." Paper presented at the International Economic History Congress, Buenos Aires, 2002.

Martins Filho, Amilcar, and Roberto B. Martins. "Slavery in a Nonexport Economy: Nineteenth-Century Minas Gerais Revisited." *Hispanic American Historical Review* 63, no. 3 (1983): 537–68.

Mattos, Ilmar Rohloff de. *O tempo saquarema*. São Paulo: HUCITEC, 1987.

Mattoso, Katia de Queiróz. *Bahia, Século XIX: Uma província no império*. Rio de Janeiro: Editora Nova Fronteira,1992.

———. *To Be a Slave in Brazil*. New Brunswick, NJ: Rutgers University Press, 1986.

McCusker, John, and Phillip Morgan. *The Early Atlantic Economy*. Cambridge: Cambridge University Press, 2001.

Mello, Pedro Carvalho de. "The Economics of Labor in Brazilian Coffee Plantations, 1850–1888." PhD dissertation, University of Chicago, 1977.

———. "Rates of Return on Slave Capital in Brazilian Coffee Plantations, 1871–1881." In *Without Consent or Contract. Technical Papers: The Rise and Fall of American Slavery*, vol. 2, ed. Robert Fogel and Stanley Engerman, 63–79. New York: W. W. Norton, 1992.

Mello, Zélia Maria Cardoso de. *Metamorfoses da riqueza: São Paulo, 1845–1895*. São Paulo: Hucitec, 1982.

Metcalf, Alida. *Family and Frontier in Colonial Brazil: Santana de Parnaíba, 1580–1822*. Berkeley: University of California Press, 1992.

Miller, Joseph C. *Way of Death: Merchant Capitalism and the Angolan Slave Trade, 1730–1830*. Madison: University of Wisconsin Press, 1988.

Mintz, Sidney. *Caribbean Transformations*. Baltimore, MD: Johns Hopkins University Press, 1974.

Moya, José. *Cousins and Strangers: Spanish Immigrants in Buenos Aires, 1850–1930*. Berkeley: University of California Press, 1995.

Nazzari, Muriel. *The Disappearance of the Dowry: Women, Families, and Social Change in São Paulo, Brazil, 1600–1900*. Stanford, CA: Stanford University Press, 1991.

Needell, Jeffrey "Party Formation and State-Making: The Conservative Party and the Reconstruction of the Brazilian State, 1831–40." *Hispanic American Historical Review* 81, no. 2 (May 2001): 259–308.

———. *A Tropical Belle Époque: Elite Culture and Society in Turn-of-the-Century Rio de Janeiro*. Cambridge: Cambridge University Press, 1987.

North, Douglass. *Institutions, Institutional Change, and Economic Performance*. New York: Cambridge University Press, 1990.

O'Rourke, Kevin, and Jeffrey Williamson. *Globalization and History: The Evolution of a Nineteenth-Century Atlantic Economy*. Cambridge, MA: MIT Press, 1999.

Owensby, Brian. *Intimate Ironies: Modernity and the Making of Middle-Class Lives in Brazil*. Stanford, CA: Stanford University Press, 1999.

Paiva, Clotilde de, and Herbert Klein. "Freedmen in a Slave Economy: Minas Gerais in 1831." *Journal of Social History* 29, no. 4: 933–62.

Paiva, Eduardo França. *Escravidão e universo cultural na colônia: Minas Gerais, 1716–1789*. Belo Horizonte: Ed. UFMG, 2001.

Paiva, Eduardo França, and Carla Maria Junho Anastásia. *O trabalho mestiço: Maneiras de pensar e formas de viver, séculos XVI a XIX*. São Paulo: Annablume, 2002.

Pimenta, Tânia Salgado. "Barbeiros-sangradores e curandeiros no Brasil (1808–1828)." *História, Ciência, Saúde—Manguinhos* 5, no. 2 (1998): 349–72.

———. "Entre Sangradores e doutores: práticas e formação médica na primeira metade do século XIX." *Cad. Cedes, Campinas* 23, no. 59 (2003): 91–102.

Prado Júnior, Caio. *História Econômica do Brasil*. São Paulo: Brasiliense, 1998.

Reis, João José. "O cotidiano da morte no Brasil oitocentista." In *História da vida privada no Brasil. Império: A corte e a modernidade nacional*, ed. Luiz Felipe de Alencastro, 95–141. São Paulo: Companhia das Letras, 1997.

————. *Death Is a Festival: Funeral Rites and Rebellion in Nineteenth-Century Brazil*. Chapel Hill: University of North Carolina Press, 2003.

Reis, João José, and Eduardo Silva. *Negociação e conflito: Resistência negra no Brasil escravista*. São Paulo: Companhia das Letras, 1989.

Relatorio apresentado ao exm. Sr. Presidente da provincial de São Paulo pela commissão central de estatística. São Paulo: Typ. King, 1888.

Ribeiro, Gladys. *A liberdade em construção: Identidade e conflitos antilusitanos no primeiro reinado*. Rio de Janeiro: Relume-Dumará, 2002.

Russell-Wood, A. J. R. *The Black Man in Slavery and Freedom in Colonial Brazil*. London : Macmillan, 1982.

Sabato, Hilda. *The Many and the Few: Political Participation in Republican Buenos Aires*. Stanford, CA: Stanford University Press, 2001.

Salvucci, Richard. "Mexican National Income in the Era of Independence." In *How Latin America Fell Behind: Essays on the Economic History of Brazil and Mexico, 1800–1914*, ed. Stephen Haber, 216–42. Stanford, CA: Stanford University Press, 1997.

Schlichthorst, Carl. *Rio de Janeiro wie es ist*. Hannover, Germany: Hahn, 1829.

Schultz, Kirsten. *Tropical Versailles: Empire, Monarchy, and the Portuguese Royal Court in Rio de Janeiro, 1808–1821*. London: Routledge, 2001.

Schwartz, Stuart. "The Colonial Past: Conceptualizing Post- *Dependentista* Brazil." In *Colonial Legacies: The Problem of Persistence in Latin America*, ed. Jeremy Adelman, 175–92. New York: Routledge, 1999.

————. "Patterns of Slaveholding in the Americas: New Evidence from Brazil." *American Historical Review* 87, no. 1 (1982): 55–86.

Silva, Maria Beatriz Nizza da. *História da família no Brasil colonial*. Rio de Janeiro: Editora Nova Fronteira, 1998.

Silva, Marilene Rosa Nogueira da. *Negro na rua: A nova face da escravidão*. São Paulo: HUCITEC, 1988.

Silveira, Ricardo Antonio Rocha. "The Distribution of Wealth in Brazil—The Case of Rio de Janeiro: 1870s to 1980s." PhD dissertation, UC Berkeley, 1985.

Slenes, Robert. "The Demography and Economics of Brazilian Slavery, 1850–1888." PhD dissertation, Stanford University, 1975.

————. *Na senzala, uma flor: esperanças e recordações na formação da família escrava, Brasil Sudeste, Século XIX*. Rio de Janeiro: Nova Fronteira, 1999.

Soares, Carlos Eugênio Líbano. *A capoeira escrava e outras tradições rebeldes no Rio de Janeiro (1808–1850)*. Campinas: Editora UNICAMP, 2002.

Soltow, Lee. *Distribution of Wealth and Income in the United States in 1798*. Pittsburgh, PA: University of Pittsburgh Press, 1989.

Stein, Stanley. *Vassouras: A Brazilian Coffee County, 1850–1890*. Cambridge, MA: Harvard University Press, 1957.

Stein, Stanley, and Barbara Stein. *The Colonial Heritage of Latin America: Essays on Economic Dependence in Perspective*. New York: Oxford University Press, 1970.

Summerhill, William. *Order Against Progress: Government, Foreign Investment, and Railroads in Brazil, 1854–1913*. Stanford, CA: Stanford University Press, 2003.

Thornton, John K. *The Kongolese Saint Anthony: Dona Beatriz Kimpa Vita and the Antonian Movement, 1684–1706*. Cambridge: Cambridge University Press, 1998.

Toplin, Robert Brent. *The Abolition of Slavery in Brazil*. New York: Atheneum, 1972.

Triner, Gail D. *Banking and Economic Development: Brazil 1889–1930*. New York: Palgrave, 2000.

Vedder, Richard K. "The Slave Exploitation (Expropriation) Rate." *Explorations in Economic History* 12 (1975): 453–58.

Versiani, Flávio, and José R. O. Vergolino, "Slave Holdings in Nineteenth-Century Brazilian Northeast: Sugar Estates and the Backlands." Paper presented at the International Economic History Congress, Buenos Aires, 2002.

Walsh, Robert. *Notices of Brazil in 1828 and 1829*, vols. 1 and 2. Boston: Boston Press, 1831.

Zimmerman, Kari. "Advertising Gender: The Division of Labor in Rio de Janeiro's Working Class, 1850–1890." Paper presented at the Rocky Mountain Conference on Latin American Studies, Phoenix, 2003.

INDEX

113–21; commercial code in, 82, 198n. 3; economic growth of, 2, 7–8, 13, 16, 21, 22, 23–25, 46–69, 70–76, 95, 117 162; elite class in, 17, 42, 51–52, 66, 79, 193n. 57, 199n. 5; entrepreneurs in, 13, 35, 55, 74, 91, 109–11, 113–21; financial institutions in, 24, 83, 95; government in, 24, 117; houses in, **34,** 34–36, **35;** immigrants in, 14, 68–69, 86, 89, 91–92; institutional change in, 13, 22–23, 70–76, 95, 167; population makeup of, 17–18, 21, 46, 52, 189n. 1; Portuguese court in, 12, 13, 22–23; property rights in, 82, 167; property values in, 33–34, 39–41, 52, 55, 56, 58–60, 62–63, 67–69, 74, 79–82, 88–89, 107–8, 167, 196n. 25; residential patterns in, 31–38, 51–55, 79–82, 193n. 57; rural districts surrounding, 42, **53;** service economy of, 24, 27–28, 109–11, 113–21, 167; slavery in, 15, 17–18, 20, **21,** 23, 32–33, 52, 75, 94, 107–8, 167–70, 215n. 10; social structures of, 2, 7–8, 13, 23, 26–31, 38–39, 46–69, 70, 79, 91–92, 114, 147, 167; stock market and, 87–89, 160–62, 164; tenements (*cortiços*) in, 80–81, 117–18; trade in, 23–24, 46, 59, 70, 71, 74, 86, 166; urban growth in, 24, 46, 68, 70–76, 79, 167; urban milieu of, 51–55, 88; wages in, 24, 68–69, 72, 76, 204n. 9;

wealth in, 39–45, 56–60, 70–95, 108–13, 180–83
Rio de Janeiro Province, 6, 46, 70, 71, 86, 91

Saint Anthony: Kingdom of Kongo and, 124–25; of Moraria, 124
Salvador, Brazil, 74
São Paulo: dowries in, 162–63; economic development in, 162; real estate in, 81; slaves and, 47; trade in, 14, 23, 70, 86, 96, 166, 199n. 15
Schlichthorst, Carl, 43
Schwartz, Stuart, 6
Silva, Antonio Fernandes da, 51, 131–35, 137–40, 142–45, 210n. 40
Silva, João Baptista Moreira da (husband of Ignacia Dutra), 110, 125, 131–34, 137, 139, 205n. 31, 210n. 37
Silveira, Ricardo Antonio Rocha, 176–78
slave rental market, 47–50, 60–65, 72, 75, 101–3
slave trade, 19–21, 23–24, 46, 190n. 17; suppression of, 11, 22, 70, 74–78, 84–86, 94, 100, 167
slaveholdings, 3, 99; barriers to, 84, 98–101; middling (*see* middling slaveholders); patterns of, 77–78, 84, 175–78; rate of savings of, 97–103; risks of, 65, 78; size of, 85; slave gender and, 118; social mobility and, 7–9, 21, 68, 70–71, 75, 86, 96–97, 165–66; urban, 77–78
slavery: abolition of, 3, 7, 14, 91, 93, 95, 165–66, 168, 204n. 19;

in Brazil, 5–7, 11, 17–18;
decline of, 2; elites and, 3;
freed slaves and, 3; gender
and, 29; institution of, 77,
168; in Rio de Janeiro (*see*
Rio de Janeiro); rural, 6,
17–18, 87, 120; social
mobility and, 3–4, 7–8,
11–13, 21, 167; suppression
of, 11–12, 59; urban, 6–7, 21,
87, 120–21; wealthholders
and, 3
slavery: Middle Passage, the,
19–21
slaves: advertisements for, 47–50,
61, 64, 75, 102; African,
19–21, 94, 101–2, 113, 190n.
12, 204n. 16, 208n. 14; age
of, 85; agency of, 63–64, 78,
175; barber, **28**, 93, 112–13,
117, 137; Brazilian-born,
102; conditions for, 20;
corporal punishment of, **26**,
116, **116**; costs of raising,
102; death and, 127–28, **129**;
distribution of, 60, 175–78,
193n. 58, 215n. 10; domestic,
18, 47–48, 61, 65; earnings
of, 47, 60–68, 75, 101–3;
economic importance of,
42–43, 84–91; expropriation
of, 101–3; family and, 148;
female, 27, 47–48, 118, 160;
first purchase of, 97–98;
frailty of, 63–64; free (*see*
freed slaves); labor market
for, 47; male, 48, 61, 118;
middling wealthholders
and (*see* middling
slaveholders and);
occupations of, 47;
plantation, 46, 61; porter, 28,
30; prices of, 24, 40, 43–45,

55, 58–59, 69, 74–77, 79,
85–86, 97–101, 105, 117, 155,
167, 197n. 36, 198n. 50, 201n.
45, 214n. 7; purchases, 100;
rate of return on, 60–65,
97–100, 101–3, 105, 116–17,
191n. 37, 197n. 43, 203n. 8;
rental of (*see* slave rental
market); resistance of, 7, 93,
101, 204n. 16; runaway, 50,
63–64, 102, 137, 198n. 49;
rural, 6, 17–18, 87, 120, 202n.
48; savings rates and,
98–103; self-purchase by, 18,
68, 100; skilled, 49, 68, 119;
social structure and wealth
and, 75, 96–97; spirituality
of, 124–25; urban, 18, 21,
24–25, 47–50, 61, 63–64,
120–21, 202n. 48; urban
wages and, 98–100
southeastern Brazil: economy of,
12, 70–76, 86–87, 165;
slavery in, 7, 165
Stein, Stanley, 91
street vendors, 27
Summerhill, W., 70

Walsh, Robert, 15–16, 20
wealth, 90, 92, 96; alternative
pathways to, 103–8; civil
status and, 156, 158–64;
distribution of, 42, 44, 56,
58–59, 75, 76–77, 163, 166,
183, 200n. 23, 215n. 10;
financial, 82–83, 88–89, 92,
94–95; forms of, 39–45,
59–60; growth of, 72–76,
200n. 20; inequality of, 75,
76–77, 84, 164, 166, 180,
183–84; inherited, 96–97,
164; paths to, 96–121; real
estate, 39–41, 56, 58–60, 68,